Choosing the Right School for Your Child

Choosing the Right School for Your Child

A Guide to Selected Elementary Schools
in the Washington Area

Blythe Lyons
and
Missy Janes

MADISON BOOKS
Lanham • New York • London

Published by Madison Books
4720 Boston Way
Lanham, Maryland 20706

3 Henrietta Street
London WC2E 8LU England

Distributed by National Book Network

The paper used in this publication meets the minimum requirements of American National Standard for Information Sciences—Permanence of Paper for Printed Library Materials, ANSI Z39.48–1984. ♾™
Manufactured in the United States of America.

5 4 3 2 1

Library of Congress Cataloging-in-Publication Data

Lyons, Blythe.
Choosing the right school for your child : a guide to selected elementary schools in the Washington area / Blythe Lyons and Missy Janes.
p. cm.
1. Elementary schools—Washington (D.C.)—Directories. 2. Private schools—Washington (D.C.)—Directories. 3. School, Choice of—Washington (D.C.) I. Janes, Missy. II. Title.
L903.W36L96 1990
372.9753'025—dc20 90–31678 CIP

ISBN 0–8191–7682–6 (alk. paper)

British Cataloging in Publication Information Available

To our children
Ted and Michael
Pack and Maxine

May their school experiences be
well suited and successful!

Contents

Acknowledgments

We offer our sincere thanks to friends, associates, parents, schools, and educational professionals who have generously donated their time to help us. Our early supporters and questionnaire advisers deserving thanks are Suzanne Babcock, Maxine Freund, Malcolm Gauld, Pamela Gould, Ibby Jeppson, Chris Kloman, John Mackenzie, Mary Roberts, Patricia Scallan, Isabelle Schuessler, Elaine Shadler, Karen Strimple, and Jim Weiss. We appreciate the work of those who tested the questionnaire, especially the Ellis School of Pittsburgh, Pennsylvania. Many parents who helped us build mailing lists and fine tune the parent questionnaire deserve recognition: Darcy Weber, Andrea Chafetz, Karen Leslie Ross, Kim Chester, and David and Pat Arnaudo.

With gratitude we recognize the authors who generously agreed to write the essays in this book: Patricia O. Quinn, Diane Dunning Trunzo, Judith Denton Jones, Vicki Rab, Patricia Lemer, and Diane Wilson. The written words have been typed beautifully by Kim Wheeland, Dorothy Albritton, and Terri Boddorff. The sage legal and strategic advice given by Geoffrey Stewart has been invaluable. We are also grateful for the efforts made by the communications office of the District of Columbia public school system.

And last but not least we thank our husbands, Jed and Bill, who have supported our endeavor.

Introduction

As parents beginning to look at elementary schools for the first time, we found the number of excellent choices to be both exciting and overwhelming. But the task of calling schools for brochures, going on tours, and deciding what made each school stand out became overwhelming. No wonder so many people tend to consider the same schools each year—researching all of the options is a monumental task.

We decided to write a book for parents by parents. We are not education experts. We have tried to provide answers to the questions parents have by asking the schools and other parents at each school to provide information based on their first-hand experiences. We did not want to give readers our analysis of each school, but rather a look at the school from those who know it best. Therefore, our information is taken from parents' and schools' questionnaires.

It is our judgment, however, that there are many different, wonderful, and academically excellent schools in the Washington, D.C., metropolitan area. Most important, we hope parents will believe, as we do, that a so-called good school is not what other people say is a good school. It is a school that fits your child's learning style, personality, and needs, as well as your family's philosophy and goals.

To this end, we have decided not to rate the schools or make a list of the "best" ones. The fact that a school is reviewed in this book does not imply that it is better than a school that is not reviewed. How then did we choose the schools for inclusion in this book?

A combination of criteria were used in choosing schools. For non-public schools, we limited the selection to schools either located inside the Beltway or having a significant number of students who live inside the Beltway. Some of the schools that met these criteria were not reviewed due to a lack of school and/or parent participation in our survey. Due to policies in the District of Columbia public school system, we received limited permission to interview school principals and, therefore, many schools we would have reviewed are not included. In all other public school jurisdictions, we were denied permission to interview school principals and, with the exception of some Montgomery County schools, decided that the profile could not be written without the schools' cooperation. Selected Montgomery County schools are profiled because the county publishes a significant amount of information about its schools, and parents were most generous with their time in completing our surveys and answering additional questions.

Even if the schools in your area or those of interest to you are not included, the essays and profile format should help you comparatively evaluate such schools. We do regret, however, that we were unable to review more schools.

We have taken a three-pronged approach to acquiring the information contained in the profiles.

First, with the help of advisers, we developed two questionnaires. Included among our advisers were teachers from public, parochial, and independent schools representing a variety of subjects: a child development specialist; an educational consultant; school heads; a Ph.D. in special education; school board trustees; a questionnaire specialist; other professionals; and parents.

In developing the questionnaires, we prepared several drafts, subjected these drafts to an advisers' review, and developed an out-of-area pilot test on a number of schools for the final draft of the school questionnaire.

The questionnaire had two versions: one for the school administrator and one for parents, teachers, and others to complete. We asked every school to complete the survey and a number of parents and teachers from each school to do the same.

Because the questionnaires and responses to it are confidential, copies are not included in this book. We can say that the parents' survey asked questions about parental involvement, school philosophy and goals, school head and faculty, facilities, services and extracurricular opportunities, the curriculum, and general opinions. The school version asked for general information, student body statistics, philosophy, goals and practices, registration or admissions and financial aid information, curriculum, the athletic program, facilities and services, faculty, and school head profile.

Second, we personally visited an extensive number of Washington area schools. Dozens of schools were recommended by parents and educators and we followed up on each one.

Third, throughout the course of this project, we interviewed as many people as possible to guide and advise us.

We prepared the profiles based on information contained in school brochures and the schools' and parents' surveys. We decided that the profiles would focus only on the positive aspects of the schools, not on their weaknesses. Each school was given the opportunity to challenge, comment upon, and edit our draft profiles. While some schools did not choose to do so, the majority of school profiles have been read carefully by the school prior to publication.

The terms in the profiles are defined below; those not defined are self-explanatory.

Enrollment: Gives the enrollment for lower and middle schools and for the entire school; for example, K–12. In many public schools, the boy-girl enrollment was not available and is not generally relevant since the school administrator does not make a conscious decision to have a particular ratio.

Birthdate req.: Public schools will accept all students whose age meets the published date of birth deadline. Other schools state the general birthday requirement, but may have other practices; it is best to inquire about the age range in each class.

Head profile: Provides information about the current school head. In some cases information was provided by parents, not the school.

Costs: A cost range for N, PreK, or K through the highest elementary grade is given, for the '89–90 school year. Some public schools charge tuition for out-of-state students; refer to the admissions/registration section.

School: While some schools include higher grades, the profile focuses on the elementary grades or "lower and/or middle school" and never past grade six.

Parents say: Refers to parents' general comments that did not fit into another category.

Extended day: Lists the morning arrival and/or evening departure hours for the program.

Major entry grade(s): Gives the grade to which most students apply; this category is not relevant to public schools.

Parent fund raising: Refers only to monies raised by parents, typically the PTA, and not by the school for development, annual giving, etc.

Transportation: Includes school-provided bus service or independent contractor service.

After-school activities: Differs from extended day care and means parent-paid-for classes, lessons, or sports activities offered on the campus by the school or parent association.

Neighborhood: The one(s) in which the school is located.

Curriculum: Based on information provided by the school or parents; outlines highlights of the academic program.

Faculty features: Lists the numbers, tenure, turnover (M = minimal, N = normal, I = increased lately), and types of available teachers; part-time status is indicated in parentheses.

Philosophy and character: Attempts to characterize the school based on its philosophy, student body characteristics, and special activities at the school.

Parent involvement: Defines the level of parent participation at the school and includes typical volunteer opportunities available.

Special qualities: Refers to unique programs, philosophy, location, and student body characteristics at the school and is based on judgments made by the school, parents, and/or the authors.

NA: not applicable.

U: unavailable.

Sports news: Lists sports taught in weekly physical education class; does not include after-school sports programs.

Registration/admissions: Describes process, tests, and documents required and gives availability of financial aid, if relevant.

Special spots: Lists the school's indoor and outdoor facilities, rooms, and expansion plans, if any.

Parent wish list: Gives only those services, programs, or facilities most often mentioned in the parents' questionnaires.

Where next: refers to the schools most often attended by graduates of the school; if a school goes through grade 12, college placements are not given.

This book comprises four parts: Part One presents essays by local educational professionals and the authors on choosing a school based on your child's personality and learning style, kindergarten readiness, the parents' role in the early education process, the benefits of a public school education, the school admission process, private school financing options, a school evaluation checklist, and a look at matching a child's personality to a school. Part Two contains the profiles as described above. Part Three offers a chart divided into fourteen categories comparing all of the schools in this book. Part Four provides an extensive array of lists that characterize various aspects of the schools covered in this book, including sources for additional information or counseling.

We hope this book will serve as an introduction to the local elementary schools and broaden your approach to the important and difficult task of selecting a public, parochial, or independent school for your child. Selecting the right school might be an arduous task but we can be thankful that there are so many options from which to choose. Many parents who completed our survey commented that they enjoyed the chance to think more about their children's schools and all of the aspects that make them unique. It is our wish that you and your child will benefit from our compilation of thoughts and facts to take advantage of the opportunities available. Best of luck to all!

Part One

Thoughts on Getting Ready

Making the Right Match

Diane Dunning Trunzo

Parents of school-age children in the Washington, D.C., metropolitan area are fortunate to have available to them many fine educational options. Despite the range of choices, selecting the right academic and social setting for a child can be one of the most important and stressful challenges any parent faces. For those parents who choose an independent school option, the challenge is often compounded by an unfamiliar admissions process and heavy competition for limited spaces in the most desirable schools.

Unfortunately, there is no proven formula for choosing the right school, or for gaining a place at the school of one's choice. Making decisions about school is never an exact science. Rather, the process is more of an art that lies not in the prestige of a school or in standardized test results, but in trying to make the best match between a child's strengths and needs and the school's expectations and offerings.

How then does a parent make the best match between a school and a child? As a director of admissions, I offer the following guidelines for making appropriate educational choices and understanding the admissions process.

1. OBSERVE YOUR CHILD

Although it is difficult for parents to be unbiased about their children, I suggest that you step back and think about your child as

---

Diane Dunning Trunzo is director of admissions at St. Agnes School in Alexandria, Virginia. She is also the 1989–90 chair of the Association of Independent Schools of the Greater Washington Area Admission Steering Committee. Previous experience includes ten years of teaching in public and independent schools. She is the mother of two young sons.

objectively as possible. It might help to imagine yourself as an anthropologist using the technique of a "participant observer."

While observing your child, consider the following questions:

- What activities does your child find interesting or enjoyable?
- In what areas does your child seem to excel?
- What tasks does your child find difficult or unpleasant?
- What style of learning seems most comfortable for your child?
- How does your child interact in small and large peer groups?

Share your observations with other trusted adults who know your child such as current teachers, day care providers, relatives, and friends. Discuss the consistencies and discrepancies in your perceptions.

This exercise is an essential first step to all that follows. Understanding your child's strengths and needs will allow you to determine which schools can challenge those strengths and nurture those weaknesses, while simultaneously building self-esteem.

2. DO YOUR HOMEWORK EARLY

Many parents are surprised to discover how early most families apply. Generally, you need to begin the formal application process the fall before you hope to enroll your child. Some parents find it helpful to do preliminary homework before the time comes to submit an application.

You should call the admissions office to request a school catalogue and inquire about any upcoming open house or similar events. Other sources of valuable information are the recommendations of friends and colleagues, educational consultants, and independent school directories.

When reviewing the materials and recommendations, consider the following questions:

- What is the overall philosophy of the school?
- Is the approach traditional or progressive?
- What academic and extracurricular programs are offered?

- What are the qualifications of the faculty? Of the head of the school?
- What other services are available: Financial aid? Loans? Monthly payment plans? Transportation? Extended day?

Gathering answers to these questions will help you to narrow the options you consider appropriate for your child and your family.

3. VISIT SEVERAL SCHOOLS

Most of the information you collect through your reading and conversations will be reliable. However, it is unwise to base your judgment on reputation or one family's perception of a school. A personal visit is a must.

To arrange your visit, call the admissions office in advance to make an appointment. Some schools set up individual tours; others schedule group tours for specific dates. (Be sure to ask whether your child should accompany you on these visits.) Keep in mind your child's age and personality. Some children enjoy going to new places while others feel overwhelmed, especially if they visit too many schools in a short time span. Most schools require the child to visit once an application has been submitted.

During a school visit, consider:

- How comfortable do you feel in this school environment?
- Do children and staff appear happy and enthusiastic about learning?
- Could you imagine your child working with the students and teachers you see?
- Does the written philosophy seem consistent with what you observe?
- Are there specific topics for which you need clarification or confirmation?

Trust your instincts. Each school has a distinct "feel" and only a personal visit will enable you to experience the intangible qualities that comprise the emotional atmosphere of a school.

4. UNDERSTAND THE PROCESS

In order for a child to be considered for admission, most independent schools require: a formal application, an interview and/or visit, standardized testing, written teacher and personal recommendations, and the child's current school record. Admission decisions are typically made by an admissions committee comprised of administrators and teachers who review all of the information submitted. Decision letters are generally mailed in March.

What matters most?

All parts of the process matter but no one piece of information is *the* most important piece. Making judgments about young children is always a complex and difficult task. Admissions officers have responded by developing a careful and thorough process. This process allows the admissions committee to identify candidates who are most likely to flourish in their particular school environment and to determine whether their school can meet the candidates' needs.

What happens in the interview?

Interviews provide valuable information but rarely determine the decision. I advise parents to prepare children by explaining that you are visiting schools as a family to decide which ones might be best for yours. Let your child know that an adult at the school will want to get to know each child and may ask general questions about interests, school, and family life. As parents, you should be prepared to portray your child's strengths and needs honestly and to articulate what you hope a school will provide for your child.

How is testing used?

Standardized testing and informal batteries measure a child's school readiness (for kindergarten and first grade) and cognitive abilities and achievement levels in reading and mathematics (for older students). One low score would not cause immediate rejection, nor would one high score guarantee acceptance. In most cases, test results are consistent with a pattern of development evident in other portions of a candidate's folder. Each school knows the range of scores that predict success in its program. Therefore, performance on admissions tests is used judiciously by the admissions committee to make an appropriate match between a candidate and the program offered.

Are additional recommendations helpful?

Padding a child's folder with numerous personal recommendations, or one from a well-known person who is basically unfamiliar with your child, is not advisable. In fact, it can be a red flag. One thoughtful letter from someone who genuinely knows your child is much more effective. Most independent schools guarantee the confidentiality of teacher recommendations and therefore do not make these accessible to parents.

5. KEEP YOUR PERSPECTIVE

Being a parent of two young children, I recognize how difficult it is to maintain perspective about one's offspring. Remember however, that not every school is right for every child. It is critical that a child never be made to feel that only one school is acceptable. As we are all aware, children are astute interpreters of their parents' feelings. If a parent truly views admissions as a matchmaking process, the child probably will feel the same way. A parent's approach, along with a school's sensitivity, can protect a child from any undue pressure.

If your child is not offered a place at a particular school, it may be a blessing in disguise. When a chosen school cannot meet the specific needs of a child, the child will pay the cost academically and emotionally. This is true even if the school has an outstanding reputation or the child is a highly motivated student.

On the positive side, information gained during the admissions process may prove invaluable for all future educational planning. Some parents feel a tremendous sense of relief when they are able to identify the source of a learning difficulty they have suspected. On many occasions, I have been touched by parents who overcome deep disappointment about a decision by focusing on their child and taking the necessary steps to address the needs that were revealed.

Although admissions professionals spend enormous amounts of time and care trying to make the best match between school and child, other factors also influence decisions.

From a given applicant pool, the admissions committee attempts to create a class that is balanced in gender and/or age, that is diverse, and in which all the skills of individual children mesh as a group. In addition, many schools give some preference to siblings or legacies. Because an admissions committee uses both explicit and intuitive measures, mistakes are also inevitable.

It is therefore possible that a qualified child may not be admitted for reasons beyond the control of parents. It helps to accept this as a reality that accompanies competition for limited spaces. A family's choices may be altered by an admissions decision but they will never be eliminated.

Having worked through the admissions process with numerous families, I firmly believe that viewing the process as an art of match-making will serve the best interest of the child as well as reduce the anxiety families may feel when applying to an independent school. After all, we are all in this together to ensure that each child receives the best education parents and schools can provide.

Learning Styles and School Styles

Patricia S. Lemer

With more than 300 private schools and 5 jurisdictions to choose from in the metropolitan Washington, D.C., area, one of the most important factors that must be considered in making a placement is a child's learning style. By the time a child is four or five, his preferences for some activities over others are clearly defined. We all know the child who can sit and color for hours, staying neatly within the lines of preprinted coloring books, and making the sky blue, the trees green, and people's hair brown or yellow. This child's style is quite different from the one who prefers blank paper, magic markers, paste, and stickers to make his *own* pictures. With blocks and Legos™, some children make marvelously creative constructions tapping into their own imagination, while others are justly proud of copying the model pictured on the box. Then there is the child who cannot sit still for more than two minutes to draw or build anything and prefers riding his bicycle for hours, running around the yard, and going back and forth from one end of the playground to the other. And there is the little scientist who before he enters kindergarten can classify rocks and dinosaurs at a high school level and read maps accurately. There are children who love to be read to, and there are others who wiggle and squirm while you're reading and want to look at the book themselves. There are those who jabber to themselves and others as they play, and there are those who are quiet for so long that you are sure they are either dead or doing something awful, like fingerpainting on the walls.

Patricia S. Lemer, M.Ed., has been in private practice for more than 10 years as a diagnostician and advocate for children experiencing school problems. She is the mother of a 15-year-old daughter.

One of the luxuries of living in a large city is that just as children have their individual styles, so do schools. This is usually a result of the administration, the board of trustees, the location, and the physical plant. One can assume with some certainty that a school with a dress code (or uniforms) is somewhat more traditional in its approach to instruction than one without such constraints. A school with desks lined up neatly in rows, with the teacher engaging all of the students together will be a better fit for the child who can sit for lengthy periods of time than the wiggleworm. Conversely, bright students who provide their own sense of structure and have good organizational skills often do better in a less traditional school, where they are given the opportunity to discover things on their own. In fact, in an environment that is too structured, they feel stifled, and the chance for rebellion in response to too much authority is pretty high. An urban school with a small campus is less likely to have a strong athletics program to accommodate the needs of a budding trophy winner. On the other hand, a school in the suburbs with acres of playing fields may not venture out on field trips to the Smithsonian Institution or the Kennedy Center as frequently as one on Capitol Hill or Connecticut Avenue.

In general, there are four types of learners requiring four different styles of teaching to accommodate their unique approaches to materials. However, no child or school has one pure style; a variety of preferences are evidenced from subject to subject, teacher to teacher, student to student, and grade to grade.

1. The *highly focused, goal-oriented student* can learn almost anywhere you drop him. He sits still for lengthy periods of time and does what is expected. He likes rules and is responsive to worksheets, drill, memorization, and recitation. His favorite subjects are math, science, and geography, and his arts and crafts projects are not too original. He hates subjects for which he sees no use. He thrives in a traditional school that may be parochial and/or have a dress code. He does well with his own desk, is usually quiet and hard-working. In a school for him, children are usually all working on the same assignment at the same time. Grades are given, and teachers "take off for spelling." Handwriting is an individual subject, and papers must be neat or done over if they are not. Walls hold art, but many of the pictures look the same.

2. The *cerebral, budding scientist* is the type of student whose favorite word is "why." He loves to explore possibilities, find new ways to use materials, classify information, and discover the answer. He is

likely to argue frequently with the teacher, and will drive a traditional teacher who is trying to follow a lesson plan crazy and make her feel stupid. He loves playing with words, finding the quickest way to do a math problem in his head, hates drill and subjects that are repetitious and "boring" (another one of his favorite words).

The school for this student bustles with noise and activity. Rather than children sitting at individual desks, one may see tables. There are examples of what is being studied all around: globes, maps, hornets' nests, abacuses, large pads for creative writing. The teacher may split a large group into smaller units to discover a principle or to create a project. There may be much talking, with the teacher walking around supervising. Grades are dependent on content, not mechanics; the teacher may or may not care about handwriting and spelling.

3. Another type of student is more *people-oriented* than subject- or object-conscious. This student needs a warm, harmonious learning environment. He will like a subject if he likes the teacher and thinks the teacher likes him. The atmosphere must be democratic and allow for group discussions, role playing, and drama. It is not easy for this particular student to memorize. He loves creative writing and hates math. He needs to be respected, listened to, and—above all else—loved. Music, art, poetry, and drama are inherent parts of the science, social studies, and reading programs. Assemblies take place frequently, and children are hugged and kissed for excellent performances. There is a casualness and a lack of concern about time, as opposed to people, and sometimes parts of a planned curriculum might not happen if another unit on something exciting exceeds its allotted time. Grading is based primarily on effort, not product. Children are given an opportunity to be themselves, be immature, and take time to grow up.

4. Finally, there is the student who is the most misunderstood child in the classroom, who must *learn by doing.* He needs hands-on experience; he must live a subject to make it meaningful. All the lectures and textbooks are wasted on him without projects, objects, and machines. If forced to learn by listening rather than doing, he will become the class clown, the drifter, or the one who appears not to care. Because he is "hands-on" by nature, he loves P.E., art, and theater. The school for him offers unlimited experiences. Field trips are frequent. Reenacting the Civil War or Edison's experiments with electricity takes the place of reading about these events. Math is learned by cutting, cooking, measuring, playing store, and using a calendar or clock. The reading and writing curricula are not separate

from those of the content subjects. If a student participates, whatever he does is acceptable. There may be no grades at all. Teachers are often part-time and experts in their fields. Learning by doing permeates the school.

To repeat, no student or school is purely one type, and the best schools have components of each style to accommodate each type of learner. But, if you look carefully at both your child and an individual school, you will find a dominant style that will help you make a match. It is paramount that a student be in a place where he feels comfortable. A child who is in the wrong type of school can hurt as much as a child in ill-fitting shoes.

Last, keep in mind that one of the most difficult placements for a traditional parent to make is to put a less traditional learner in an unstructured learning environment. Frequently, parents will say, "He has to learn to conform eventually; he might as well learn now!" This is not true. For a child marching to a different drummer, placing him in an authoritarian school could not only make him a reluctant learner, but damage his self-esteem as well. Not all wiggleworms need structure; many do well without it. A rose in a school for daffodils will not become a daffodil, but rather a wilted rose! Respect your child's own style, and be grateful that you have so many options that you can be sure to make a good match for him.

If Your Child is . . ., Then . . .

Patricia O. Quinn, M.D.

In choosing a school it is always important to seek as good a match for your child as possible. The following are some suggestions of things to look for as you make your school observations.

If your child is active or needs space, look closely at:

size of classroom
playground equipment
amount of time for active play
individual workspace/desk
flexibility of teacher

If your child is disorganized, look closely at:

existing structure/routine
amount of independent work
organization of teacher
amount of time spent waiting

Patricia O. Quinn, M.D., is a developmental pediatrician who has practiced in the Washington area since 1972. She was formerly Director of Medicine at Georgetown University Child Development Center. Dr. Quinn specializes in child development and psychopharmacology. In her private practice, she sees high-risk infants and young children and follows patients through their school years. Dr. Quinn works extensively in the areas of attention deficit disorder, hyperactivity, learning disabilities, and mental retardation, and has published widely in these fields.

If your child is creative, look closely at:

amount of routine/free play
creative use of toys
amount of student-directed activities

If your child is distractable, look closely at:

number of children in class
individual desk/workspace
quiet, organized setting
amount of clutter

If your child is quiet, or needs positive feedback, look closely at:

tone of program
comments on displayed papers
temperament of other children
encouragement by teacher

If your child is slow in fine motor area, look closely at:

amount of writing per day
type of artwork expected
availability of computer

If your child is mildly learning disabled, look closely at:

adaptability/flexibility of program
creative teaching strategies
individualized instruction

In general, is the teacher approachable . . . professional . . . encouraging . . . flexible . . . organized . . . respectful . . . touching . . . How does she give directions? . . . . What is her tone of voice? . . . Does she make eye contact?

Look at books, worksheets, dittos, availability of equipment and books to the children. . . . How are holidays celebrated? . . . What is the amount of parent involvement? . . . . How is science taught (hands on/dittos/books/nature walks, etc.)?

Look at notes on the board, comments on papers. . . . How is the classroom arranged (desks vs. tables, organized space vs. clutter, etc.)?

Were all the children in the class the same and would your child fit in?

In all of this, remember you are looking for a program where both you and your child feel comfortable. You know your child better than anyone. Trust your instincts, as a parent, when making your choices. Don't be pressured by tradition, convenience, family, friends, or a school's reputation. There is a school for each child.

In conclusion, no decision is final, and if a school isn't right for whatever reasons, you can and should be willing to change. Be open, explore, and above all have fun!

Ready for Kindergarten? Simple Tests to Help You Decide

Victoria Y. Rab

I still remember my first day of kindergarten. My mother and my aunt walked me to school. The building was enormous and the hall seemed endless. When we got to the door of the classroom, I took one look and ran. My aunt, who was the more experienced parent, bribed me back with a pack of Lifesavers. My teacher was very nice but it didn't make any difference. With Lloyd, another reluctant recruit, I stood next to her and cried all morning. Was I ready for kindergarten? Did my mother make the right decision? My birthday is in late September so my mother did not have to send me.

I went on to enjoy kindergarten and was not bothered by being one of the youngest in my class. But what was the right decision for me might not have been right for another child. And times have changed; kindergarten is different. In 1962 only 50 percent of U.S. five-year-olds went to kindergarten. Today, it is the rare child who does not attend. In addition, many children have had one or more years of day care or nursery school and some of the concepts that used to be taught in kindergarten are now covered in preschool. As a result, many parents look for kindergarten to go beyond what their children have already learned. Children learn numbers and letters and are often reading by the end of the year.

How can you tell if your child is ready for kindergarten this year or if it would be better to wait another year?

Parents often ask me: Should he know his colors and letters? (Most

---

Victoria Rab, M.Ed., is a child development specialist with Children's Medical Associates, Inc., Alexandria, Virginia, and director of a federally funded in-service training project at George Washington University. She is the mother of two daughters, 9 and 12.

do.) Should he be able to tie his shoes? (Not necessarily—many learn in kindergarten.) Should he be interested in reading? (Some are reading when they start school; others have little interest in even trying.) Should he be able to play unsupervised with other children? (Yes, for short periods of time.)

But even these factors are only part of the answer. One often-neglected element is the importance of a good "match" between the abilities of the child and the expectations of the kindergarten. For example, will your child be expected to read by the end of kindergarten or is the emphasis on socialization and developmentally appropriate tasks?

When I visit a kindergarten, children are frequently working in small groups. The teacher moves from group to group providing assistance as needed, but the children are expected to work independently. Most children are intent on their tasks but some of them look lost. They may be playing with a button on their sweater, sucking their thumb, or poking the child next to them.

My youngest child Lisa went to kindergarten when she was five and a half. She had enjoyed preschool and I felt confident that she was ready. On the second day she came home with a tummy ache. This continued for several days. We went to the pediatrician who, to my horror, diagnosed "school phobia." After several long discussions, Lisa told me that the teacher had put her in a group with three very loud and disruptive boys. She was frightened. A conversation with the teacher resulted in a move to a more sedate group, and Lisa began to love school.

As you consider all possibilities, remember that the decision you make need not be irrevocable. Although it is easier to choose right the first time, it is always possible to withdraw your child or change schools if things are not going well.

There are a few simple tests to help you decide whether your child is ready for kindergarten. The key considerations are:

- degree of social maturity
- attention span
- distractability
- memory
- level of preacademic skills

- ability to understand and follow directions
- ability to play without too much supervision
- summer or fall birthdate

SOCIAL MATURITY

One of the first things to consider as you think about your child's readiness for kindergarten is his degree of social maturity. Watching your child with other children and adults can give you valuable information about his personal style of interaction. How does he get along with other adults? Can he tell another adult about his activities and accomplishments? How does he play with other children? How does he negotiate disagreements with other children? Is he comfortable playing with one child but shy in larger groups? How does he behave at his friends' birthday parties? Is he comfortable without a parent close by? Can he choose his own play activities at home and play by himself?

Josh was five years old in May. He has wanted to go to school since he was two. At the neighborhood pool he told anyone who would listen, "My name is Josh; this is my lunchbox, and I'm going to kindergarten." Josh had a great time with his friends playing soccer on the lawn, buying ice cream, and splashing each other in the pool. He was obviously ready.

At age four, Emily went to nursery school. In the carpool she never talked to the other children. At school she played only in the dress-up corner. On the playground she stood and watched the other children. Yet each day when her mom asked about school, Emily was effusive. She loved school. She couldn't understand why she couldn't go on weekends. Emily, too, although she has a different personal style, will probably do well in kindergarten.

Being either a social butterfly or a shy wallflower is not necessarily positive or negative. Rather, you want your child to develop the social skills needed to negotiate a variety of situations. Watch what happens at a friend's birthday party. If your child stands by herself and watches the party activities, you might be concerned. Afterwards, if she tells you that she just didn't feel like playing with all of those new children right away, you would be less concerned. You want to know that your child is aware of her feelings and can talk about them. This means that when your child gets angry at a party or at home she can say that she's angry before she grabs the toy. She can tell her friend not to push rather than shoving back or crying to her mother each time. Children differ as much as adults do in the way they handle themselves in social situations.

Josh is always the life of the party. He walks in the door announcing, "I'm here!" and off he goes. Jennifer walks in the door clinging to her mother's leg. Thirty minutes later she still hasn't budged. When her mother urges her to play, she clings more tightly and begins to cry. Emily, too, stays close to her mother. But when she sees another child she knows, she joins the party, checking every now and then to make sure her mother is still there.

Clearly, Josh has the social skills he will need for kindergarten. Emily may also, but she will need the patient support of her mother and teacher. But Jennifer, who is overwhelmed in a new situation, may not be ready. She may need more time before she is able to be on her own confidently.

ATTENTION SPAN, DISTRACTABILITY, AND MEMORY

Attention span, distractability, and memory are important for kindergarten success. A review of research studies on the warning signs of school failure by Marvin Simner suggests that a child who has difficulties in these areas may have problems in kindergarten.

- Is your child able to focus his attention on one thing and ignore distractions?
- Can he remember and follow a series of at least three directions?
- Does he have a good memory for details in stories?
- Can he tell you easily and precisely about past activities and events?
- If he goes to preschool, does he participate eagerly and enthusiastically?

PREACADEMIC SKILLS

If you answer no to more than one of the following questions, you might want to consult your child's teacher or your pediatrician.

- Can he recognize more than five upper-case letters?

- Can he recognize the numbers one through nine?
- Does he talk about abstract concepts? (For example, is he interested in how engines work, or why airplanes fly?)
- Can he copy several letters or numbers correctly?

UNDERSTANDING AND FOLLOWING DIRECTIONS

Your child has probably been able to follow simple directions since he was little more than a year old. He could bring you his shoes or get the ball any time you asked. By age three or four, your child probably developed selective hearing. While he understood what you asked, he may not have responded. So while he understood such specific requests as, "Put your shoes and coat on so we can leave" or "Finish your breakfast, we're late for school," he did not cooperate all the time.

In kindergarten, directions are given to the whole class—"Put your crayons away and go get your coats." Children need to be able to listen and understand directions given to a group, and they must be able to remember more than one direction at a time.

If your child is in preschool, you can ask the teacher about his ability in this area. At home you might try these easy tests: From another room, ask your child to bring you your shoes or some other object. For example, you might be in the kitchen and ask your child, who is in the living room, to bring you your slippers and the broom. Ask your child to help put away the toys, wash his hands, and come for a snack. Routines without reminders will be part of everyday life in school.

PLAYING WITHOUT SUPERVISION

Your child should be able to play in groups of twos and threes with minimal adult supervision and intervention. He should be able to understand and follow simple rules of behavior. For example, you might overhear him tell a friend firmly, "No grabbing, I had it first."

BIRTHDATE

Despite the clues you might get from all these tests, age seems to be the best predictor of a child's early school performance. The surprising finding of educational researchers is that the most important factor in a child's success in kindergarten is chronological age—the older the child, the better he does. In kindergarten through second grade, these differences are very noticeable. This means, generally, that a five-year-old with an earlier birthday is likely to do better than a five-year-old whose birthday is close to the cutoff date for kindergarten. Some children are reading by the end of kindergarten while others don't read until second grade. These differences in academic skills seem much less noticeable by third grade.

Kindergarten teachers in general seem pleased by the trend to send children to kindergarten later. They feel that children who are older are generally more successful. Many parents are also comfortable with waiting. One mother whose son is now in second grade told me, "There was a period when I thought we'd made a mistake, but now I'm so happy we waited." At age four her son Andrew was in a preschool program and was doing well. But he was rather small for his age and somewhat quiet. His parents began to realize that he didn't have to go to kindergarten in the fall. Andrew's father had a December birthday and regretted that he had been sent to school early. Andrew's parents were able to find a school that had a prekindergarten program that Andrew loved. Now in second grade, Andrew is not the oldest in his class nor is he bored. His teacher gives him research projects when he finishes his work early, and Andrew finds his homework a breeze. When asked if she worried about Andrew being bored, his mother replied, "I don't believe that. He still likes to listen to the stories I read to his younger brother even though he can read them by himself."

I asked one teacher if she had ever had a child who was bored, or who she felt should have attended kindergarten earlier. She answered with an unqualified no. "There is so much for them to learn," she said. "They broaden their understanding." She feels strongly that the curriculum is varied and flexible enough to accommodate even the academically advanced child.

This teacher does not hesitate to retain children who she feels are not ready for the first grade. She believes that another year of kindergarten is better than an unsuccessful year in first grade. She says that the children she has held back go on to do well and suffer no ill effects. However, some researchers disagree. A study in *American Educator* (Summer, 1988) by Lorrie A. Shepard, chairman of research and evaluation methodology at the University of Colorado, and Mary Lee Smith of Arizona State University, shows that children do suffer emotionally and socially by being held back in kindergarten. They argue that children should be promoted because retaining them "does nothing to boost their subsequent academic achievement." They also feel that many kindergarten curricula are inappropriate in their emphasis on early reading and academics. They suggest that if the curriculum were more appropriate, fewer children would fail.

Some children seem "over ready" for kindergarten and present their own kinds of dilemmas for the concerned parent. These children may already be starting to read even though they will not be five until close to the kindergarten cutoff date. Parents ask me:

- If I don't send her to kindergarten this year, won't she be bored?
- If I don't send her to kindergarten this year, won't she be behind academically?
- If she goes this year and doesn't do well, can't she just repeat kindergarten?

These are important questions, but more information is needed before they can be answered.

- Has she attended a preschool or play group? If so, did she enjoy it?
- What recommendation has her teacher made?
- Are her friends going to kindergarten?
- Is a transition program available?
- How old will the average child in her kindergarten class be?
- What does the kindergarten teacher or school principal advise?

If she enjoyed preschool, her teacher concurs, and she will not be the youngest in her class, kindergarten may be appropriate. But if you and her teacher are not sure and there is a good prekindergarten or transition program available, it might be wise to wait another year.

ACTIVITIES YOU CAN DO WITH YOUR CHILD

Few parents are in a position to change what is taught in kindergarten. What you can do is help your child develop the skills necessary for success in kindergarten. Allow him the time to mature socially and emotionally so that when he approaches the kindergarten experience with eagerness and enthusiasm you know he is ready.

One of the things you can do is play with your child. Stanley Greenspan, author of *First Feelings*, recommends something called "floor time." This means getting down on the floor, allowing the child to choose the toys or activities, and playing for 15 to 20 minutes. The child leads, the parent follows. The only rules are no hitting and no breaking. The time belongs to the child. It gives him an opportunity to initiate activities and your interest helps him follow through.

Creating stories with your child can help him develop the memory and thinking skills he will need to read. This can be as simple as both of you telling about what happened when you went to the zoo. Or it can become an elaborate series of imaginative adventures. My father used to tell me bedtime stories about Morris the Monkey. I still remember his adventures in the Ungle Bungle Jungle.

Coloring with fat crayons and finger painting will help your child develop the small muscles in his hands and fingers that he will need for writing. Encourage him to draw people and shapes rather than letters and numbers.

Of course, books are always a wonderful way to teach your child about the joys of reading. The books should be about things that interest your child. Some fairy tales may be too abstract or scary for a preschool child. All of the Dr. Seuss books were favorites of my daughters. Reading to your child should be a special time. You can read at dinner, bedtime, or any other quiet moment.

In summary, with an open mind and careful consideration of your child's social development, you will be prepared to make the best decision for your preschooler. Kindergarten, whether now or later, should be a successful, secure experience.

Making Order Out of the Jungle Gym: Not Just a School's Job!

Missy Janes

Busy parents with stressful, demanding schedules are finding it important for the school selection process to focus on issues of philosophy and style. School does provide the routine and the academic programs to safely tame our toddler tigers and further refine their skills for success as civilized citizens. Parents have a great responsibility, however, to share the process with their child's school. Quality and order come to the jungle gym when each child's education is seen as a daily partnership between home and school. Perhaps this precept is useful to keep in mind when looking for a school.

Every day, parents lead their little untamed ones through a variety of adventures. As guides, they may be cautious or daring, creative or practical, witty or pedantic. Whatever their style may be, the safari is a memorable experience. Ask yourself if it is consistent at home and at school.

By seizing the moment, parents create fun and make mystery, music, or even math of seemingly mundane opportunities. They can take advantage of their magical qualities and turn a who, what, when, where, why question into an exciting team investigation. They can develop curious minds by asking "what if," and choreographing a made-up problem using organized and logical steps. A positive attitude

---

Missy Janes a native of Middleburg, Virginia, earned a degree in Elementary Education from Goucher College in Baltimore. Her teaching experience includes work with children with communication disorders, hospitalized infants, and toddlers. She was the Art Coordinator at the National Geographic Society until leaving to start her own company in children's wear. She lives in Washington, D.C. with her husband and two small children.

toward learning grows outside of school as much as, and sometimes more than, in school.

A slightly creative or unusual approach, a sense of humor, a touch of the ridiculous, or a case of simple curiosity can motivate almost anyone. Would you or the school you are considering, go for a walk in the rain? Would you draw in the mud or discuss evaporation? Breaking into song at the height of controversy or in the doldrums of a long drive is effective at changing a mood and can jolt the creative juices while at the same time calling on memory, rhyming, and cadence. Are you thinking of creative ways to deal with behavior and transitions? Does the school you are visiting? The point is to leap a step ahead and inspire curiosity, resourcefulness, and organization by our own example. Listen, ask questions, and talk to those capable little apprentices and they will develop into good communicators. Give them a chance to make choices and to make mistakes. By being grateful and genuine, and showing trust, you will help them gain confidence and a sense of self.

But given the fact that parents must turn their progeny over to the teachers, again the question arises, which school is best for my child?

Take one very busy playground and examine its contents. Kids are happy doing what kids do best—playing hard while learning. Digging in piles of sand, swinging like monkeys, roaring like lions, singing like birds, they are busy at primitive tasks but absorbing information about themselves, their environment, and their effect on others.

Here is an opportunity to identify some valuable characteristics concerning your child's unique character and behavior. How do other children relate to your child and what is his or her response? Do unfamiliar adults or children illicit different reactions? What distinguishes their manner, vocabulary, eye contact, and so on? In what situations does your child feel most relaxed, interested, and inspired? Does he or she prefer focusing on play with one friend in one corner of the sandbox or galloping around the entire play space with a gang of friends? Is your child more comfortable with set rules and boundaries or happier with less rigidity? Make a test of your judgments by matching various style categories with different children you can easily observe. Ask their parent where they happen to go to school and whether they feel it has been a good choice for such a personality. What other activities, places, household habits have been successful?

In the process of figuring out what makes your own children tick, and while evaluating the pros and cons of various schools, it is also a good time to ask yourself if you are doing the most you can outside of school. Extra activities can provide valuable opportunities for learning a new skill, making special friendships, or relating to a non-academic role model. Quiet time and free play at home can be a time to unwind, escape the conflicts of a group, and provide a chance to construct something without interruptions of other children or routine. The whole picture is what really counts for each child. There are many transitions in a day of seemingly mundane proportions of time which can be used to advantage.

Parents have a big responsibility! Our job spans all of the transitions in a day, a year, and a life. Quality and order come to the jungle gym when each child's education is seen as a partnership between home and school while a caring, respectful relationship is developed and cultivated between parent and child.

Keep in mind the following jungle juice recipe and ask yourself whether the schools you are visiting are measuring the ingredients appropriately for you and your child:

- Love those wild tigers.
- Respect and support the cautious and daring lions.
- Stay open-minded and flexible for those birds of a different feather.
- Laugh and have fun with all those curious, silly little monkeys. The taming is tedious; the rewards are worth it!

Benefits of a Public School Education and How to Improve It

Judith Denton Jones

Parents who place a high value on education can influence their local school's program to ensure that it is academically challenging. Children learn a great deal about each other, about diversity of family backgrounds, and about tolerance for others in a well-run public school. These experiences are an important part of their growing up, and are important ingredients in the development of their future world view and practice of citizenship.

Given the complex social problems facing adults in our country, it is important to educate children in an environment that exposes them to social diversity and encourages them to learn tolerance and caring for others. Even if public schools in some areas do not have all the facilities of the "best" private schools, or as many good teachers as in the "best" private schools, that does not mean that public education is not the "best." The ingredients of the "best" education include the development of neighborhood ties, social tolerance, and leadership abilities, not just academic competitiveness and social exclusivity. In the long run, we need to judge our schools by their output of socially concerned and technically competent citizens.

Over the past ten years, the Washington, D.C., public school system has shown flexibility and a willingness to improve in response to parental pressure and educational crisis. Parents who have participated in these efforts have had the satisfaction of seeing educational

---

Judith Denton Jones is an urban sociologist with experience in policy planning, evaluation studies, and community research. She has taught at American and George Washington universities and is the author of *Six School Complex: A Successful Innovation in Washington, D.C. Public Schools*.

quality improve not only for their own children, but also for many other children in the city. While not everyone can become a parent activist, it is amazing how small contributions by many parents add up to significant change over time.

Within the D.C. public schools significant progress has occurred over the past decade in offering both better quality programs and a wider variety of educational options. D.C. pioneered early childhood education in the early 1970s when it established half-day prekindergarten programs for four-year-olds. Prekindergarten is now a full-day program and DCPS hopes to extend it to three-year-olds in the near future. In cooperation with the Department of Human Services, DCPS has established several therapeutic nurseries for handicapped two- and three-year-olds in school buildings.

Implementation of the competency-based curriculum, which began in 1978, has led to large gains in student achievement at the elementary level, as well as providing a system of teacher accountability. DCPS, along with many other school systems, is now working to improve the curriculum for older children in order to teach them better cognitive and critical thinking skills. School systems are also looking at ways of restructuring schools to encourage friendlier, more stimulating environments where personal relationships among students and teachers can be fostered more easily.

In a large metropolitan area where schools do vary in their ability to train students well both academically and socially, how should parents proceed to find and help develop good schools? Moving to an area whose schools have a reputation for being "good" may not be a feasible or desirable option for many families. In the Washington, D.C., metropolitan area, a number of options exist, depending on a family's location. There are magnet schools, alternative schools, citywide programs, and clusters of schools for which enrollment does not depend strictly on living in a defined school boundary. Montgomery and Prince George's (P.G.) counties have established several magnet schools, and variations on "gifted and talented" programs are often available. In P.G. County, there are a K-8 creative and performing arts magnet school in Landover; Montessori classes in three public schools; the Academic Center at Beltsville; four traditional/classical academies; a science, mathematics, and technology program at six elementary schools; two French immersion schools; and a talented and gifted program at eight different elementary schools. D.C. schools allow parents to request "special permission" to send children to an elementary or junior high school outside their residential districts.

Unfortunately, due to increasing enrollment at some elementary schools, the new options may not be available to all applicants.

Before parents turn away from public schools, I urge them to look carefully and realistically at their children's needs, and at the options and alternatives that might be available. The effort you extend on behalf of your own child's education may also enrich the lives of other children in the metropolitan area for years to come.

Parents should make the effort to visit local schools personally to judge the quality of teaching and learning, rather than rely on rumor, reputation, or second-hand knowledge from neighbors. I especially urge visiting with an open mind because of the pervasive anxiety about urban public education that exists in Washington as well as in other urban areas. Such anxieties tend to influence people's attitudes negatively, so that evidence to the contrary is never sought or, if it is available, is ignored. Perceptions of the quality of education at the junior and senior high school levels seem to affect parental decisions about enrolling or keeping their children in public elementary schools, yet these perceptions are often based on hearsay. Personal investigation is essential, and so are perhaps discussions with neighboring families in areas where large numbers of children attend private schools.

Shifting demographic patterns will continue to affect our public education system, as the challenge to promote greater ethnic and racial integration in some areas grows with the expected increase in children from Hispanic, Asian, and black families over the next 20 years. In addition, the U.S. Census Bureau predicts a significant increase in net migration to the area from 1990 to 2010, resulting in a continuing increase in school-age children, even after the passing of the "baby boomlet" wave through high school around the year 2000. Most of the families and workers moving to the metropolitan area over the next 20 years are expected to settle in the suburbs, especially those in the so-called outer ring, although all jurisdictions are expected to experience significant population growth.

During these decades we will be faced with continued in-migration of foreign refugees, growth of poverty among female-head households of all races, growing discrepancies of income and opportunities among families, and a decreasing percentage of children in our society. All of these trends highlight the need to improve the education that the majority of children will experience, so that they can become well-educated, socially caring individuals capable of helping to solve pressing social problems.

Strong and continued population growth creates significant opportunities for parents to influence the development of public education in their neighborhoods. School boards should be looking at new ways to respond to growth, minimize transportation needs, manage ethnic group tensions, provide "choice" among programs, and meet the needs of society's extremes—the gifted and the impoverished students—as well as the average ones. Through the dedication of parents, teachers, and administrators, compassion and competence can be combined in public education programs, creating enhanced opportunity for all.

Pressure from parents to increase the number and variety of options is an important element in getting educational bureaucracies to change and improve. As long as a school has a "territorial monopoly," feedback from parents has less impact and competitive pressure from alternative programs is ignored more easily. Competitive pressure from other public schools can push principals and staff to improve the educational program, learning atmosphere, and even, to some extent, the maintenance of physical facilities.

There is considerable discussion among educators right now about expanding the choices parents have among various public school options. Efforts to increase choice are directed not only toward attracting a wider range of children to public schools, but also toward improving the quality and variety of educational programs available in public school systems.

The participation of parents from all social and racial strata is needed to help solve the difficult problems facing urban school systems today. And while not every parent can or should become an education activist, efforts to maintain and improve our public education programs will be necessary for increasing numbers of us, if the original and still important goals of universal free public education are to be achieved in the decades to come.

Admissions Testing

Patricia S. Lemer

Completing applications and sending a precious child off to be tested for admission to private schools can be two of the most anxiety-producing activities a parent can undergo—but they don't need to be. Once parents understand the process thoroughly, they can feel confident about where their child will fit best.

Admissions testing takes a variety of forms, depending on the age of the child and the style of the particular school being applied to. The general purpose of testing is to have a uniform measure by which to compare the performance of a child applying in a given grade with that of other applicants, as well as with students already in attendance. Individual schools have a good idea of which aptitudes and abilities will predict success in their environment.

For young children (ages three to six), most schools use the *McCarthy Scales of Children's Abilities*. Children do not view this as a test, and it should not be presented to them as such, but rather as appealing activities and games. The examiner is with a child for 45 minutes to an hour and asks him to do such things as answer questions, complete phrases, define simple words, draw a few figures, throw, catch, hop, skip, balance, build with blocks, and complete puzzles. These tasks evaluate the preschooler's evenness of development and readiness for academic materials.

In older children (those above age six) evaluation is somewhat more sophisticated and the student is more aware of being tested. Frequently a *Wechsler Intelligence Scale for Children* (WISC-R) or a *Wechsler Pre-School and Primary Scale of Intelligence* (WPPSI) is used. A child should be encouraged not to worry if there are things he cannot do. The format is basically the same as the McCarthy Scales: questions and answers as well as manipulative materials such as blocks and puzzles. In addition, the child may be asked to read, write, and complete some mathematical calculations.

Most schools use standardized evaluation instruments such as the *McCarthy*, *WPPSI*, and *WISC-R*, which yield standard scores and percentile ranks. Some, however, have compiled informal batteries containing bits and pieces of standardized tests that they have found to be good predictors of success in years past. If your child has been given any of the standardized instruments prior to application for admission, you may be able to avoid additional testing. Ask the examiner what to do before you sign up for another evaluation. A retest in less than a year invalidates results.

The location of the testing and availability of test results also vary from school to school. Some schools request that parents contact a central testing agency to have a child evaluated. In this case, the family pays a fee directly to the agency (usually about $75), and the agency forwards the results to the schools of the parent's choice. Other schools test on site, and the testing fee may be extra or included as part of the application fee. These schools will usually be happy to share results with other schools as well. Testing can also be done by a recognized private individual, who may charge slightly more but who can advise you on appropriate schools based on the results.

Ask a school, agency, or individual whether parents routinely receive a report of a child's testing, and, if so, when. This information can be helpful in making an informed decision. If results can only be obtained after the admissions process is over, it may be too late to apply elsewhere.

It is important to keep the testing in perspective; it is only one part of the application process. If a child does well, his acceptance is not assured. Similarly, if he does poorly, he is not eliminated outright. Other factors such as his personality, his teacher's comments, and his compatibility with current students are also taken into consideration.

Last, think positively. If a child is not admitted to a particular school, there may be good reasons. Testing may shed light on an area that needs some attention, and early intervention can be started. It would not be appropriate for a child to be in a school where he would not feel good about himself. The testing process will allow you to go forth as an informed consumer looking for the best match between your child and a nurturing learning environment.

The Financial Side of Independent Education

Diane R. Wilson

Independent education has many advantages. The fact that you are reading this book indicates that you are considering an alternative to public education for your child. The many benefits of independent education will quickly become evident to you as you read the articles in this guide and explore the individual school profiles. In fact, if you were to begin a list of the pluses and minuses of independent education, one of the very few minuses would be cost. Because independent education is not supported by local, state, or federal tax dollars, the burden of financing this sector falls to you, the product's consumer.

It is critical that you make your school decisions based first and foremost on the question, "Which school is going to be right for my child?" It is unrealistic of us in the independent sector of education, however, to deny the fact that you are also going to be asking yourself, "Can I afford this school once I've decided that it meets my child's educational needs?" This article is written to help educate you about the financial end of the school selection process. It will focus on three basic issues: how to find out about financial matters during the admissions process; what financial aid entails and how to enter the financial aid system; and how to assess any other financing options a school may offer.

Diane R. Wilson has been director of admissions and financial aid at the Sidwell Friends School in Washington, D.C., since 1984. Prior to that, she was director of admissions and financial aid at Hood College in Frederick, Maryland.

HOW TO FIND OUT ABOUT FINANCIAL MATTERS DURING THE ADMISSIONS PROCESS

Most schools have a section about costs, financial aid, and other financial issues in their general descriptive brochures. Some have a separate brochure about financial aid as well. This is the place to start your search for information about financial matters. Here are some questions that you shouldn't hesitate to ask an admissions officer as you discuss a particular institution:

What is your tuition this year? Is the kindergarten tuition higher than the prekindergarten tuition? Is the tuition for this year's first grade more than the kindergarten tuition? Most schools charge the least for PreK, more for K, and still more for grades 1 through 6.

How much has your tuition been increasing from year to year? What sort of percentage increases do you anticipate in the next few years? Most schools in the Washington area have been increasing their tuition rates by significantly more than the rate of inflation.

What does your tuition actually cover? What other fixed charges are there? What other expenses are involved? A school's tuition can cover instruction only, or it can include every cost the family incurs. Things to inquire about specifically include lunch costs, books and other supplies, and activity fees. You may also need to consider the cost of transportation, uniforms, social activities, etc.

What is your tuition payment schedule? Most independent schools require much more than 50 percent of the year's tuition by mid-July, if not sooner. Be sure you know when the first payment is due, as well as when the balance of the tuition is required.

What is your enrollment deposit? If your child is offered a place at a particular school, you will be expected to pay a deposit to hold his place. The earlier in the admissions season a child is accepted, the sooner you are going to have to pay this deposit. Some schools require only a few hundred dollars to hold the place; others charge more than $1,000. A large required deposit, plus a bill for 70 to 80 percent of the balance of the tuition due by July 1, can catch parents off guard the first year they are involved with the school.

What are your annual giving expectations? Many schools assess every family an annual giving charge. Others ask families to contribute to the extent that they are able. All schools hope that as many families as possible will contribute to the fund-raising initiatives of the school, as tuition revenues do not generate all the income needed to run the school in any given year.

Do you offer any sort of tuition discount plan for siblings? Some schools charge full tuition for the first child in a family enrolled in their school, and then less for siblings.

FINANCIAL AID PROGRAMS

The vast majority of independent schools are committed to having a diverse student body, and they intentionally seek students from varied economic backgrounds. Recognizing that all or part of a year's tuition will certainly be an economic impossibility for many families, schools offer financial assistance to those families they want in the school but who cannot afford to pay the entire cost. Financial assistance is frequently referred to as scholarships or financial aid. Scholarships are financial rewards for a particular strength that a student might possess, and they are not generally based on a family's need for the money. Most independent schools no longer offer scholarships to their students, especially in the elementary and middle school years. At the high school level, some schools do offer scholarships for academic achievement or athletic ability, among other talents.

Financial aid is awarded to a family based solely on its inability to pay all of the stated tuition. Receipt of financial aid should not feel like a stigma to the family receiving it. Schools know that not every family is going to be able to afford their total cost. They offer financial aid to make it possible for families from all economic levels to be part of the school community. Generally, very few members of the school community are aware of who the financial aid recipients are in a student body. No distinctions are made between financial aid recipients and other students.

Most financial aid programs are based on the belief that families have an obligation to pay the educational expenses of their children to the extent that they are able. The purpose of the financial aid program is to fill the gap between the actual cost of a year's tuition and what a family realistically can afford to pay.

To determine a family's contribution toward a year's expenses, most schools use the needs analysis service of the School and Student Service for Financial Assistance (SSS), based in Princeton, New Jersey. By filling out the Parent's Financial Statement of SSS, a family provides information about its income, assets, size, educational and other extraordinary expenses, retirement needs, etc. Every family applying for financial aid is evaluated according to the same criteria, thus providing an equitable base for the distribution of the school's resources. Once a family's income and assets are protected to provide for a modest standard of living as defined by the Bureau of Labor Statistics, a portion of any remaining resources may be expected to be available for school tuition. If a school determines that you are able to pay less than its tuition, it will try to offer you aid to help you with the remainder.

Questions you should keep in mind as you evaluate a particular school's financial aid program include:

Is the need for financial aid a factor in making admissions decisions? Most schools try to make what are called "need blind" admissions decisions. This means that they do not discriminate in their acceptances against families that might not be able to pay the full tuition.

Does your school have financial aid for prekindergarten, kindergarten, and/or elementary school age children? Many schools, particularly those that go beyond the early elementary years, have made the decision to make their aid dollars accessible to the older children in their school. This may mean that they have very limited, if any, aid available for the youngest members of the school community.

What forms are required to apply for financial aid? Most schools will use the Parents Financial Statement of the School and Student Service for Financial Assistance. Some will ask you to send your completed form to Princeton; others will want to send it directly to their financial aid officer. Some schools also have their own financial aid application form, which asks specific questions not asked on the Princeton form. Almost all schools also require a copy of your most recent IRS 1040 form, to verify the income information you have provided on your Parents' Financial Statement.

What are the financial aid deadlines? Applying early, and definitely before any published deadlines, is crucial in order to be considered for financial aid. Most schools will want to have paperwork submitted well before March 1 of the year for which you are applying.

Is financial aid offered to every family that qualifies for it? Some schools have very limited funds and they are not able to award assistance to all students who qualify. If this is the case, how are distinctions made as to who receives aid and who does not?

If my child is accepted, when can I expect to hear about financial aid? Some schools will notify you of your financial aid award in the acceptance letter. Others wait until later in the spring before notifying you of any aid award. No school should require you to pay an enrollment deposit until it has informed you of your financial aid position.

FINANCING OPTIONS BEYOND FINANCIAL AID

Recognizing that many families who can afford to pay their tuition may have cash flow problems or other situations that make it difficult for them to adhere to the school's tuition payment schedule, most independent schools offer a variety of payment plans and financing options for parents. These include noninterest-charging monthly payment plans, prepayment plans, one-year tuition loans, or longer-term tuition loans. Some of these plans are school-based; others are offered through outside financial institutions. Most schools will answer general questions about the types of plans available, but will send only descriptive literature about the specific plans used by that school after a child has been accepted for enrollment.

Payment plans enable a family to pay the year's tuition in several monthly installments, usually beginning in the summer prior to the school year in question. Although interest is not charged on the unpaid tuition, there is usually a service fee charged for participating in this type of plan.

Prepayment plans are a type of tuition savings account set up by established financial institutions. A family begins paying a predetermined amount into the plan on a monthly basis several months before the school year begins. The money paid into the plan earns interest on its accumulated balance. The financial institution uses the accrued funds to pay the tuition bills for the family as they come due.

One-year tuition loans are offered to parents of a particular independent school by many local lending institutions in the school's community. The school makes the loan application available to the parents, who then apply directly to the lending institution. The interest rate on the loan is usually more favorable than that charged by the lending institution for regular consumer loans. A family's creditworthiness is considered in approving these loans. The loan is paid off in monthly installments beginning just before the school year begins. The bank pays the funds needed to pay the tuition directly to the school prior to any tuition due dates.

Longer-term tuition loans work in the same way as one-year loans, except that families contract to borrow much larger sums of money based on their projected tuition needs for a several-year period. The interest rates charged on these longer-term loans are generally more than on the one-year loans, and are in line with other types of consumer loans.

SUMMARY

The process of considering the financial concerns of independent education has three parts: 1) the costs of a school and how to assess them during the admissions process; 2) financial aid and how to apply for it; and 3) other options for financing tuition payments. The question of a school's costs can be determined by asking questions of the admissions officer during the interviewing period. Financial aid may be necessary for a family. If so, the SSS in Princeton is often called upon to help determine the amount needed. But in each case, the parents must carefully question the school's staff regarding aid availability, qualification requirements, and the applications process. Finally, schools and other financial institutions may offer other options, such as monthly payment plans, prepayment plans, one-year loans, long-term loans, or home equity lines of credit. Regardless of need, all parents should assess financial questions carefully before applying to a particular school.

Checklist for Choosing Your Child's Elementary School

Blythe Lyons

Parents in the Washington, D.C., metropolitan area are blessed (or cursed) with an overwhelming choice of elementary schools. In the District of Columbia alone there are approximately 120 public schools. Add to that an equal number of independent and parochial schools within or close to the Beltway, and the dilemma becomes obvious.

The process of choosing the right school for your child has several steps, including determining your family's educational goals and values; learning about early childhood education issues; assessing your child's educational needs; gathering information about the schools; and narrowing the choices through personal tours and assessment.

First, in determining goals and values, it is important to decide between public and private, sectarian and nonsectarian schools. The earlier essay by Judith Jones discusses the many benefits of choosing public schools in the D.C. area. Second, the essays and reference lists of books, articles, and organizations in this book can provide a good start to learn about early childhood education issues. During this process you should learn about the Montessori education philosophy. Third, ask yourself if your child would thrive in a formal, traditional school or one with a discovery learning approach, a small or large school, a city or a sprawling country-style campus, etc. Read about learning styles and teaching strategies. Listen carefully to the com-

---

Blythe Lyons, a native of Pittsburgh, Pennsylvania, is a graduate of the Edmund A. Walsh School of Foreign Service at Georgetown University. She has been employed as a researcher and writer at the Atlantic Council of the United States and as a Senior Consultant at International Energy Associates, Limited. She currently resides in Washington, D.C. with her husband and two sons.

ments of your child's teacher about your child's learning style. These indicators can help you to decide on the type of school to look for.

The next step is to begin the information-gathering process. Calling friends and listening to playground discussions can give you important clues. If you have decided to consider independent schools, call as many of them as is reasonably possible in September or early October to request brochures and open house dates. Allow yourself plenty of time. Even if you are looking at private schools, visit your local public school; its open house date(s) will be published in the newspaper. In addition, many public school principals are willing to arrange for visits to their schools. Make some initial choices after reading the schools' literature and then schedule school tours. It is important to do this early in the fall, since some schools may cut off applications if enough qualified students have applied.

The hardest part of the school selection process is getting a feeling for the school during a one- or two-hour tour. Every tour is different—some focus on curriculum while others just give a general school overview. After seeing a few schools, you will begin to pick out the differences more easily and understand the nuances and qualities that make each school unique. Perhaps you might start off with the schools that aren't at the top of your list to practice the art of school tours.

A checklist is provided to help you develop your own set of criteria for evaluating schools. When you have developed your list, make several photocopies of it and take it with you on each school tour. Most important, don't let the desire to get everything answered keep you from the main task of looking at, feeling, and sensing what is taking place at the school.

While it's easy to say, "go with your gut feeling," often that's the only way to make a decision when overwhelmed with so much information. Trust your intuition and don't apply to a school unless you feel reasonably confident that it would be the right match for your child.

School Evaluation Checklist

GRADES AND SCHOOL HOURS

• Is there a preK program? Is it full- or half-day?

• Is kindergarten full- or half-day? Is there a transition class available if your child turns out not to be ready to go to the next grade level?

• Which grades have the most openings?

• Do you want a school that includes G3, G6, G8, or G12?

• When do most students leave to go on to the next school?

• What are the regular hours? Is there an early dismissal day?

• Is an extended-day program available? If so, is it also available on days off and during vacation periods?

• If the elementary school also has a middle and upper school, can you tour these divisions as well?

ENROLLMENT

• Is the school large or small? Does each grade have one or several sections?

• Are there expansion plans?

• What is the boy-girl ratio? How well is it maintained in upper grades?

• Where do students go next?

• What neighborhoods do students come from?

• Are the classes "old" or is there a wide range of January–December birthdays?

PHILOSOPHY AND SCHOOL CHARACTER

• What does the school say about its philosophy? What do other parents say about the school's focus?

• What is the school's religious orientation, if any? Will your child be required to attend religious services or classes?

• What is the racial, cultural, economic, and religious diversity of the student body and teachers?

• Are students involved in community service activities?

• Is it an urban/suburban/rural school?

• What is the dress code?

• How do the students and teachers relate to each other? For example, are they addressed by first or last name?

• What is the age range of teachers? How many are male? How many female?

• What type of counseling is available?

• What is the school's atmosphere?

• What is the quality of discussion—noisy, busy chatter, silence?

COSTS

• Application, testing, registration, or tuition fees

• Payment plans, loan availability, financial aid (full- or partial-tuition only)

• Extra fees: books, lunch, bus, extended day, extracurricular activities

• Expectations for further financial contributions

• PTA dues

• Is there an additional cost for tutoring, remedial work, or extra time with a resource teacher?

CURRICULUM

• Does the catalogue describe the course of study? If not, ask the admissions staff or principal's office for more information.

• What is the reading curriculum, when does the formal program begin, what textbooks and teaching methods are used?

• What is the math curriculum? Are manipulatives and other materials available? How are workbooks used?

• What kind of social studies program is offered?

• Are there enrichment teachers, tutors, remedial teachers, etc., on staff?

• What is unique about the curriculum?

• Who teaches science? How often? Is the approach hands-on? Is there a lab?

• What is the level of music instruction? By whom is music taught? How often is it given?

• Are computers available? What is taught? Are they integrated into the math, reading, and science programs? How many students per computer in a class?

• What is the approach to the language arts program?

• How often is P.E. taught? Where, by whom, and what is the focus?

• Are the arts programs integrated into the core subject areas?

• When does homework begin and how much time will it take?

• Is foreign language instruction available and when? Does the teacher speak only the language being taught while in the classroom? Are there language labs?

• Do teachers adapt to many learning styles (auditory, visual, tactile)?

• What is the grading and reporting system?

• How is the school day organized? How much time is allotted for free play?

• Is the academic program departmentalized or based on homeroom teaching?

PARENTAL INVOLVEMENT

• Can parents volunteer and, if so, what are the opportunities?

• Is there pressure to volunteer?

• What is parents' influence on school affairs?

• Who governs the school?

• Does the school rely on parent fund raising for operating costs, salaries, scholarships, teaching materials, equipment?

FACILITIES

• What does the campus look like?

• What do classrooms look like (organized, cluttered, interesting, colorful, comfortable, inviting)?

• Is there visual stimulation? Are classrooms sunny or dreary? What is the desk configuration? What is displayed on classroom and hallway walls?

• Is the play area large enough, safe, up-to-date?

- Even if facilities are great, are they being used by the children?
- What does the library look like? Is it cozy, well stocked, used for other purposes, staffed by a librarian?
- Are computers available in classrooms and/or a special room?

REGISTRATION/ADMISSIONS

- Registration date or application deadline (Is early submission important?)
- What is the step-by-step process?
- What tests are required? Are tests from other schools accepted?
- What documents must be presented at time of registration?
- What are the procedures for applying to a public school that isn't within your home school's boundary?
- On what basis is an admissions decision made (age; prior educational exposure; religion; first-come, first-served; tie to the school; test results; teacher recommendation; other recommendation)?

OTHER FACTORS

- How far is the school from your home?
- How will your child get to and from school? How do most other students go back and forth?
- What after-school programs are available?

WHAT MAKES SCHOOL UNIQUE

- Sectarian or nonsectarian and any corresponding implications for curriculum and school life
- A particular approach in the curriculum
- Facilities
- Diversity of teacher and student body
- Size of school and grades
- Unusual programs
- School spirit, ambiance
- Caliber of teachers
- School head
- Teaching styles
- Educational philosophy
- Degree of parent involvement

Part Two

School Profiles

The Alexandria Country Day School

2405 Russell Road, Alexandria, VA 22301
703/548-4804
HEAD: Joan C. Barton

Basics

Year founded: 1983
Enrollment: 104
  Boys: 69
  Girls: 35
Grades: PreK–8
Major entry grade: K
Birthdate req.: 4½ yrs. by Sept.
Arrival: 8:30 a.m.
Dismissal: 3:10 p.m.
Early dismissal: 1x/quarter on Wed.
Extended day: 6:00 p.m.
Costs: $2500–$4650
Parent fund raising: $15,000–$20,000
Transportation: no
Lunch: yes
After-school activities: yes
Camp: no
Dress code: none
Neighborhood: Rosemont/Beverly Hills areas of Alexandria

Special Qualities

Small school offering small classes and individual attention.
Dedicated faculty.
Traditional classroom setting.

Philosophy and Character

Independent, nonsectarian, coed elementary school.
Dedicated to providing small classes, individualized attention, excellent faculty and family atmosphere.
Offers traditional classroom with standard curriculum.
Weekly assembly program.
Students perform for senior citizens, give supplies to homeless shelters, and tutor homeless.
Class size ranges from 8–14 students with one section per grade.

99% students from VA, 1% MD.
10% minority enrollment.
Mostly upper-middle-class families.

Curriculum

Curriculum includes English, communication skills, math through algebra, social studies, science, health.
Drama program.
Enrichment classes in computer science.
Spanish instruction starting K.
Band and chorus participation by students.
Homework begins G2 with 15 min. increasing to 1 hr. by G6.

Special Spots

x	Computer room
x	Science lab
	Dedicated music room
x	Music practice room
	Gymnasium
	Dedicated art room
	Ceramic studio
x	Auditorium
	Tennis court
	Pool
	Playing fields
	Enrichment rooms
x	Library (2500 volumes)
	Language lab
	Dance studio
x	Separate lunchroom
x	Kitchen
x	Infirmary
	Conference room
	Multipurpose room
x	Expansion plans (expand minority enrollment, improve boy/girl ratio, look for new building)

Sports News

P.E. Instruction

	Swimming
x	Basketball
	Gymnastics
	Dance
	Softball
	Skating
x	Soccer
	Volleyball
	Creative movement

Weekly P.E. class

2	PreK
2	Transition
3	Kindergarten
3	First
3	Second
4	Third
4	Fourth
5	Fifth
6	Sixth

After-School Activities

Enrichment program.

Registration/Admissions

Dr. Sylven Beck, 703/820-5661.
Parent requests information and arranges for tour and interview.
Student visits classroom and is evaluated using Gesell, Otis, Lennon.
Admission priority given to siblings, previous applicants.
Rolling admissions policy.
Financial aid available by applying to SSS in Princeton, 7 tuitions given 1988–1989.

Where Next

Bishop Ireton, St. Mary's, Gonzaga, Madeira, St. Timothy's, Choate.

Head Profile

B.A., 2 M.A. degrees, Ph.D.; 20 years of teaching and 10 years of administrative experience. Head of Country Day since 1982. Involved with students, teaching, administration, and parent relations, among others.

Faculty Features

1	No. male teachers
16	No. female teachers
N	Turnover (25%)
4	Typical tenure (yrs.)
	Art teacher
	Vocal music teacher
x	Instrumental music teacher
	Counselor/psychologist
	Nurse
x	Language teacher
x	Math teacher
	Reading teacher
x	P.E. teacher
x	Remedial reading teacher
x	Remedial math teacher
	Speech therapist
x	Full-time science teacher
	Enrichment teacher
	ESL teacher
x	Tutor
	Assistant teachers

Parents Say

School gives children close, personal attention.

Parent Wish List

More computer time, more foreign language time.

Parent Involvement

PTL is active.
Volunteer activities include help with computer, library programs, art aide, admissions, and in enrichment program.

Your Notes

The Barrie School

3500 Layhill Road (N-3); 2400 Bel Pre Road (G4–12)
Silver Spring, MD 20906
301/871-6200
HEAD: Timothy David Seldin

Basics

Year founded: 1932
Enrollment: 356 (N–6); 478 (N–12)
Boys: 193
Girls: 163
Grades: N2–12
Major entry grade: N3, N4, 1, 4
Birthdate req.: 2 yrs.
Arrival: 9:00 a.m.
Dismissal: 3:30 p.m.
Early dismissal: no
Extended day: 7:00 a.m.–6:00 p.m.
Costs: \$3200–\$5275
Parent fund raising: \$150,000
Transportation: yes
Lunch: no
After-school activities: yes
Camp: yes
Dress code: none
Neighborhood: Silver Spring/Layhill

Special Qualities

41-acre wooded campus.
Model Montessori school.
Nonsectarian, coed, integrated school.
Strong in humanities and sciences.
Combination of Montessori and outdoor activities.
Individually paced course of study, grouping students of different ages.
School sponsors graduate school program offering M.A. in Montessori education in conjunction with Trinity College.

Philosophy and Character

Humanistic international country day school.
Educational approach based on work of Montessori, Adler,

Freud, Piaget, Dewey, and outdoor education movement.
Children active in service and community projects.
Emphasis on individual reaching full potential.
Students address teacher by first name.
School closed for major Christian, Jewish, and federal holidays.
Approximately 25 2-year olds, 150 3- to 5-year-olds with 5 sections. G1–3 has about 40 students per grade with 4 sections and G4–6 has about 25 students per grade with 3 sections each.
Diverse international student body with 21% non-U.S. citizens; 38% minority enrollment.
91% from MD, 8% from DC.

Curriculum

Integrated thematic approach.
Recognizes and addresses different learning styles.
Students work with teachers for 2- to 3-year periods.
Reading begins with phonetic approach.
Classes contain children of 3-year age span.
Hands-on (manipulatives) approach to math.
Science is hands-on and includes introduction to botany and zoology through ecological studies, using 41-acre wildlife habitat campus.
Two computers per classroom: MacIntosh and Apple.
Spanish begins PreK; French or Spanish offered G1 up.
History and world culture taught age 3 up with several international festivals and celebrations as the high points of every year.
Kodaly and Orff approaches to music.
Formal art begins in K with all classrooms containing art center.
Homework begins G1 with 1 hour by G2.

Special Spots

x	Computer room (50 computers)
x	Science lab (3)
x	Dedicated music room (2)
x	Music practice room
x	Gymnasium (2)
x	Dedicated art room (3)
	Ceramic studio
x	Auditorium
x	Tennis court (4)
x	Pool (2)
x	Playing fields (2)

_____ Enrichment rooms
__x__ Library (2 elementary)
__x__ Language lab
_____ Dance studio
__x__ Separate lunchroom
__x__ Kitchen
__x__ Infirmary
__x__ Conference room
__x__ Multipurpose room
__x__ Expansion plans (place G4–12 at N–3 campus; expand G7–12 enrollment)

Sports News

P.E. Instruction:

_____ Swimming
_____ Basketball
__x__ Gymnastics
_____ Skating
__x__ Soccer
_____ Volleyball
__x__ Creative movement, dance, gymnastics

Weekly P.E. class:

__3__ Pre-K
__3__ Transition
__3__ Kindergarten
__3__ First
__3__ Second
__3__ Third
__3__ Fourth
__3__ Fifth
__3__ Sixth

After-School Activities

Sports: tennis, volleyball, softball, basketball, track, soccer, riding; scouts; music lessons; dance.

Registration/Admissions

Susan Cohen, 301/871-6200.
Thurs., 9:30 a.m., Open House.
Applications accepted Oct.–April.
Barrie obtains 3 recommendations.
Barrie only tests G1-up, using Woodcock, Johnson achievement, Peabody vocabulary, and other tests.
G1 up student full-day visit.
Parents interview with director or admissions director.
Test results shared.
Notification within 2 weeks of completed interviews.
$85,000 financial aid 1988–89.
Apply for aid using Princeton form, deadline 4/15.

Where Next

Approximately 85% elementary students continue through G12.

Head Profile

Tim Seldin's mother founded Barrie. At Barrie since 1968, 18 years as headmaster. Graduated from Barrie; B.A., Georgetown University; M.Ed., American University; trained in counseling psychology; Montessori certificate. Focuses on students, faculty relations, communicating with parents, and providing educational leadership for school.

Faculty Features

2	No. male teachers
23	No. female teachers
M	Turnover (6–9%)
8–10	Typical tenure (yrs.)
x	Art teacher
x	Vocal music teacher
x	Instrumental music teacher
x	Counselor/psychologist
x	Nurse
x	Language teacher
x	Math teacher
x	Reading teacher
x	P.E. teacher
	Remedial reading teacher
	Remedial math teacher
	Speech therapist
x	Full-time science teacher
	Enrichment teacher
	ESL teacher
	Tutor
	Assistant teachers

Parents Say

Headmaster very accessible. Facilities are outstanding. Excellent extended-day service. School has strong sense of community.

Parent Wish List

Indoor theater, broader music and art curriculum, upgrade facilities for G4 up.

Parent Involvement

Volunteers welcomed and encouraged.

Can join Parent Advisory Board. Building and Grounds Committee, Computer Advisory Group.

Can assist with fund raisers, field trips, tours, and others.

Your Notes

Beauvoir

3500 Woodley Road NW, Washington, DC 20016
202/537-6492
HEAD: Mary T. Moreland

Basics

Year founded: 1933
Enrollment: 355–358
  Boys: unavailable
  Girls: unavailable
Grades: N4–3
Major entry grade: N4, K
Birthdate req.: Oct. 1*
Arrival: 8:00–8:20 a.m.
Dismissal: 3:00 p.m.
Early dismissal: Fri. 1:00 p.m.
Extended day: 7:00 a.m.–6:00 p.m.
Costs: $6430
Parent fund raising: $130,000
Transportation: limited
Lunch: yes
After-school activities: no
Camp: yes
Dress code: simple, neat, comfortable
Neighborhood: National Cathedral

Special Qualities

Individual attention.
Nurturing environment.
Learning Alternatives Team.
Traditional school.
Involved parents.
Expansive Cathedral campus.
Ends at G3.
Outstanding facilities.

Philosophy and Character

Large, coed, independent school affiliated with Protestant Cathedral Foundation.
Traditional, nurturing philosophy.
Emphasizes love of learning, building sense of personal worth, and individual responsibility while caring for others.
Encourages good parent-school relations.

---

*Beauvoir is cautious in admitting children with late birthdays.

Parents feel emphasis is on developing self-esteem.
PreK class contains 60 students with 4 sections, others have 80 students with 4 sections.
Volunteering and annual giving strongly encouraged.
Community service entails clothing and food collections.
G1–3 attend monthly chapel; children and teachers prepare chapel with various themes.
Religious environment with focus on values.
19% minority enrollment.

Curriculum

Developmental program for PreK–K with emphasis on learning concepts through playful activities; exposure to art, music, media, library, computer.
Formal reading program begins G1.
Computers introduced at PreK level.
Homework begins G2, 20 minutes 2x/week.
Two parent-teacher conferences per year.
No foreign language instruction.

Special Spots

x	Computer room
x	Science lab
x	Music practice room
x	Gymnasium
x	Dedicated art room
x	Ceramic studio
x	Auditorium
	Tennis court
x	Pool (camp)
x	Playing fields
x	Enrichment rooms
x	Library
	Language lab
	Dance studio
x	Separate lunchroom
x	Kitchen
x	Infirmary
x	Conference room
	Expansion plans

Sports News

P.E. Instruction

	Swimming
	Basketball
x	Gymnastics
x	Dance
	Softball
	Skating
x	Soccer
x	Creative movement

Weekly P.E. class

2	Pre-K
	Transition
2	Kindergarten
4	First
4	Second

__4__ Third
_____ Fourth
_____ Fifth
_____ Sixth

After-School Activities

None

Registration/Admissions

Clare Amend, Admissions Director.
Request brochure in fall.
Tour with other families by appointment.
Applications available at tour.
School visit by child-group session for PreK–1 and class visit for G2–3.
Assessment testing available at Beauvoir.
Application due end of Jan.
Decision by March 20.
Siblings are given priority in N4 with applications due in mid-Oct.
Financial aid available with information reviewed at Princeton and Beauvoir.
Testing results after decisions can be discussed upon request.
Beauvoir seeks "old" children (i.e., early-year birthdays) for PreK and K classes.
Financial aid available.

Where Next

St. Albans, National Cathedral School, Georgetown Day School, Holton Arms, Holy Trinity, Landon, Maret, Mater Dei, Potomac, St. Patrick's, St. Stephen's, Stone Ridge, local public schools.

Head Profile

Mrs. Moreland has been at Beauvoir since 1979. Degree from Bucknell; M.Ed. from Johns Hopkins. Formerly lower school principal of Baltimore Friends School.

Faculty Features

__0__ No. male teachers
__42__ No. female teachers
__N__ % turnover
__u__ Typical tenure
__x__ Art teacher
__x__ Vocal music teacher
__x__ Instrumental music teacher (and instrumental)
__4__ Counselor/psychologist*

*Learning Alternatives faculty.

__x__ Nurse
_____ Language teacher
_____ Math teacher
_____ Reading teacher
__x__ P.E. teacher (2)
__x__ Remedial reading teacher
_____ Remedial math teacher
_____ Speech therapist
__x__ Full-time science teacher
__x__ Enrichment teacher (media)
_____ ESL teacher
__x__ Tutor

Parents Say

Beauvoir has warm, nurturing environment that provides children with individual attention. Parental involvement is expected. Facilities are excellent.

Parent Wish List

Music lessons, soccer team, decreased parental involvement.

Parent Involvement

Very active Beauvoir Parents Association.

Opportunities include work in library, newsletter, hosts for events and fund raisers such as fall used clothing sale, auction, book fair, school photos, and others.

Parents asked to sign up for volunteer opportunities each September.

Parents make up majority of governing board.

Your Notes

Browne Academy

5719 Telegraph Road, Alexandria, VA 22310
703/960-3000
HEAD: Lois R. Ferrer

Basics

Year founded: 1941
Enrollment: 265
  Boys: 132
  Girls: 133
Grades: PreK–8
Major entry grade: N, K
Birthdate req.: 3 yrs. by Dec. 31
Arrival: 8:15 a.m.
Dismissal: 3:30 p.m.
Early dismissal: no
Extended day: 7:00 a.m.–6:00 p.m.
Costs: $4400–$5150
Parent fund raising: $30,000
Transportation: yes
Lunch: yes (PreK and Lower School)
After-school activities: yes
Camp: yes
Dress code: none
Neighborhood: Wilton Woods area of Alexandria

Special Qualities

Spacious and country-like campus.
PEAK program for gifted and talented students.
Individualized plan for each child: composed of goals, teaching style, developmentally appropriate academic activities.

Philosophy and Character

Independent, coed, and nonsectarian.
Each child is unique.
Provides flexible learning environment.
Developmental academic program.
Comprehensive extended-day program provided.
Approximately 90 students in preschool with 4 sections. K–2

have 30–45 students per class with 2 sections per grade. G3–8 averages 10–20 students per class with one section.

Diverse student body with 19% minority enrollment, 92% students from VA, 4% DC, 4% MD.

Curriculum

Program of Enrichment Activities for Kids (PEAK), K–8.

Pre-school emphasizes intellectual development, self-help, social skills, physical development, reading and math readiness, computer introduction.

All students have language arts at same period with ability (not grade) level grouping; individualized approach.

Reading: phonetic approach, Ginn reading series and phonovisual.

Math: Math Stack and Heath mathematics series.

Science: Silver Burdett; science fair participation required for G4–8.

Computer: preschool readiness software K–3, LOGO; G4–8 word processing.

Music, French, art offered.

French introduced in PreK.

Special Spots

__x__ Computer room
__x__ Science lab
__x__ Dedicated music room
_____ Music practice room
_____ Gymnasium
__x__ Dedicated art room
_____ Ceramic studio
__x__ Auditorium (amphitheater)
_____ Tennis court
__x__ Pool
__x__ Playing fields
_____ Enrichment rooms
__x__ Library (3000 volumes)
_____ Language lab
_____ Dance studio
__x__ Separate lunchroom (G5–8)
__x__ Kitchen
__x__ Infirmary
_____ Conference room
_____ Multipurpose room
__x__ Expansion plans (multipurpose building)

Sports News

P.E. Instruction
__x__ Swimming
__x__ Basketball
_____ Gymnastics
__x__ Dance
__x__ Softball
_____ Skating

_x_ Soccer
___ Volleyball
_x_ Creative movement

Weekly P.E. class
_2_ PreK
_2_ Transition
_2_ Kindergarten
_2_ First
_2_ Second
_2_ Third
_2_ Fourth
_2_ Fifth
_5_ Sixth

After-School Activities

Drama, cooking, newspaper, creativity lab, chorus, computers, sports, FRIDAY clubs, library, study hall.

Registration/Admissions

Admissions director Leah S. Brixey.
Call for brochure.
Appointment for parent interview, Open House visit, school tour.
Submit application with birth certificate.
Applicant is interviewed.
Testing required for K–8, with a separate evaluation for preschool.
Rolling admissions process; notification when file complete.
Financial aid given, $88,000 in 1988–89.

Where Next

St. Stephen's, St. Agnes, St. Mary's, Bishop Denis J. O. Connell, Bishop Ireton, Thomas Jefferson.

Head Profile

At Browne Academy since 1975. Registered nurse; B.A., M.A., Ph.D. Previous experience at Baldwin Schools, Creative Country Day Schools, PA and NY public schools.

Faculty Features

_1_ No. male teachers
_27_ No. female teachers
_3_ % turnover
_6_ Typical tenure (yrs.)
_x_ Art teacher (2)
_x_ Vocal music teacher
_x_ Instrumental music teacher
___ Counselor/psychologist
_x_ Nurse
_x_ Language teacher (2)

_____ Math teacher
__x__ Reading teacher (2)
__x__ P.E. teacher (2)
__x__ Remedial reading teacher
_____ Remedial math teacher
_____ Speech therapist
_____ Full-time science teacher
__x__ Enrichment teacher
_____ ESL teacher
__x__ Tutor
_____ Assistant teachers

Parents Say

unavailable

Parent Wish List

Addition of 9th grade.

Parent Involvement

Association of Parents and Teachers involved in library, fund raisers, hospitality, room parents, parent education. Parents participate in space planning, sex education curriculum, special events, and PR.

Your Notes

Burgundy Farm Country Day School

3700 Burgundy Road, Alexandria, VA 22303
703/960-3431
HEAD: Gerald L. Marchildon

Basics

Year founded: 1946
Enrollment: 250
Boys: 130
Girls: 120
Grades: PreK–8
Major entry grade: PreK, K, 1, 4
Birthdate req.: 4 yrs. by Oct. 1
Arrival: 8:30 a.m.
Dismissal: 3:00 p.m.
Early dismissal: no
Extended day: 6:00 p.m.
Costs: $5650–$6250
Parent fund raising: $23,000
Transportation: yes
Lunch: no
After-school activities: yes
Camp: yes
Dress code: comfortable
Neighborhood: Alexandria

Special Qualities

Child-centered philosophy.
Hands-on manipulative learning approach.
Integrated curriculum.
Nurturing environment.
Rural setting with farm on campus, woods.
Transition class.
Cooperative nature of school.

Philosophy and Character

Cooperatively owned by parents, staff, founders.
Education is cooperative enterprise requiring students, teachers, and parents to work together.
Committed to nurturing and perpetuating independence and curiosity, integrating basic skills, and extending concepts into higher-level thinking.
Classes range in size from 15–30. G1 up has two class sections per grade.
School strives for racial and cultural diversity: 19% minority enrollment.

Majority students (65%) from VA, 16% DC, 19% MD.

Curriculum

300-acre wildlife campus in WV, used spring/fall.
French and Spanish instruction.
Swimming lessons 4 weeks each spring and fall.
Science program is theme-oriented and uses on-campus woods, pond, stream; yearly science fair.
Mixed age grouping G1–5 considering academic and developmental needs and male-female ratio.
Parents actively participate in class.
Reading: daily, literature-oriented, phonics stressed in spelling work, ability reading groups, phonovisuals program in K, Great Books program.
Math: emphasizes understanding of concepts, uses manipulatives and pictorial material.
Computer begins in K with LOGO introduction.
Elementary grades each have 2 teachers, small group instruction, with ability grouping in math and reading, special teachers for music, P.E., art, drama, library, languages.

Special Spots

__x__ Computer room
__x__ Science lab (Middle School)
__x__ Dedicated music room
_____ Music practice room
_____ Gymnasium
__x__ Dedicated art room (2)
__x__ Ceramic studio
_____ Auditorium
_____ Tennis court
__x__ Pool
__x__ Playing fields
__x__ Enrichment rooms
__x__ Library (7000 volumes)
__x__ Language lab (2)
_____ Dance studio
_____ Separate lunchroom
_____ Kitchen
__x__ Infirmary
__x__ Conference room
__x__ Multipurpose room
__x__ Expansion plans (upgrade classrooms, science labs, and Middle School faculty)

Sports News

P.E. Instruction
__x__ Swimming
__x__ Basketball
_____ Gymnastics
_____ Dance
__x__ Softball
_____ Skating

_x_ Soccer
_x_ Volleyball
___ Creative movement
_x_ Tennis

Weekly P.E. class
_2_ PreK
_2_ Transition
_2_ Kindergarten
_3_ First
_3_ Second
_3_ Third
_3_ Fourth
_3_ Fifth
_3_ Sixth

After-School Activities

Karate, dance, gymnastics, art, piano.

Registration/Admissions

Natalie Hall.
Fall and spring Open House.
Individual tour by appointment.
Application due by Feb. 1 or as space permits.
PreK–G1 applicants given developmental test at school by Specific Diagnostics.
G2 up take WISC-R and WRAT.
Results given to parents after school decision.
Teacher recommendation form and transcripts required.
Siblings given admission priority.
Financial aid given, send SSS form to Princeton: $58,000 given 1988–89.

Where Next

Local public schools (50%), Georgetown Day, Field, Canterbury, Edmund Burke, Madeira, Maret, Bishop Ireton, Gonzaga, Thomas Jefferson.

Head Profile

New head June 1989; B.A. in history, Southern Illinois U., 1960; M.S. in counseling/guidance, 1962; assistant headmaster at North Country School, Lake Placid, NY.

Faculty Features

_2_ No. male teachers
_23_ No. female teachers
_N_ turnover
_5_ Typical tenure (yrs.)
_x_ Art teacher (3)
_x_ Vocal music teacher
___ Instrumental music teacher
___ Counselor/psychologist
___ Nurse

__x__ Language teacher (2)
_____ Math teacher
_____ Reading teacher
__x__ P.E. teacher
__x__ Remedial reading teacher (as needed)
__x__ Remedial math teacher (as needed)
__x__ Speech therapist (as needed)
_____ Full-time science teacher
__x__ Enrichment teacher
_____ ESL teacher
__x__ Tutor (from Kingsbury Center)
_____ Assistant teachers

Parents Say

unavailable

Parent Wish List

unavailable

Parent Involvement

Active parent participation in all areas of school life.

Your Notes

Capitol Hill Cluster (Peabody and Watkins)

12th and E Streets SE, Washington, DC 20003
202/724-4714
HEAD: Veola M. Jackson

Basics

Year founded: Peabody, 1890; Watkins, 1962

Enrollment:	P: 223	W: 447
Boys:	112	232
Girls:	111	215

Grades: PreK–4
Major entry grade: na
Birthdate req.: Dec. 31
Arrival: 9:00 a.m.
Dismissal: 3:00 p.m.
Early dismissal: no
Extended day: 7:00 a.m.–6:00 p.m.
Cost: na
Parent fund raising: $80,000
Transportation: limited
Lunch: yes
After-school activities: yes
Camp: no
Dress code: none
Neighborhood: Capitol Hill

Special Qualities

Highly motivated staff.
Enrichment program for gifted and talented.
Step up enrichment program.
Diverse inner-city school.
Energetic, positive, friendly atmosphere.
Student performance above the national norm on standardized tests.
Cooperative Nursery of Capitol Hill housed at Peabody for 3-year-olds.
Special education programs for students with learning disabilities and communicative disorders.

Philosophy and Character

Strives to encourage every child to work up to highest standard of achievement, not forgetting the behavior necessary for personal growth and improvement.

Student body is economically, racially, and socially diverse (Peabody 75% black, 25% white; Watkins 89% black, 11% white).

Emphasizes challenging curriculum with many enrichment activities—i.e., foreign language and trips to Discovery Theater.

Frequent, special assemblies to reward student performance.

PreK class has approximately 80 students in 4 sections. Other grades range from 100–130 students with 5 or 6 sections per class.

Large proportion of out-of-boundary students (about ⅔ of student body).

Curriculum

CTBS test scores:* 3rd grade
Reading: 54 percentile
Math: 76 percentile
Language: 63 percentile
Science: 52 percentile

Creative approach to traditional academic curriculum.

"Emergent Literacy" reading program; reading curriculum diverse.

Creation of a literate environment using silent and oral reading, dramatizations, predictions and thematically connected art projects, nightly reading at home.

Hands-on science, with Arts and Science Center.

PreK–G2 "FLEX" foreign language experience: exposure to language, culture, foods, etc.

G3 Spanish language introduced.

Competition encouraged, prizes awarded for number of books read, award performances at assembly for teachers and students, science fair, spelling bee, history day, Olympics of the Mind.

Gifted and talented program.

Homework begins in K.

Musical theater.

Site for student teaching from area universities.

Watkins also has PreK–G4 with magnet program focusing on early childhood education, sponsors before- and after-school program, Capitol Hill Cooperative Nursery School, and arts and science center.

Special Spots

__x__ Computer labs
__x__ Science lab (Watkins)
__x__ Dedicated music room
__x__ Music practice room
_____ Gymnasium
__x__ Dedicated art room

*May 1989 results.

x Ceramic studio
x Auditorium (Watkins)
___ Tennis court
___ Pool
x Playing fields
x Enrichment rooms
x Library
x Language room (Spanish)
x Dance studio
x Separate lunchroom
x Kitchen
___ Infirmary
x Conference room
x Multipurpose room
___ Expansion plans

Sports News

P.E. Instruction
___ Swimming
x Basketball
___ Gymnastics
x Dance
___ Softball
___ Skating
x Soccer
x Volleyball
___ Creative movement

Weekly P.E. class:
1 PreK
1 Kindergarten
1 First
1 Second
1 Third
1 Fourth
1 Fifth
1 Sixth

After-School Activities

PTA operates programs at Watkins and Peabody—drama and cooking, art, cheerleading, student council, science.

Registration/Admissions

April is registration month for DC public schools.

Watch for newspaper notification or bulletin.

Proof of residency, birth certificate, immunization record are required.

PreK classes fill up quickly and children enrolled on first-come, first-served basis.

Wise to sign up during scheduled registration period.

Apply for out-of-boundary admission at school; acceptance is limited.

Out-of-state admission requires tuition of $1880–$2727.

Where Next

Stuart Hobson (Cluster's Middle school), Gonzaga, Sidwell, Maret, Field, Capitol Hill Day, Baneker, Eastern, School Without Walls.

Head Profile

Principal at Watkins since 1973; 27 years in education in DC; received Capitol Hill Community Achievement Award, recognized by mayor for service to DC public schools. Recipient of First Annual Superintendent Incentive Award for Administrators. Assistant principals administer the individual schools.

Faculty Features

8	No. male teachers
46	No. female teachers
N	% turnover
u	Typical tenure
x	Art teacher
x	Vocal music teacher
x	Instrumental music teacher
x	Counselor/psychologist
x	Nurse
x	Language teacher (Spanish and French)
x	Math teacher
x	Reading teacher
x	P.E. teacher
x	Remedial reading teacher
x	Remedial math teacher
x	Speech therapist
x	Full-time science teacher
x	Enrichment teacher
	Tutor
x	Assistant teachers

Parents Say

Principal is purposeful, inspiring, dynamic, innovative, strong in initiating new programs, curriculum development, and administration. Very favorable reports. Parents voiced some concern over trying to run Peabody and Watkins simultaneously. Peabody less of a neighborhood school with busing necessary.

Parent Wish List

More P.E. instruction and a gymnasium.

Intramural basketball, social studies.

Library open after school.

Improve communication between school and home.

Better playground.

Parent Involvement

Strong influence in development of cluster 1985–86 and school policy.

Participation in school invited as field trip chaperone, class assistant, and for special project.

Fund-raising activities include Capitol Hill Classic (10K), auction, bake sales to fund book purchases, classroom equipment, special programs.

Very diverse attitudes and participation.

Your Notes

Capitol Hill Day School

210 South Carolina Avenue SE, Washington, DC 20003
202/547-2244
HEAD: Catherine Peterson

Basics

Year founded: 1968
Enrollment: 213
  Boys: 92
  Girls: 121
Grades: PreK–8
Major entry grade: PreK
Birthdate req.: Oct. 1
Arrival: 8:10 a.m.
Dismissal: 3:00 p.m.
Early dismissal: Wed., 2:00 p.m.
Extended day: 6:00 p.m.*
Costs: $4800–$5900
Parent fund raising: $100,000
Transporatation: yes
Lunch: no
After-school activities: yes
Camp: yes
Dress code: none
Neighborhood: Capitol Hill

Special Qualities

Every parent is voting member of school corporation, which elects board of trustees.
Good relationship between parents and teachers.
Core curriculum.
Academic emphasis.
Interesting after-school programs coordinated with Levine School of Music and Capitol Hill Arts Workshop.
Early music and language instruction.
Small, attractive, homey environment with creative use of rented DC public school building.

---

*Also available early dismissal days, teacher workdays, conference days, and spring break.

Philosophy and Character

Nondenominational, independent school.
Governed by trustees elected by parents.
Commitment to a diverse student body, interaction with parents.
Experience-based approach to learning.
Academic program that stimulates intellectual curiosity.
Class size is 23–24 students per grade with one section for all grades but an additional small section for PreK and K.
Neighborhood school: 97% students from DC.
Diverse student body with approximately 22% minority enrollment.

Curriculum

Subjects at each grade level organized around a core of social studies and science activities.
Washington resources widely used to augment studies.
Reading taught daily, starting G1; literature-based with phonics in younger grades.
Strong math program taught by homeroom teacher; focuses on patterns and relationships.
Science emphasizes scientific method and is taught in homeroom.
French instruction begins in PreK.
LOGO taught in computer class starting in K.
Music, art, drama strong—Orff instruments taught.
Homework begins in G3.
Field education coordinator, school uses metropolitan area as classroom.

Special Spots

__x__ Computer room
__x__ Science lab (with animals)
__x__ Dedicated music room
_____ Music practice room
__x__ Gymnasium (off-campus, rented)
__x__ Dedicated art room
__x__ Ceramic studio
_____ Auditorium
__x__ Tennis court (public)
_____ Pool
__x__ Playing fields (public)
_____ Enrichment rooms
__x__ Library
_____ Language lab
_____ Dance studio
_____ Separate lunchroom
__x__ Kitchen
_____ Infirmary
_____ Conference room
_____ Expansion plans

Sports News

P.E. Instruction

___	Swimming
x	Basketball
___	Gymnastics
___	Dance
x	Softball
___	Skating
x	Soccer
x	Volleyball
___	Creative movement
___	Tennis

Weekly P.E. class:

2	PreK
___	Transition
2	Kindergarten
2	First
2	Second
2	Third
2	Fourth
2	Fifth
2	Sixth

After-School Activities

Levine School of Music classes.
Recorder instruction.
Gymnastics.
Pottery and crafts, drama, cooking, and sports: tennis, swimming, ice hockey, skating, soccer.

Registration/Admissions

Open House visit or by appointment.
Applications due Feb. 28.
Playgroup visit for PreK–1 applicants or full-day class visit.
Testing by Marilyn Ringenberg, Kingsbury or SDT.
Recommendation forms submitted.
Decisions by end of March.
Test results may or may not be released.
Priority given to siblings and students who have applied previously.
1988–89 financial aid totaled
$85,000–$100,000; forms submitted with application.

Where Next

Edmund Burke, Field, Georgetown Day, Gonzaga, Madeira, Maret, National Cathedral, Sandy Springs Friends, Sidwell Friends, Washington Ethical School, Washington International School.

Head Profile

Director since 1985. B.A., Smith; M.Ed., Goucher. Teaching experience at Germantown Friends and Newton public schools. Important duties include, among others, faculty relations, supervising programs, communicating with parents, and policy development. Extremely highly rated by parents. Teaches math (developed math curriculum for Fairfax County public schools).

Faculty Features

2	No. male teachers
24	No. female teachers
N	Turnover (10–20%)
8	Typical tenure (yrs.)
x	Art teacher (2)
x	Vocal music teacher
	Instrumental music teacher
x	Counselor/psychologist
	Nurse
x	Language teacher
x	Math teacher (G6 up)
	Reading teacher
x	P.E. teacher
	Remedial reading teacher
	Remedial math teacher
x	Speech therapist
x	Full-time science teacher (G5–8)
	Enrichment teacher
	ESL teacher
x	Tutor (from Kingsbury Center)
	Assistant teachers
x	Coordinator of field studies

Parents Say

School head is competent, calm, problem solver. School offers hands-on learning experience with individual attention and challenging classes. Age-appropriate community activities pursued.

Parent Wish List

Gymnasium

Parent Involvement

Volunteer opportunities include board committees, fund raising, classroom support.
Volunteering strongly encouraged.
Parents directly influence school policies.
Parent support groups.

Your Notes

Capitol Hill Montessori School

701 5th Street SE (P.O. Box 15176), Washington, DC 20003
202/543-3727
HEAD: Grace Hanks

Basics

Year founded: 1964
Enrollment: 75
Boys: 40
Girls: 35
Grades: N–G4
Major entry grade: na
Birthdate req.: 18 mos.
Arrival: 8:45 a.m.
Dismissal: 11:45 a.m., 3:00 p.m. (depending on grade)
Early dismissal: 1st Fri. of each month, 12:00 noon
Extended day: 7:30 a.m.–6:00 p.m.
Costs: $2600–$4500
Parent fund raising: $20,000
Transportation: yes
Lunch: no
After-school activities: yes
Camp: yes
Dress code: none
Neighborhood: Capitol Hill

Special Qualities

Problem-solving approach.
Positive attitudes of faculty and staff.
Children are helpful and supportive toward classmates older or younger.
Creative, charismatic educational director.
Children challenged and encouraged but not pressured.

Philosophy and Character

Located in old Lenox School at 5th and G Street, S.E.
Racial integration (50%).
Parent co-op with parent board of directors.
Philosophy is based on creating an independent, focused, self-sufficient, caring individual.

The school works to build self-esteem and individualizes curriculum to each child's potential.

Individual birthdays are recognized by celebrating the accomplishments of birthday child.

Two formal conferences per year with as many informal discussions as necessary.

Fifty students with 2 sections in the primary class and one section of 12–13 students for both N and elementary classes.

Curriculum

Montessori curriculum incorporates many facets of learning into the daily classroom.

Curriculum: science, music, language, computer, p.e., art, math, reading.

Trained Montessori teacher focuses on the child.

Learning pace is established by child who is allowed under guidance to discover through exploration and accomplishment.

Spanish is introduced in the primary program.

Special Spots

__x__ Computers (2) ("Computat" 1x/wk)
__x__ Science lab
__x__ Dedicated music room
_____ Music practice room
_____ Gymnasium
_____ Dedicated art room
_____ Ceramic studio
_____ Auditorium
_____ Tennis court
_____ Pool
__x__ Playing fields
_____ Enrichment rooms
__x__ Library
__x__ Language lab
_____ Dance studio
_____ Separate lunchroom
__x__ Kitchen
_____ Infirmary
_____ Conference room
_____ Multipurpose room
_____ Expansion plans

Sports News

P.E. Instruction
_____ Swimming
_____ Basketball
__x__ Gymnastics
__x__ Dance
_____ Softball
__x__ Skating
_____ Soccer
_____ Volleyball
__x__ Creative movement

Weekly P.E. class:
__5__ N
__5__ Primary
__5__ Elementary

After-School Activities

Dance, photography, cooking, gymnastics, music, crafts, field trips, sports.

Registration/Admissions

Very low pressure—no testing.
Two personal interviews, one for child to visit class, one for parent to observe Montessori approach.
Advance registration deadline is March 1.
Financial aid available; use school and Princeton forms; $20,000 given.

Where Next

Burgundy Farm, Capitol Hill Day, Mater Amoris, Georgetown Day, Maret.

Head Profile

Mrs. Hanks has over 30 years professional experience working with and for children. She was selected after a national search and comes to CHMS from California, where several of her previous programs, including child-abuse prevention, children's coalitions, Head Start, and remedial, were recognized with awards. Her many offices held include chairman of the California Conference on Children and Youth and her appointment as delegate to the White House Conference on Children and Youth.

Faculty Features

__2__ No. male teachers (aides)
__8__ No. female teachers
__10__ % turnover
__9__ Typical tenure (yrs.)
_____ Art teacher
__x__ Vocal music teacher
_____ Instrumental music teacher
_____ Counselor/psychologist
_____ Nurse
__x__ Language teacher
_____ Math teacher
_____ Reading teacher
_____ P.E. teacher
_____ Remedial reading teacher
_____ Remedial math teacher
_____ Speech therapist
_____ Full-time science teacher
_____ Enrichment teacher
_____ ESL teacher

_____ Tutor
_____ Assistant teachers

Parents Say

Tremendous amount of one-on-one personal attention given as teachers float through classroom of combined ages. Easy, natural transitions. Teachers have a quiet but powerful influence on students as they flourish socially, personally, and academically.

Parent Wish List

Stronger P.E. program, more computers for older children, more recreational facilities, new facility, program to continue through all elementary grades.

Parent Involvement

All families have a 30-hour co-op responsibility as part of membership contract.
Participation is very high in all areas of school from classroom to fund raising to office, finance, maintenance, field trips, etc.
The school is very much a family place. Fund raisers for scholarships include: craft fair, Christmas bazaar, auction, 5K race.

Your Notes

Charles E. Smith Jewish Day School of Greater Washington

1901 East Jefferson Street, Rockville, MD 20852
301/881-1400
HEAD: R. Geraldine Nussbaum (Lower School)

Basics

Year founded: 1965
Enrollment: 582 (Lower School)
  Boys: 302 (K–6)
  Girls: 280 (K–6)
Grades: K–12 (K–6 Lower School)
Major entry grade: K, 1, 7
Birthdate req.: 5 yrs. by Nov. 30
Arrival: 8:15 a.m.
Dismissal: 3:00 p.m.
Early dismissal: Fri., 2:15 p.m.
Extended day: no
Costs: $4655
Parent fund raising: $50,000
Transportation: yes
Lunch: no (except 1x/week)
After-school activities: yes
Camp: yes
Dress code: neat, clean
Neighborhood: Rockville

Special Qualities

Jewish educational institution.
Caring environment where "community" is felt.
Integration of Judaic studies into the curriculum.
Individual approach to teaching students.

Philosophy and Character

Co-ed, independent, college-prep Jewish school.
School mission is to educate students for their fullest participation as Jews and as citizens.
Boys wear *kippah* and standards of Kashrut are maintained.
Students encouraged to partici-

pate in community service projects.
School community spirit is fostered.
Parents expected to contribute to school.
Grade size varies from 16 in K and 69–100 in G1–6 with 3–4 sections.
100% students are Jewish; 20% international students, 80% students from MD, with 10% each from VA, DC.
Most students from middle-class families.

Curriculum

Dual curriculum of general and Judaic studies beginning in K.
Reading: program begins in K with sight, key word, and phonics.
Writing is encouraged with daily journal and production of literary magazine.
Science: hands-on, taught in classroom and by science teacher 1x/week.
Hebrew taught from K up.
Social studies focuses on Israel and world awareness.
Prayers said daily.
Art in art room.
Special music teacher.
Homework begins G1.
Computer education: LOGO, math, and language arts.
Enrichment and Hebrew remediation.

Special Spots

__x__ Computer room
__x__ Science lab
_____ Dedicated music room
_____ Music practice room
__x__ Gymnasium
_____ Dedicated art room
_____ Ceramic studio
__x__ Auditorium
_____ Tennis court
_____ Pool
__x__ Playing fields (use of JCC fields)
_____ Enrichment rooms
__x__ Library
_____ Language lab
_____ Dance studio
_____ Separate lunchroom
__x__ Kitchen
_____ Infirmary
_____ Conference room
_____ Multipurpose room
__x__ Expansion plans (redo K playground)

Sports News

P.E. Instruction
_____ Swimming
__x__ Basketball

_____ Gymnastics
_____ Dance
_____ Softball
_____ Skating
_____ Soccer
_____ Volleyball
_____ Creative movement

Weekly P.E. class:
_____ Pre-K
__1__ Transition
__3__ Kindergarten
__4__ First
__4__ Second
__4__ Third
__4__ Fourth
__4__ Fifth
__3__ Sixth

After-School Activities

Hands-on science, computer, 4-H.

Registration/Admissions

Susan Ritzer.
Applications accepted 14 months in advance with rolling admissions process.
Group family tours given in fall.
Parent interviews arranged after receipt of application.
PreK report and application required.
Developmental screening done by school counselors and teachers, results shared.
Admissions priorities given to siblings.
Notification by March 15.
Can accept some learning disabled and handicapped students.
Financial aid is available based on need.
Approximately 22–24% of students in K–12 are receiving aid.

Where Next

Students remain at CES/JDS.

Head Profile

Lower School principal: B.A., Barnard College; M.A., New York University; Judaic Studies, Teachers' Institute at Stern College, Yeshiva University; Ph.D. candidate, University of Maryland. Formerly served as principal, Hebrew Academy of Texas in Houston.

Faculty Features

__0__ No. male teachers
__52__ No. female teachers

M % turnover
10–15 Typical tenure (yrs.)
x Art teacher
x Vocal music teacher
___ Instrumental music teacher
x Counselor/psychologist (5)
x Nurse
x Language teacher
x Math teacher
x Reading teacher
x P.E. teacher
x Remedial reading teacher
x Remedial math teacher
x Speech therapist (by contract)
___ Full-time science teacher
x Enrichment teacher
x ESL teacher (several)
___ Tutor
x Assistant teachers

Parents Say

unavailable

Parent Wish List

unavailable

Parent Involvement

Active PTA sponsors meetings, raises funds, enlists volunteers.

Volunteer opportunities include library, school celebrations, workshops, new parent orientation, social activities, field trips, tutoring, helping in classroom.

Your Notes

Chevy Chase Elementary School

4015 Rosemary Street, Chevy Chase, MD 20815
301/657-4994
HEAD: Pat D. Abrunzo

Basics

Year founded: 1936
Enrollment: 325
  Boys: unavailable
  Girls: unavailable
Grades: 3–6*
Major entry grades: na
Birthdate req.: 5 yrs. by Dec. 31
Arrival: 8:55 a.m.
Dismissal: 2:55 p.m.
Early dismissal: no
Extended day: 7:00 a.m.–6:00 p.m.
Costs: na
Parent fund raising: u
Transportation: yes
Lunch: yes
After-school activities: yes
Camp: no
Dress code: none
Neighborhood: Chevy Chase

Special Qualities

Magnet School program.
Teachers meet individual students' needs.
Good music program.
Chorus program.
Computer and AV labs.

Philosophy and Character

Public school in Montgomery County located on 4 acres of land in heart of Chevy Chase.
Provides overnight field trips which complement curriculum.
Students go to Rosemary Hills for K–2, then CCE.
Grades range in size from 72–90.
Approximately 37% minority enrollment.

*Rosemary Hills Elementary School, a K–2 school, feeds into Chevy Chase.

Curriculum

Gifted and talented program for "arts."
Study skills emphasized.
Homework assigned nightly.
French and Spanish classes offered before school.
P.E. class 1x/week is augmented by 1–2 recesses per day.

Special Spots

x Computer room
x Science lab
x Dedicated music room
_____ Music practice room
x Gymnasium
x Dedicated art room
_____ Ceramic studio
_____ Auditorium
_____ Tennis court
_____ Pool
x Playing fields
_____ Enrichment rooms
x Library
_____ Language lab
_____ Dance studio
x Separate lunchroom
x Kitchen
x Infirmary
x Conference room
_____ Multipurpose room
x Expansion plans

Sports News

P.E. Instruction
_____ Swimming
_____ Basketball
_____ Gymnastics
_____ Dance
_____ Softball
_____ Skating
x Soccer
_____ Volleyball
_____ Creative movement

Weekly P.E. class
_____ PreK
_____ Transition
_____ Kindergarten
_____ First
_____ Second
1 Third
1 Fourth
1 Fifth
1 Sixth

After-School Activities

Hands-on science, sports instruction, gymnastics.

Registration/Admissions

Registration at school throughout school year.
Documents required: birth certificate, immunization

record, transcript if appropriate.

Non-U.S. citizens enroll through International Students Admissions Office, 301/230-2843.

May request transfer to out-of-boundary school at home school from Jan. 1–April 30.

Where Next

Westland Intermediate.

Head Profile

Acting principal from Montgomery County Public Schools headquarters.

Faculty Features

7	No. male teachers
20	No. female teachers
u	% turnover
15	Typical tenure (yrs.)
x	Art teacher
x	Vocal music teacher
x	Instrumental music teacher
x	Counselor/psychologist
	Nurse
	Language teacher
	Math teacher
x	Reading teacher
x	P.E. teacher
	Remedial reading teacher
	Remedial math teacher
x	Speech therapist
	Full-time science teacher
	Enrichment teacher
x	ESL teacher (2)
	Tutor
	Assistant teachers
x	Resource room teacher
x	Media specialist

Parents Say

Facilities are very good. School has a special choir—best in the region.

Parent Wish List

No comments given.

Parent Involvement

Active PTA.

Volunteer opportunities: health aide, at lunch hour, fund raising, library aide, room parent, choir assistant.

Fund raisers include Garden Tour, Fun Night; funds raised pay for choir activities and extras for teachers.

Your Notes

Concord Hill School

6050 Wisconsin Avenue, Chevy Chase, MD 20815
301/654-2626
HEAD: Eleanor Chatfield-Taylor

Basics

Year founded: 1965
Enrollment: 90
  Boys: 47
  Girls: 43
Grades: N–3
Major entry grade: N, K
Birthdate req.: Dec. 1
Arrival: 8:40 a.m.
Dismissal: 12:15 p.m., 3:00 p.m. (depending on grade)
Early dismissal: Fri., 12:15 p.m.
Extended day: no
Costs: $3565–$4715
Parent fund raising: $40,000
Transportation: no
Lunch: no
After-school activities: no
Camp: under consideration for PreK
Dress code: none
Neighborhood: West Chevy Chase

Special Qualities

Sweet, warm, loving environment.
Small school giving individual attention in traditional structured classroom.
Antiquarian Book Fair.
Tuition lower than many comparable schools.

Philosophy and Character

School designed for early childhood years.
Small, caring environment—developmental approach.
Challenge but not pressure children.
Educational program designed to develop skills, ideas, and attitudes essential to constructive and rewarding life.

Student population rather homogeneous.
Each grade has one section and ranges in size from 10–18.

Curriculum

Classrooms filled with good materials/perceptual activities.
Half-day N–K.
Program for N and PreK stresses socialization, creative projects, field trips, music, stories.
K program includes play time, reading and math readiness.
G1 emphasizes math and reading skills, Scott Foresman basal readers, ability groups in reading.
Social studies introduced K.
Science is hands-on, no lab.
Music and art teachers; exposure to rhythm instruments, variety art media.
Many museum and concert field trips.

Special Spots

_____ Computer room
_____ Science lab
__x__ Dedicated music room
_____ Music practice room
_____ Gymnasium
_____ Dedicated art room
_____ Ceramic studio
_____ Auditorium
_____ Tennis court
_____ Pool
_____ Playing fields
_____ Enrichment rooms
__x__ Library (2000 volumes)
_____ Language lab
_____ Dance studio
_____ Separate lunchroom
_____ Kitchen
_____ Infirmary
__x__ Conference room
__x__ Multipurpose room
_____ Expansion plans

Sports News

P.E. Instruction
_____ Swimming
_____ Basketball
_____ Gymnastics
_____ Dance
_____ Softball
_____ Skating
_____ Soccer
_____ Volleyball
__x__ Creative movement
__x__ Ball skills

Weekly P.E. class
recess PreK and N
_____ Transition
recess Kindergarten
__4__ First

4	Second
4	Third
	Fourth
	Fifth
	Sixth

After-School Activities

None

Registration-Admissions

Request brochure.
Appointment for individual tour, classroom observation, and interview with Director.
Complete application and arrange for completion of teacher recommendation and sending transcript N–3.
Applicant visit during end Jan.–early March; 45 min. for N–K and full morning G1–3.
Readiness testing for G1 and reading and math achievement test for G2–3, all during applicant visit.
Rolling admissions for N–K and notification mid-March for G1–3.
No financial aid given at present time.

Where Next

Parochial and public schools, Holton Arms, Landon, Potomac, St. Albans, Grace Episcopal, Maret, McLean, National Cathedral, National Presbyterian, Sidwell Friends, Stone Ridge, St. Patrick's, Washington Episcopal.

Head Profile

Washingtonian. Director of Concord Hill since 1967. A.B., child study from Vassar. Committed and personable. Knows every student well.

Faculty Features

0	No. male teachers
10	No. female teachers
M	% turnover
12	Typical tenure (yrs.)
x	Art teacher
x	Vocal music teacher
	Instrumental music teacher
	Counselor/psychologist
	Nurse
	Language teacher
	Math teacher
	Reading teacher
	P.E. teacher
	Remedial reading teacher
	Remedial math teacher
x	Speech therapist (from Ridley & Fill)

_____ Full-time science teacher
_____ Enrichment teacher
_____ ESL teacher
__x__ Tutor (from Kingsbury Center)
__x__ Assistant teacher (1)

Parents Say:

Indoor facilities are outstanding. Highly favorable opinion of headmistress. Very accessible. Personal, family-oriented admissions process. School not overly academic.

Parent Wish List

Larger outdoor play space.

Parent Involvement

No formal PTA. Loyal parent body now raising funds through capital campaign. No annual giving. Fund raisers include Antiquarian Book Fair, Fall Cocktail Party.

Parents run library and Spring Golf Tournament.

Your Notes

Congressional School of Virginia

3229 Sleepy Hollow Road, Falls Church, VA 22042
703/533-9711
HEAD: Jay Roudebush

Basics

Year founded: 1939
Enrollment: 330
  Boys: 115
  Girls: 115
Grades: N–8
Major entry grade: K, 1, 5, 6, 7
Birthdate req.: 5 yrs. by Oct. 31 for K*
Arrival: 8:30 a.m.
Dismissal: 3:05 p.m.
Early dismissal: no
Extended day: 7:00 a.m.–6:00 p.m.
Costs: $4000–5200
Parent fund raising: $30,000
Transportation: yes
Lunch: yes
After-school activities: yes
Camp: yes
Dress code: uniform
Neighborhood: Falls Church, Annandale

Special Qualities

Traditional educational approach.
Diverse student body.
Strong science program.
Wonderful facility and site.

Philosophy and Character

Traditional school located on a 40-acre, safe and secure campus.
Strives for positive moral and ethical climate.
Honor code: "Respect for oneself, respect for others, and respect for the property of others."
Balanced programs with close attention to student progress.
Class size is no larger than 20. Older grades have one section and younger grades have 2–3 sections.

---

*Six weeks old for infant care; 2½ for Nursery.

Students 98.5% VA, 1% DC, .5% MD; 10% Afro-American, 10% Asian-American, 5% Hispanic-American, 5% Middle Eastern.
30% use extended day.

Curriculum

Science: strong area with 2 labs; science fair for PreK–8; "scientific method" cornerstone of program.
Reading: basal readers, phonics, introducing literature-based "write to learn" program.
Math: taught by classroom teachers G1–4.
French: G1–8, Spanish: G5–8.
Computer: K–2 familiarity; G3–8 BASIC instruction.
Music: 2–3x/week in music studio G1–8, 2x/week PreK.
Art: 2x/week in art studio G1–8.
Homework: G2, 3—½ hr; G4—1 hr; G5—1½ hrs.
Athletics: based on participation, teamwork.

Special Spots

x Computer room
x Science lab (2)
x Dedicated music room
___ Music practice room
___ Gymnasium
x Dedicated art room
___ Ceramic studio
x Auditorium
___ Tennis court
x Pool
x Playing fields
___ Enrichment rooms
x Library (5000+ volumes)
___ Language lab
___ Dance studio
x Separate lunchroom
x Kitchen
x Infirmary
x Conference room
x Multipurpose room
x Expansion plans (increase enrollment to 400–425)

Sports News

P.E. Instruction
x Swimming
x Basketball
___ Gymnastics
___ Dance
x Softball
___ Skating
x Soccer
x Volleyball
___ Creative movement
x Bowling

Weekly P.E. class
2 PreK
2 Kindergarten

3	First
3	Second
3	Third
3	Fourth
5	Fifth
5	Sixth

After-School Activities

Drama, sports, "Science encounters."
CAC (Capitol Athletic Council)—network of independent schools that compete G5–8.

Registration/Admissions

Stephen J. Whiteley.
Rolling admissions.
Individual tour with or without student.
Submit application and $50.
Arrange for test (McCarthy scale for G1 or younger; WISC-R for G2 or older) at Kingsbury or Assessment Associates.
Submit recommendation form.
Student must visit at some point during process.
No financial aid.

Where Next

Georgetown Prep, Bishop O'Connell, Washington International, Thomas Jefferson, St. Stephen's School, National Cathedral, Madeira, Potomac, Field School, Georgetown Day.

Head Profile

Two years at Congressional as head, 10 years at Sidwell Friends (4 as principal of Middle School); M.Ed., American University, 1981; B.A. Occidental, 1964; 5 years teaching at Robert Louis Stevenson School, Pebble Beach, CA. Goals: 1) establish strong school-family ties; 2) build comprehensive "hands-on" educational program; 3) ensure each child gets attention and support needed to be successful; 4) strengthen school's stature in community; 5) attract and retain outstanding teachers. Coaches basketball.

Faculty Features

4	No. male teachers
25	No. female teachers
	Assistant teachers
M	Turnover (10%)
5	Typical tenure (yrs.)
x	Art teacher
x	Vocal music teacher

_____ Instrumental music teacher
_____ Counselor/psychologist
__x__ Nurse
__x__ Language teacher
__x__ Math teacher
_____ Reading teacher
__x__ P.E. teacher
_____ Remedial reading teacher
_____ Remedial math teacher
_____ Speech therapist
__x__ Full-time science teacher
_____ Enrichment teacher
_____ ESL teacher
_____ Tutor

Parents Say

A traditional school in a safe environment, with strong parental involvement. Head is confident, fair, firm, forward-looking.

Parent Wish List

unavailable

Parent Involvement

Parents Organization sponsors meetings and workshops, staffs fund raisers, and publishes newsletter.
Volunteer opportunities in library, as guest speakers, chaperones, room parents.

Your Notes

John Eaton Elementary School

34th and Lowell Streets NW, Washington, DC 20016
202/282-0103
HEAD: Patricia Greer

Basics

Year founded: 1911
Enrollment: 403
Boys: 250
Girls: 150
Grades: PreK–6
Major entry grade: na
Birthdate req.: 5 yrs. by Dec. 31
Arrival: 9:00 a.m.
Dismissal: 3:00 p.m.
Early dismissal: no
Extended day: 7:00 a.m.–6:00 p.m.
Costs: na
Parent fund raising: $50,000
Transportation: no
Lunch: yes
After-school activities: yes
Camp: no
Dress code: none
Neighborhood: Cleveland Park

Special Qualities

Enthusiasm for new ideas.
Committed faculty, administration, and parents.
Children from diverse backgrounds work together and are challenged academically.

Philosophy and Character

A model school of the National Network of Successful Schools.
Process approach to learning emphasized.
Strive for dynamic program that is always changing and improving.
Good citizenship in a diverse environment.
Interest and respect for bilingual and multilingual programs.
Successful math curriculum exempted school from city requirements.
Style of leadership turns problems into programs.
Grades range in size from 40–60 with 25 in the PreK class.

Curriculum

CTBS Test scores* G3 G6

Reading:	G3 72 percentile
	G6 76 percentile
Math:	G3 83 percentile
	G6 86 percentile
Language:	G3 90 percentile
	G6 80 percentile
Science:	G3 78 percentile
	G6 70 percentile

Computer: developing overall approach.

Math: strong process learning approach (problem solving, thinking skills, discovery by capitalizing on curiosity, e.g. graphing data about classmates).

Science: hands-on exploration, experimentation, and discovery-resource room filled with dismantled telephones, jars of bugs.

Writing: process approach—brainstorm ideas, draft, edit, revise . . . publish.

Reading: good program with Junior Books.

Foreign language begins in G3 with Spanish. A before-school program offers language at an earlier age and French.

Special Spots

_____ Computer room
__x__ Science lab
__x__ Dedicated music room
_____ Music practice room
_____ Gymnasium
__x__ Dedicated art room
_____ Ceramic studio
__x__ Auditorium (PE and Cafeteria)
_____ Tennis court
_____ Pool
__x__ Playing fields
__x__ Enrichment rooms
__x__ Library (7000 volumes)
_____ Language lab
_____ Dance studio
_____ Separate lunchroom
__x__ Kitchen
_____ Infirmary
__x__ Conference room
__x__ Multipurpose room (with stage)
_____ Expansion plans

Sports News

P.E. Instruction

_____ Swimming
__x__ Basketball
__x__ Gymnastics
__x__ Dance
__x__ Softball
__x__ Skating
__x__ Soccer
__x__ Volleyball
__x__ Creative movement

*May 1989 results.

Weekly P.E. class

1	Pre-K
	Transition
1	Kindergarten
1	First
1	Second
1	Third
1	Fourth
1	Fifth
1	Sixth

After-School Activities

Cleveland Park after-school program: ceramics, gymnastics, computer, drama.
Parents say "excellent."

Registration-Admissions

April is registration month in DC public schools.
Watch for newspaper notification or bulletin.
Proof of residency, birth certificate, immunization record are required.
PreK classes fill up quickly and children enrolled on first-come, first-served basis.
Wise to sign up during scheduled registration period.
Apply for out-of-boundary admission at school; acceptance is limited. Out-of-state admission requires tuition of $1880–$2727.

Where Next

Alice Deal, Maret, Sidwell Friends, St. Albans.

Head Profile

Principal at John Eaton since 1976. Five years as program coordinator prior to principalship. DC recipient of Washington Post Distinguished Educational Leadership Award (Fall, 1987). Received Officers Incentive Award from DCPS for innovative program (1988). Member of Principals Institute of Harvard University.

Faculty Features

2	No. male teachers
29	No. female teachers
M	% turnover
15	Typical tenure (yrs.)
x	Art teacher (2)
x	Vocal music teacher
	Instrumental music teacher
x	Counselor/psychologist
x	Nurse

__x__ Language teacher (G5 Latin; G3 Spanish)
__x__ Math teacher (2)
__x__ Reading teacher (2)
__x__ P.E. teacher
__x__ Remedial reading teacher
__x__ Remedial math teacher
__x__ Speech therapist
__x__ Full-time science teacher
_____ Enrichment teacher
__x__ ESL teacher (2)
_____ Tutor
__x__ Assistant teachers (3)

Parents Say

Principal is confident, respected, dynamic, strong in administration, curriculum development, and initiating new programs.

Parent Wish List

A computer lab and computers in every classroom.
More emphasis on athletics.
Flexibility to move classroom teachers when strength apparent in specialty area.

Parent Involvement

Parents are greatly involved and responsible for placing more emphasis on various subjects, by having extra art teacher, developing new math curriculum, working with computers in classroom, before-school programs in Spanish and French, Great Books, and computers; Community Outreach projects, volunteering special skills and fund-raising events.
HSA-Home School Association.

Your Notes

Georgetown Day School

4530 MacArthur Boulevard NW, Washington, DC 20007
202/333-7727
HEAD: Gladys M. Stern

Basics

Year founded: 1945
Enrollment: 413 (PreK–6); 971 (PreK–12)*
  Boys: 204 (PreK–6)
  Girls: 209 (PreK–6)
Grades:*
Major entry grade: PreK, 1, 7
Birthdate req.: none
Arrival: 8:00 a.m.
Dismissal: 3:00 p.m.
Early dismissal: no
Extended day: 3:15–6:00 p.m.
Costs: $7632–$8436
Parent fund raising: $368,000
Transportation: no
Lunch: no
After-school activities: yes
Camp: no
Dress code: none
Neighborhood: Palisades, upper Wisconsin Avenue (high school)

Special Qualities

Diverse student body.
Country campus in Luray, VA.
Highly academic orientation.
Learning lab.
Students address teachers by first name.
Nontraditional atmosphere.
Individualization of teaching.
Extensive use of city resources.

Philosophy and Character

Parent-owned, nonsectarian.
Governed by board of trustees elected by parents.
Instruct students in academic disciplines, arts, and physical education in atmosphere supportive of each individual.
Teaching very "hands-on," less

*GDS is divided into Lower School (PreK–4), Middle School (5–8), and High School (9–12).

rote learning and more self-discovery.
Friday assemblies and four annual festivals for Christmas, MLK Day, Seder, Grandparents Day.
Goal to have diverse student body and faculty.
PreK class has 12 students in one section, K increases to 36 with 2 sections, G1 has 48 with 2 sections, G2 has 54 in 3 sections, and G3–6 have 64 students with 4 sections.
G4 participates in Martha's Table.
Very child-oriented, builds confidence, success.
First integrated school in 1940s.

Curriculum

Science: focus on hands-on experiments, life cycles and earth science 2x/week.
Math: problem solving and basic skill acquisition.
Art: introduction to materials, artistic self-confidence, 2x/wk.
Computers: brought into PreK–K; LOGO in lab.
Cooperative learning approach for PreK–K.
No foreign language until G5.
Drama class G1 up.
Reading in small groups, start with Open Court materials, phonics, begin to read G1.
Learning lab offers diagnostic services and remedial help.
No grades until G7, parent conferences in November, written reports December to June.

Special Spots

_x_ Computer room
_x_ Science lab
_x_ Dedicated music room
_x_ Music practice room
_x_ Gymnasium
_x_ Dedicated art room
_x_ Ceramic studio
_x_ Auditorium
___ Tennis court
___ Pool
_x_ Playing fields
___ Enrichment rooms
_x_ Library
_x_ Language lab
_x_ Dance studio
___ Separate lunchroom
_x_ Kitchen
___ Infirmary
_x_ Conference room
_x_ Multipurpose room
___ Expansion plans

Sports News

P.E. Instruction
___ Swimming

x Basketball
x Gymnastics
x Dance
x Softball
___ Skating
x Soccer
x Volleyball
___ Creative movement

Weekly P.E. class:
x PreK
___ Transition
x Kindergarten
x First
x Second
x Third
x Fourth
x Fifth
x Sixth

After-School Activities

None

Registration/Admissions

Francis Permenick.
Appointment for parent interview and tour.
Submit application, transcript, and recommendations.
Applicant visits school; 1 hr. PreK, ½ day K, full day G1 up.
Testing administered during school visit.

Financial aid given: $675,000 for 1988–89.
Apply to school by Feb. 15.

Where Next

Most students continue through G12.

Head Profile

Gladys Stern succeeded Edith Nash as the third director of Georgetown Day School in 1975. She has been associated with the school since 1955.

Faculty Features

30 No. male teachers
99 No. female teachers
10 % Turnover
___ Typical tenure
x Art teacher
x Vocal music teacher
x Instrumental music teacher
___ Counselor/psychologist
___ Nurse
x Language teacher
x Math teacher
___ Reading teacher
x P.E. teacher
___ Remedial reading teacher

____ Remedial math teacher
_x_ Speech therapist
_x_ Full-time science teacher
_x_ Enrichment teacher
____ ESL teacher
____ Tutor
_x_ Assistant teachers
_x_ Computer
_x_ Drama

Parent Involvement

Parents encouraged to volunteer.
Opportunities include library volunteer, classroom aide, playground and office helpers.
Fund raisers: country market day, spring auction; fund school activities.

Parents Say

Thoughtful, strengths include curriculum development, new programs, and teaching.

Parent Wish List

Bus, more sports, activities after school, continue large scholarships for very diverse student body.

Your Notes

Grace Episcopal Church Day School

3601 Russell Road, Alexandria, VA 22305
703/549-5067
HEAD: Shirley N. Tyler

Basics

Year founded: 1959
Enrollment: 91
  Boys: 49
  Girls: 42
Grades: N–3
Major entry grade: N, K
Birthdate req.: 3 yrs. by Sept. 30
Arrival: 8:45 a.m.
Dismissal: 12:00 noon (PreK), 3:00 p.m.
Early dismissal: no
Extended day: 7:30 a.m.–5:30 p.m.
Costs: $850–$4600
Parent fund raising: $3500–$6000
Transportation: no
Lunch: no
After-school activities: occasional
Camp: no
Dress code: comfortable attire
Neighborhood: Beverly Hills, Warwick Village, North Ridge

Special Qualities

Emphasis on values and Christian education.
Atmosphere allows for individual growth.
Low pupil-teacher ratio.
Teachers are competent and caring.
Prayers and grace said daily.
Strong in language arts, reading, math.
Extended-day program.

Philosophy and Character

Small coed preschool and primary parochial grade school.
Located in education wing of Episcopal church, suburban Alexandria.
Provides nurturing environment

and well-rounded education, fostering an awareness of God, His world, and sense of responsibility to others.
Weekly chapel service.
Religious holidays are celebrated, non-Christian holidays discussed.
All classes have 1 section; enrollment varies yearly and by class with 24 in N and 3 in G3.
Age-appropriate giving to community service projects.
99% students from VA.
Recently 15% minority enrollment, down from 30%.
Students range from moderate-income to upper-income families with majority in upper-middle now.
35–40% use extended-day service.

Curriculum

Focus on reading and language-related skills.
Developmental preschool program.
Reading, readiness program in PreK and K emphasizes readiness and love of books.
Houghton-Mifflin (HM) basal readers, SRA, Great Books, and phonics stressed in elementary reading program.
Language arts stresses process and creative writing—"whole language."
Math objectives: computational, conceptual, and analytical skills using HM program, computers, manipulatives.
Science in homeroom with texts, projects, teaching scientific method.
Religion G1–3 required.
Music class G1–3, N–K: rhythm band and instruments.
Art class G1–3 1x/week.
Homework begins G1 with 15 min. increasing to 1 hr. by G2.
No foreign language.

Special Spots

x	Computer area (in library)
	Science lab
x	Dedicated music room
	Music practice room
	Gymnasium
	Dedicated art room
	Ceramic studio
x	Auditorium
	Tennis court
	Pool
	Playing fields
	Enrichment rooms
x	Library (2000 volumes)
	Language lab
	Dance studio
	Separate lunchroom
x	Kitchen

_____ Infirmary
_____ Conference room
_____ Multipurpose room
_____ Expansion plans

Sports News

P.E. Instruction:
_____ Swimming
_____ Basketball
_____ Gymnastics
_____ Dance
_____ Softball
_____ Skating
_____ Soccer
__x__ Creative movement

Weekly P.E. class:
_____ Pre-K
_____ Transition
_____ Kindergarten
__3__ First
__3__ Second
__3__ Third
_____ Fourth
_____ Fifth
_____ Sixth

After-School Activities

Programs sometimes contracted.

Registration/Admissions

Director Shirley N. Tyler.
Ongoing application process; recommended to apply by Jan. 15.
Tour available.
Child interviews with director.
No PreK testing.
School administers screening tests for G2 and 3.
School recommendation and $45 application fee required.
Admission priority given to siblings, alumni children, parishioners.
Can accept limited number of students with mild learning or physical disability.
Limited financial aid based on need is given: $20,000 in 1988–89.
Apply to school director.

Where Next

St. Agnes, St. Stephen's, Maury, MacArthur, Barrett, Mt. Vernon, Polk, National Cathedral School.

Head Profile

Master's. Director since 1975. Teaches religion occasionally.

Faculty Features

__0__ No. male teachers
__8__ No. female teachers

N	Turnover (15%)
4–5	Typical tenure (yrs.)
x	Art teacher (part-time)
x	Vocal music teacher (part-time)
	Instrumental music teacher
	Counselor/psychologist
	Nurse
	Language teacher
	Math teacher
	Reading teacher
	P.E. teacher
	Remedial reading teacher
	Remedial math teacher
	Speech therapist
	Full-time science teacher
	Enrichment teacher
	ESL teacher
	Tutor
x	Assistant teachers (3)

Parents Say

Provides nurturing, academic environment.

Parent Wish List

More computer purchases and classes.

More emphasis on art and music.

Foreign language instruction.

Parent Involvement

School board establishes policies; faculty and parental input is encouraged.

Parent advisory committee meets regularly.

Parents involved in numerous ways: room parent, field trips, providing refreshments, fund raising, tutoring, etc.

Your Notes

Grace Episcopal Day School

9115 Georgia Avenue, Silver Spring, MD 20910 (N–K);
9411 Connecticut Avenue, Kensington, MD 20895 (G1–6)
301/585-3513; 301/949-5860
HEAD: Carol G. Hjortsberg

Basics

Year founded: 1960
Enrollment: 180*
  Boys: 96
  Girls: 84
Grades: N–6
Major entry grade: PreK, K
Birthdate req.: Dec. 31
Arrival: 9:00 a.m.
Dismissal: 3:00 p.m. Silver Spring; 3:15 p.m. Kensington
Early dismissal: no
Extended day: 8:00 a.m.–6:00 p.m.
Costs: $2000–$4000
Parent fund raising: $40,000
Transportation: no
Lunch: no
After-school activities: yes
Camp: yes
Dress code: uniform
Neighborhood: Silver Spring, Kensington

Philosophy and Character

Parish school of Grace Episcopal Church, governed by board of governors reporting to Vestry.
Traditional elementary curriculum emphasizing basics in reading, writing, math, science, and social studies with other enrichment programs.
Weekly worship chapel.
PreK–2 has 20–28 students per grade with two sections.
G3 up has 12–14 students per grade with one section.
Students of different religious backgrounds welcomed.

*Adding additional PreK and G3 sections 1989–90 and expanding total enrollment to 190–200.

Students mainly from NW DC and Montgomery County.
Community outreach activities pursued at community nursing home and senior center.

Curriculum

One of K sections can serve as transition year before G1.
Language arts: starts in N, phonics stressed; Houghton Mifflin basal readers, novels and plays used, grammar and spelling taught.
Math: resource teacher assists classroom teachers, Open Court text G1–6, manipulatives N–1, well-supplied math lab.
Science: hands-on N–2 with resource teacher helping classroom teacher, science teacher for G3–6 instructs in physical and natural sciences.
Spanish taught K–6 with Latin G5–6.
Computers in classrooms K–2 and word-processing LOGO instruction G3–6 by computer teacher.
Music teacher for N–G6 teaches how to read music, recorder, chimes; various music events throughout year.
Art: daily N–K; 1 hr. per week G1–6 with art teacher, spring art fair.
Religious instruction for G5–6.
Homework begins G1.
Chapel and outreach; rector conducts chapel and teaches religion.

Special Spots

__x__ Computer room
__x__ Science lab
__x__ Dedicated music room
_____ Music practice room
_____ Gymnasium
__x__ Dedicated art room
_____ Ceramic studio
_____ Auditorium
_____ Tennis court
_____ Pool
__x__ Playing fields
_____ Enrichment rooms
__x__ Library
_____ Language lab
_____ Dance studio
_____ Separate lunchroom
__x__ Kitchen
_____ Infirmary
_____ Conference room
__x__ Multipurpose room
_____ Expansion plans

Sports News

P.E. Instruction*
_____ Swimming

*Incorporated seasonally into weekly PE class.

_____ Basketball
_____ Gymnastics
_____ Dance
_____ Softball
_____ Skating
_____ Soccer
_____ Volleyball
_____ Creative movement

Weekly P.E. class

2	PreK
2	Transition
2	Kindergarten
3	First
3	Second
3	Third
3	Fourth
2–3	Fifth
2–3	Sixth

After-School Activities

Enrichment classes in science, art, computer.

Registration/Admissions

Open house in November and January.
Parent interview with administrator and tour scheduled by appointment.
Application deadline Feb. 15 with rolling admissions if space is available.
Applicants for K–6 are tested and visit classroom.
Teacher recommendations and school forms are required.
Financial aid available: submit Princeton form; $18,500 given in 1988–89.

Where Next

St. Andrew's (accepts early decision candidates), St. Albans School, St. Anselms, St. John's Military, Mater Dei, Sidwell Friends, Stone Ridge, National Cathedral.

Head Profile

Head of Grace School since 1986. B.A., M.S. Serves on boards of Association of Independent Schools of Greater Washington (AISGW) and Mid-Atlantic Episcopal School Association (MAESA). Former president of MAESA and member of National Association of Episcopal Schools Governing Board.

Faculty Features

1	No. male teachers
26	No. female teachers

N Turnover
___ Typical tenure
x Art teacher
___ Vocal music teacher
___ Instrumental music teacher
___ Counselor/psychologist
___ Nurse
___ Language teacher
x Math teacher
___ Reading teacher
x P.E. teacher
___ Remedial reading teacher
___ Remedial math teacher
___ Speech therapist
x Full-time science teacher (part-time)
___ Enrichment teacher
___ ESL teacher
___ Tutor
___ Assistant teachers
x Computer teacher
x Librarian

Parents Say

School has a warm and caring atmosphere, individualized classes, and encourages students to do best at own pace.

Parent Wish List

Transportation, more sports programs such as soccer or softball teams, on-staff resource teacher.

Parent Involvement

Hard-working PTO. School welcomes volunteers—opportunities include fund raisers such as auction or gift wrap sales, room parent, and field trip chaperones.

Your Notes

Green Acres School

11701 Danville Drive, Rockville, MD 20852
301/881-4100
HEAD: Anne T. Goodrich

Basics

Year founded: 1934
Enrollment: 290
 Boys: 145
 Girls: 145
Grades: N–8
Major entry grade: N, PreK, K
Birthdate req.: 3.3 yrs by Sept. 1
Arrival: 8:30 a.m.
Dismissal: 3:00 p.m.
Early dismissal: Wed., 2:00 p.m.
Extended day: no
Costs: \$2775–\$5550
Parent fund raising: \$100,000
Transportation: yes
Lunch: no
After-school activities: yes
Camp: yes
Dress code: none
Neighborhood: Luxmanor area of Rockville

Special Qualities

Real world, hands-on approach to learning using many varied styles, materials, environments.
Philosophy of recreating and living the experience.
Social studies provides unifying element to curriculum.
Mixed age grouping in classrooms.
Small-group instruction.

Philosophy and Character

15-acre wooded campus with Center for Performing Arts and Physical Education.
Progressive philosophy: believes children are curious about their world and learn best in informal, flexible environment and by doing, then integrate knowledge.
Individuality respected.
Classes structured to respond to different learning styles.
Group gathers for weekly assemblies.

Class size is generally between 20–30 with one section per class.
Students primarily from MD 69%, DC 30%, VA 1%.

Curriculum

Developmental approach.
Mostly heterogeneous groupings.
Language literacy begins in N with formal program in G1, phonics and all methods used to meet varied learning styles; literature-based.
Write every day—journals, poem, newspaper with editing sessions to brainstorm ideas.
Math: always hands-on before paper tests, develop logical thinking, practical applications, and how math relates to world.
Science: experimental, hands-on, many animals, gardens.
Spanish begins in G5.
Social studies theme for other subjects.
Art includes woodworking, batik, pottery.
P.E.: creative problem solving using bodies.
Recorder and computer start G3.
Narrative reports N–6, letter grades added G7–8.
Homework begins G3, ½ hr.

Special Spots

__x__ Computer room
__x__ Science lab
__x__ Dedicated music room
_____ Music practice room
__x__ Gymnasium
__x__ Dedicated art room
_____ Ceramic studio
__x__ Auditorium
_____ Tennis court
__x__ Pool
__x__ Playing fields
__x__ Enrichment rooms
__x__ Library (11,000 volumes)
_____ Language lab
_____ Dance studio
_____ Separate lunchroom
__x__ Kitchen
_____ Infirmary
_____ Conference room
__x__ Expansion plans (new 3-room classroom building 1989)

Sports News

P.E. Instruction
_____ Swimming
__x__ Basketball
__x__ Gymnastics
__x__ Dance
__x__ Softball
_____ Skating
__x__ Soccer
_____ Volleyball
_____ Creative movement

Weekly P.E. class:

1	PreK
4	Kindergarten
6	First
6	Second
5	Third
5	Fourth
3	Fifth
3	Sixth

After-School Activities

Art, ceramics, dance, computer, athletics, Brownies, photography, drama.

Registration/Admissions

Ursula Ferro.
Call for place on school tour.
Tours Wed. at 9:30 a.m., mid-Oct. to mid-Feb.
Application deadline Feb. 1.
Parent interview.
Schedule group visit for child and individual visit for G1 up.
Previous school records required.
Notification by end of March.
Financial aid $87,000 in 1988–89.
Apply to School Scholarship Service in Princeton.

Where Next

Georgetown Day, Sidwell Friends, Maret, St. Albans, Edmund Burke, St. Andrew's.

Head Profile

B.A., Wellesley, 1946; M.A., Antioch College, 1978. Five years teaching, ten years administration. At Green Acres since 1979. Strong in faculty relations, supervision of programs, and involvement with students. Believes school should provide a humane environment where learning and growing are happy and successful.

Faculty Features

4	No. male teachers
36	No. female teachers
M	Turnover
8–10	Typical tenure (yrs.)
x	Art teacher (2)
x	Vocal music teacher
	Instrumental music teacher
x	Counselor/psychologist
	Nurse
x	Language teacher
x	Math teacher
x	Reading teacher

__x__ P.E. teacher (2)
_____ Remedial reading teacher
_____ Remedial math teacher
_____ Speech therapist
__x__ Full-time science teachers
_____ Enrichment teacher
_____ ESL teacher
__x__ Tutor (arrange through Kingsbury Center)

Parents Say

unavailable

Parent Wish List

unavailable

Parent Involvement

Active participation.
Outdoor workdays.
Fall Corporation Dinner, Spring Corporation Evening, and parent-run auction.
Publish *Going Places with Children in Washington, D.C.*
Development office coordinates and produces newsletters to keep parents informed.

Your Notes

Green Hedges School

415 Windover Avenue, Vienna, VA 22180
703/938-8323
HEAD: Kathleen H. Battaglia

Basics

Year founded: 1942
Enrollment: 200
  Boys: 104
  Girls: 96
Grades: PreK–8
Major entry grade: PreK, 1, 4
Birthdate req.: 2½–3 yrs.
Arrival: 8:30 a.m.
Dismissal: 11:30 a.m. (PreK); 3:00 p.m.
Early dismissal: no
Extended day: no
Costs: $3850–$5860 (G6)
Parent fund raising: u
Transportation: no
Lunch: no
After-school activities: yes
Camp: yes
Dress code: appropriate for school, uniform on special occasions (G3–8)
Neighborhood: Windover Heights

Special Qualities

Well-rounded curriculum with emphasis on fine arts, foreign language, science, and math.
Montessori primary school with traditional school G1–G8.

Philosophy and Character

Believes happy child learns best.
Stresses both educational excellence through mastery of basics and child's development of self-discipline, motivation, and independent thinking.
Students gather each day for "opening exercise."
Strong involvement in Vienna community, joint band concerts, fairs open to public.
PreK and K grades range from 45–30 each with 3 sections,

G1–2 currently have 2 sections and G3–6 have 1 section each.
Students mainly from VA with 1% MD.
10% minority enrollment.

Curriculum

PreK–K is Montessori approach with bridge to traditional instruction in G1.
Homework begins G1.
Homeroom teachers G1–3 assisted by specialists in French, library, art, music, drama, computer, P.E.
Curriculum departmentalized G4 up.
PreK–K emphasizes independent work time, French daily, music, art, and P.E.
Reading taught daily G1–6, no "reading groups," phonics stressed, literature program focus.
Yearly drama production each grade.
Music daily using Kodaly method, many performances, recorder taught, attend concerts, after-school band and chorus.
Art incorporates skill and concept mastery with encouragement of creativity.
Weekly library classes.
Oral French introduced age 2 and continued through G8, with Latin G4 up, Spanish optional G5 up.
Computer training starts G1, intro to LOGO G2, daily computer science G5–8.

Special Spots

__x__ Computer room
__x__ Science lab
_____ Dedicated music room
_____ Gymnasium
__x__ Dedicated art room
_____ Ceramic studio
__x__ Auditorium
_____ Tennis court
_____ Pool
__x__ Playing field
_____ Enrichment rooms
__x__ Library (8000 vols)
_____ Language lab
_____ Dance studio
_____ Separate lunchroom
_____ Kitchen
_____ Infirmary
__x__ Conference room
__x__ Expansion plans: multi-purpose room

Sports News

P.E. Instruction
_____ Swimming
_____ Basketball

____	Gymnastics
____	Dance
x	Softball
____	Skating
x	Soccer
x	Volleyball
____	Creative movement
x	Field hockey, lacrosse

Weekly P.E. class

3	PreK
____	Transition
3	Kindergarten
4	First
3	Second
4	Third
5	Fourth
4	Fifth
5	Sixth

After-School Activities

Chorus, band, drama, computer club.

Registration/Admissions

Marian White 703/938-8471.
Call for brochure, tour, and interview.
Apply Oct.–Jan.
Parents arrange for submission of recommendations, transcripts, test scores.
Applicant must visit.
School administers Otis-Lennon and SAT, results available through conference meeting.
Siblings receive admission priority.
Financial aid available by application to school head, $33,800 given 1988–89.

Where Next

Sidwell Friends, Georgetown Day, Madeira, Landon, Holton-Arms, St. Stephen's, Thomas Jefferson H.S. for Science and Technology.

Head Profile

With school since 1971.

Faculty Features

1	No. male teachers
22	No. female teachers
N	% turnover (7–9%)
6+	Typical tenure (yrs.)
____	Art teacher
x	Vocal music teacher
x	Instrumental music teacher
x	Counselor/psychologist
____	Nurse
x	Language teacher (2)

_x_ Math teacher
___ Reading teacher
_x_ P.E. teacher
___ Remedial reading teacher
___ Remedial math teacher
___ Speech therapist
_x_ Full-time science teacher
___ Enrichment teacher
___ ESL teacher
___ Tutor
___ Assistant teachers
_x_ Computer science teacher

Parents Say

unavailable

Parent Wish List

unavailable

Parent Involvement

Parents organization provides volunteers for support activities, help with school events, such as fun fair, book fair.

Volunteer support for auction and annual giving.

Your Notes

The Harbor School

6601 Bradley Boulevard, Bethesda, MD 20817
301/365-1100
HEAD: Beverly M. Bonwit

Basics

Year founded: 1973
Enrollment: 150
  Boys: 94
  Girls: 56
Grades: N3–2/3
Major entry grade: 3 yrs./5 yrs.
Birthdate req.: Oct. 31
Arrival: 9:15 a.m.
Dismissal: 3:00 p.m.
Early dismissal: Fri., 12:15 p.m. (K); 2:00 p.m. (G1, 2)
Extended day: 8:15 a.m.–6:00 p.m.
Costs: $2525–$4915
Parent fund raising: $15,000–25,000
Transportation: no
Lunch: no
After-school activities: no
Camp: no
Dress code: none
Neighborhood: Bradley Hills area of Bethesda

Special Qualities

Small classes, individualized program, and independent work.
Interesting curriculum features: artist-in-residence program, National Zoo Science program, continual monitoring of reading and math group placement so never static.
Known for quality materials.

Philosophy and Character

A nonprofit, independent, coed nondenominational school serving N–G2.
A harbor is a place that is secure and protected, a place to prepare for a journey.
Key to learning based on stimulating and teaching to child's own level and own pace.
Located in church facility.

Religious holidays not celebrated.
Preventive discipline a result of room arrangements, scheduling, and clear standards.
Absence from school approved if engaged in enriching family activity.
98% of students from MD.
Walls collapse and K classrooms virtually fold up on Friday.
Flexible space.
Each classroom has desk and reading nook area.
30–40% preschool children use extended day.

Curriculum

Preschool: separate cognitive and creative arts rooms to focus activities.
Primary: full-time resource teachers to accommodate reading and math in small groups at skill level.
Thematic curriculum studying one topic in all areas.
Concrete materials used to develop math concepts.
Science hands-on, with teachers trained to use National Zoo kits.
Computer introduced in K with LOGO.
Artist in-residence program for 6-week in-depth project.
French in preschool.
Virtually no homework except spelling words.

Special Spots

__x__ Computer room
_____ Science lab
_____ Dedicated music room
_____ Music practice room
_____ Gymnasium
_____ Dedicated art room
_____ Ceramic studio
_____ Auditorium
_____ Tennis court
_____ Pool
__x__ Playing fields
_____ Enrichment rooms
__x__ Library
_____ Language lab
_____ Dance studio
_____ Separate lunchroom
__x__ Kitchen
_____ Infirmary
__x__ Conference room
_____ Expansion plans

Sports News

P.E. Instruction
_____ Swimming
_____ Basketball
_____ Gymnastics
_____ Dance
__x__ Softball

_____ Skating
_____ Soccer

Weekly P.E. class
_0_ PreK
_____ Transition
_2_ Kindergarten
_2_ First
_2_ Second
_____ Third
_____ Fourth
_____ Fifth
_____ Sixth

After-School Activities

None

Registration/Admissions

Marti Jacobs.
Open admissions policy with applications starting Oct. 1; no deadlines.
First-come, first-served basis with sibling priority.
No interviewing or testing.
Parents required to observe.
Submit an application and $35 fee.
Teacher recommendation from previous school (if applicable).
Acceptances in late Feb.
Students accepted mid-year if space available.

A few scholarships every year based on need by contacting director.

Where Next

Norwood, Holton Arms, Landon, Georgetown Day, public schools.

Head Profile

B.A. in 1951 with varied graduate level courses in education and adminstration. Taught elementary grades in public school. Also preschool teacher and administrative assistant before founding Harbor in 1973. Visits classrooms frequently, reviews curriculum weekly. Encourages students to share a project or job well done. Selects unique educational materials—a hallmark of Harbor.

Faculty Features

_0_ No. male teachers
_19_ No. female teachers
_M_ Turnover (10%)
_4–5_ Typical tenure (yrs.)
_____ Art teacher
_x_ Vocal music teacher
_____ Instrumental music teacher

_____ Counselor/psychologist
_____ Nurse
__x__ Language teacher
__x__ Math teacher
__x__ Reading teacher
__x__ P.E. teacher
_____ Remedial reading teacher
_____ Remedial math teacher
_____ Speech therapist
__x__ Full-time science teacher
_____ Enrichment teacher
_____ ESL teacher
_____ Tutor

Parents Say

Head is academically strong, flexible, caring, committed to children and their long-range welfare. School provides a "safe harbor" for children. Staff and teachers very interested in students and families.

Parents Wish List

After-school activities.
Expansion to G6.
More computers.

Parent Involvement

Volunteer opportunities: room parents, parents association committees, library, theater, book fair.
Fund raising includes elaborate 100-family estate sale.

Your Notes

Hearst Elementary School

37th and Tilden Streets NW, Washington, DC 20008
202/282-0106
HEAD: Patricia Greer

Basics

Year founded: 1932
Enrollment: 158
  Boys: 94
  Girls: 64
Grades: PreK–6
Major entry grades: na
Birthdate req.: Dec. 31
Arrival: 9:00 a.m.
Dismissal: 3:00 p.m.
Early dismissal: no
Extended day: 7:45 a.m.–6:00 p.m.
Costs: na
Parent fund raising: $12,000–$15,000
Transportation: no
Lunch: yes
After-school activities: yes
Camp: DC Recreation Dept.
Dress code: none
Neighborhood: Cleveland Park/ Woodley Park

Special Qualities

Stable faculty.
Math program is excellent and teachers are creative.
Young Astronauts, Life lab, etc.
Science programs Ft. Dupont.
Outdoor classroom.

Philosophy and Character

Parents support the school's philosophy that every child has inherent right to education and individual growth of students is important.
Large out-of-neighborhood student population.
Ethnically diverse and truly integrated student body.
Homey, small school.
Expect, believe, achieve theme for 1989–90.

Foster grandparent program with Washington Home and food drives for needy families.
Classes range in size from 14–23.

Curriculum

CTBS test scores: G3 G6

Reading:	G3	87 percentile
	G6	83 percentile
Math:	G3	82 percentile
	G6	93 percentile
Language:	G3	85 percentile
	G6	89 percentile
Science:	G3	80 percentile
	G6	84 percentile

Math: innovative, hands-on program.
Science: hands-on, process approach.
Reading: use basal readers and a great deal of literature PreK–6.
Creative writing: writing process, 1st draft, 2nd draft, edit, confer, final draft—generate own ideas.
Parent-paid art teacher, minimal program.
Environmental scientist from Catholic University.
Architectural program for G6 from UDC.

Special Spots

_____ Computer room
__x__ Science lab (resource center)
_____ Dedicated music room
_____ Music practice room
_____ Gymnasium
_____ Dedicated art room
_____ Ceramic studio
_____ Auditorium
_____ Tennis court
_____ Pool
__x__ Playing fields
_____ Enrichment rooms
__x__ Library
_____ Language lab
_____ Dance studio
_____ Separate lunchroom
_____ Kitchen
_____ Infirmary
_____ Conference room
__x__ Multipurpose room
_____ Expansion plans

Sports News

P.E. Instruction
_____ Swimming
_____ Basketball
_____ Gymnastics
_____ Dance
__x__ Softball
_____ Skating
_____ Soccer
__x__ Volleyball
_____ Creative movement
__x__ Calisthenics

Weekly P.E. class:
__1__ Pre-K
_____ Transition

1	Kindergarten
1	First
1	Second
1	Third
1	Fourth
1	Fifth
1	Sixth

After-School Activities

PTA sponsors arts, crafts, and field trips.

D.C. Dept. of Recreation sponsors some programs.

Registration/Admissions

April is registration month in DC public schools.

Watch for newspaper notification or bulletins.

Proof of residency, child's birth certificate, and immunization record are required.

PreK classes fill up quickly and children enrolled on first-come, first-served basis.

Wise to sign up during scheduled registration period.

Apply for out-of-boundary admission at school; acceptance is limited. Out-of-state admission requires tuition of $1880–$2727.

Where Next

Deal.

Head Profile

Hearst shares principal with John Eaton Elementary School.

Faculty Features

1	No. male teachers
10	No. female teachers
N	% turnover
15	Typical tenure (yrs.)
	Art teacher
x	Vocal music teacher (& theory)
	Instrumental music teacher
x	Counselor/psychologist (3x/wk)
	Nurse
	Language teacher
x	Math teacher (resource)
	Reading teacher
x	P.E. teacher (part-time)
x	Remedial reading teacher
	Remedial math teacher
x	Speech therapist (part-time)
	Science teacher
	Enrichment teacher
x	ESL teacher
x	Tutor (2 from Sidwell)

x Assistant teachers
x Aide

Parents Say

Optimistic attitude at school with feeling that it is improving and moving forward. Large percentage of working mothers and out-of-neighborhood parents leads to minimal participation; however, an upswing has been noticed.

Parent Wish List

Hot lunch.
Better science, music, and art programs.

Parent Involvement

Parents substitute teach and do fund raising.
Hardworking PTA.
Fund raisers include school fair, magazine drive, phone-a-thon, and international night.

Your Notes

Holy Trinity School

1325 36th Street NW, Washington, DC 20007
202/337-2339
HEAD: Ann Marie Santora

Basics

Year founded: mid-1800s
Enrollment: 325
  Boys: unavailable
  Girls: unavailable
Grades: N3–8
Major entry grade: N3–K
Birthdate req.: 3 yrs.
Arrival: 8:30 a.m.
Dismissal: 3:00 p.m.
Early dismissal: 1st and 3rd Thurs. of each month, 1:00 p.m.
Extended day: 7:30 a.m.–6:00 p.m.
Costs: $2200–$2600; N–K $3500
Parent fund raising: $25,000
Transportation: no
Lunch: no
After-school activities: yes
Camp: no
Dress code: uniforms G1 up
Neighborhood: Georgetown

Special Qualities

Catholic school with high academic standards and traditional values.
Diverse student body.
Location in historic Georgetown.

Philosophy and Character

Catholic parish school providing basic traditional education with emphasis on hard work, discipline, self-respect, and youthful high spirit.
Accepts non-English-speaking students.
N and PreK class range from 10–15 with 1 section; K expands to 30 students with 2 sections and other grades except G3 have 1 section.

Half of student body comes from Georgetown.

Socially, racially, and economically diverse student body, 25% non-Catholic, 12 nationalities represented.

Students participate in food and clothing drives.

Curriculum

Students grouped by ability for reading instruction.

Remedial and accelerated classes available.

Tutoring provided for learning-disabled students.

Academic program is textbook-oriented.

Homework begins G2.

Foreign language instruction begins G2.

Academic program departmentalized G5 up.

Parents help run the athletic program, G5 up use Yates Field House at Georgetown University.

Computer education begins G1.

Special Spots

__x__ Computer room
__x__ Science lab
_____ Dedicated music room
_____ Music practice room
_____ Gymnasium
__x__ Dedicated art room
_____ Ceramic studio
__x__ Auditorium
__x__ Tennis court
_____ Pool
_____ Playing fields
_____ Enrichment rooms
__x__ Library
_____ Language lab
_____ Dance studio
_____ Separate lunchroom
_____ Kitchen
_____ Infirmary
_____ Conference room
__x__ Multipurpose room
__x__ Expansion plans (hired architect to design new playground equipment)

Sports News

P.E. Instruction

__x__ Swimming (G5 up)
__x__ Basketball
__x__ Gymnastics
_____ Dance
__x__ Softball
_____ Skating
__x__ Soccer
_____ Volleyball
__x__ Creative movement

Weekly PE class

__2__ Pre-K
_____ Transition

2	Kindergarten
2	First
2	Second
2	Third
2	Fourth
	Fifth
	Sixth

After-School Activities

Athletic teams, French, ballet, gymnastics.

Registration/Admissions

Information given 9:30 am.–3:00 p.m.

Call in December or January for appointment to visit N program.

Applicants for N–K are given an interview.

Entrance testing for G1 up.

Financial aid is available with priority given to current families.

Where Next

Gonzaga, Visitation.

Head Profile

unavailable

Faculty Features

3	No. male teachers
u	No. female teachers
M	% turnover
u	Typical tenure
x	Art teacher
x	Vocal music teacher
	Instrumental music teacher
	Counselor/psychologist
x	Nurse
x	Language teacher (French, Spanish)
	Math teacher
	Reading teacher
x	P.E. teacher
x	Remedial reading teacher
	Remedial math teacher
x	Speech therapist
	Full-time science teacher
	Enrichment teacher
	ESL teacher
x	Tutor (Kingsbury Center for learning-disabled students)
	Assistant teachers

Parents Say

Parents rate principal highly. School has warm, caring environment; stresses self-respect, respect for others, and Christian values.

Parent Wish List

Gymnasium; instrumental music; more equipment for music and art programs; hands-on science program.

Parent Involvement

Home-School Association is active, but no pressure to participate.

Volunteer opportunities include fund raising, coaching, special projects.

Fund raisers include auction, gala, Christmas Bazaar; proceeds fund equipment, teacher bonuses, etc.

Your Notes

Hyde Elementary School

32nd and O Streets NW, Washington, DC 20007
202/282-0170
HEAD: George Gaudette (acting principal)

Basics

Year founded: 1900s
Enrollment: 150
  Boys: 78
  Girls: 72
Grades: PreK–5
Major entry grade: na
Birthdate req.: Dec. 31
Arrival: 9:00 a.m.
Dismissal: 3:00 p.m.
Early dismissal: no
Extended day: 7:30 a.m.–6:00 p.m.
Costs: na
Parent fund raising: $7000
Transportation: no
Lunch: yes
After-school activities: no
Camp: no
Dress code: none
Neighborhood: Georgetown

Special Qualities

Sing-alongs on Thurs.
Really good teachers.
Small, family-like atmosphere.
International student mix.
Warm, friendly, kind place to learn.
Drug and other substance-abuse awareness, tutoring available after school.

Philosophy and Character

Hyde is part of a six-school complex: the complex is an alliance of four elementary schools (Hyde, Key, Stoddert, and Mann); a middle school (Hardy); and an arts center (Fillmore). Each school has its own faculty, PTA, and campus. The complex was formed in 1974.
Developmental program of instruction.
Diverse school population of students from all over the world with very diverse academic levels as well.

About ⅓ out-of-boundary students.

Has PreK program for 4-year-olds; classes range in size from 17–24 in recent years.

Pen pals in other states.

Curriculum

CTBS test scores: G3*

Reading: 38 percentile

Math: 66 percentile

Language: 82 percentile

Science: 53 percentile

Jr. Great Books Project.

Computer lab is attended by all students 1 hr./week.

Fillmore Arts Center provides instrumental and vocal music, drama, fine arts.

ESL program available.

Monthly writing contest with prizes awarded for best scores.

Special Spots

__x__ Computer room
_____ Science lab
_____ Dedicated music room
__x__ Music practice room (Fillmore)
_____ Gymnasium
__x__ Dedicated art room (Fillmore)
__x__ Ceramic studio (Fillmore)
_____ Auditorium
_____ Tennis court
_____ Pool
__x__ Playing fields
__x__ Enrichment rooms
__x__ Library (2000+ volumes)
__x__ Language lab
_____ Dance studio
__x__ Separate lunchroom
_____ Kitchen
_____ Infirmary
_____ Conference room
__x__ Multipurpose room
_____ Expansion plans

Sports News

P.E. Instruction
_____ Swimming
_____ Basketball
_____ Gymnastics
_____ Dance
_____ Softball
_____ Skating
_____ Soccer
_____ Volleyball
__x__ Creative movement

Weekly P.E. class
__1__ Pre-K
_____ Transition
__1__ Kindergarten
__1__ First
__1__ Second

*May 1989 results.

__1__ Third
__1__ Fourth
__1__ Fifth
__1__ Sixth

After-School Activities

None

Registration/Admissions

April is registration month in DC public schools.
Watch for newspaper notification or bulletins.
Proof of residency, child's birth certificate, immunization record.
PreK: 4 by Dec. 31; K: 5 by Dec. 31.
PreK classes fill up quickly and children enrolled on first-come, first-served basis.
Wise to sign up during scheduled registration period.
Out-of-area is first-come, first-served handled at Division of Elementary Education.

Where Next

Hardy Middle School.

Head Profile

Acting principal has 18 years experience, works closely with teachers on curriculum, door always open to welcome any child, wants to give children sense of security, hopes to strength English as a second language (ESL) program.

Faculty Features

__1__ No. male teachers (principal)
__9__ No. female teachers
__M__ % turnover
__10__ Typical tenure (yrs.)
__x__ Art teacher (Fillmore)
_____ Vocal music teacher
__x__ Instrumental music teacher (Fillmore)
__x__ Counselor/psychologist (part-time)
_____ Nurse (1x/mo)
__x__ Language teacher (Spanish—part-time)
__x__ Math teacher (computer/ math resource)
__x__ Reading teacher (part-time)
__x__ P.E. teacher
_____ Remedial reading teacher
_____ Remedial math teacher
__x__ Speech therapist (2x/wk)
__x__ Full-time science teacher (½ time)

_x_ Enrichment teacher
_x_ ESL teacher
___ Tutor
_x_ Assistant teachers (3)
_x_ Special ed

Parents Say

Principal is wonderful, keeps teddy bear in office to help children having bad day, really tuned into kids, substitutes in classroom, has changed atmosphere of school tremendously.

Parent Wish List

Piano, auditorium, full-time language teacher, upgrading playground equipment, science lab, computers in all classrooms.

Parent Involvement

Very supportive; fund raisers include international dinner and annual Fall Festival; money raised goes for materials and supplies generally.

Parents assist teachers, tutor, and supervise.

Working with principal to develop science lab.

Your Notes

Janney Elementary School

42nd and Albemarle Streets NW, Washington, DC 20016
202/282-0110
HEAD: Anne Gay

Basics

Year founded: 1925
Enrollment: 285
  Boys: 136
  Girls: 149
Grades: PreK–6
Major entry grade: na
Birthdate req.: Dec. 31
Arrival: 9:00 a.m.
Dismissal: 3:00 p.m.
Early dismissal: none
Extended day: 7:30 a.m.–6:00 p.m.
Costs: na
Parent fund raising: $30,000
Transportation: no
Lunch: yes
After-school activities: yes
Camp: no
Dress code: none
Neighborhood: American University Park

Philosophy and Character

One of 15 school-based management programs (SBM), giving principal greater autonomy in curriculum development, etc.
Very child-oriented.
Providing excellent education with a strong community and neighborhood support system.
Emphasis on science fair and classroom projects.
Has PreK class with approximately 20 students, other grades range from 29–40.
VIP day for each child beginning G2.
Self-motivation and independence encouraged.
Many diplomatic families representing countries such as Italy, Hungary, Brunei, Canada, Turkey, Spain.

Iona House senior citizens contribute loving personal touch and time as readers.

Curriculum

CTBS Test Scores:	G3	G6*
Reading:	87	90 percentile
Math:	95	94 percentile
Language:	96	84 percentile
Science:	91	85 percentile

Reading is supplemented by an excellent librarian, using library in as many usual and unusual ways as possible.

Spanish is one 45-min. period/ week.

Teachers stress long-range projects such as pioneer journal.

Work individually and in small groups.

Special Spots

_x_ Computer room
_x_ Science lab
_x_ Dedicated music room
___ Music practice room
_x_ Gymnasium
___ Dedicated art room (share with music room)
___ Ceramic studio
___ Auditorium
___ Tennis court
___ Pool
_x_ Playing fields
_x_ Enrichment rooms
_x_ Library
___ Language lab
___ Dance studio
___ Separate lunchroom
___ Kitchen
___ Infirmary
___ Conference room
___ Multipurpose room
_x_ Expansion plans

Sports News

P.E. Instruction:
___ Swimming
_x_ Basketball
_x_ Gymnastics
_x_ Dance
_x_ Softball
_x_ Skating
_x_ Soccer
_x_ Volleyball
_x_ Creative movement

Weekly P.E. class:
_1_ Pre-K
___ Transition
_1_ Kindergarten
_1_ First
_1_ Second

*May 1989 results.

1	Third
1	Fourth
1	Fifth
1	Sixth

After-School Activities

(PTA) Ceramics, gymnastics, choir, drawing, ballet, science, drama.

Registration/Admissions

April is registration month in DC public schools.

Watch for newspaper notification or bulletins.

Proof of residency, birth certificate, immunization record.

PreK: 4 by Dec. 31; K: 5 by Dec. 31.

PreK classes fill up quickly, children enrolled on first-come, first-served basis.

Wise to sign up during scheduled registration period.

Out-of-area is first-come, first-served and is handled at Division of Elementary Education.

Where Next

Deal (50%), Sidwell, Maret, Georgetown Day (50%).

Head Profile

Four years with DCPS, at Janney since 1989, taught in private and parochial inner-city schools, doctoral candidate at Catholic University. Wants to update science and math curriculums with interdisciplinary approach to real world, keep process exciting and dynamic.

Faculty Features

3	No. male teachers
12	No. female teachers
N	Turnover
10	Typical tenure (yrs.)
x	Art teacher
x	Vocal music teacher
	Instrumental music teacher
x	Counselor/psychologist
x	Nurse (1x/wk)
x	Language teacher
	Math teacher
	Reading teacher
x	P.E. teacher (part-time)
	Remedial reading teacher
	Remedial math teacher
x	Speech therapist (50%)
x	Full-time science teacher
x	Enrichment teacher (also gifted/talented)
x	ESL teacher
x	Tutor

__x__ Art therapist (fee)
__x__ Aides (5)
__x__ Special ed

Parents Say

Principal is committed, imaginative, energetic, friendly, effective, open.

Parent Wish List

Stronger P.E., improved science and math, more language, make music exciting, smaller classes.

Parent Involvement

Very active PTA, "Parent Watch" project for hall monitoring, participated in selection of new principal, ideas welcome and rigorously debated; extensive volunteering in classroom.

Your Notes

Key Elementary School

Hurst Terrace and Dana Place NW, Washington, DC 20016
202/282-0113
HEAD: Mrs. Dolores Martin (acting principal)

Basics

Year founded: 1929
Enrollment: 171
 Boys: 89
 Girls: 82
Grades: PreK–5
Major entry grade: na
Birthdate req.: Dec. 31
Arrival: 8:50 a.m.
Dismissal: 3:00 p.m.
Extended day: 7:30 a.m.–6:00 p.m.
Costs: na
Parent fund raising: approx. $10,000
Transportation: no
Lunch: yes
After-school activities: yes
Camp: no
Dress code: none
Neighborhood: Palisades

Special Qualities

Strong PTA.
Japan in School and garden.
Close-knit community school.
National Geographic Japan project, which includes Sat. training for teachers, exposure to undersea exploration for kids.

Philosophy and Character

Neighborhood school.
Friendly, personable, low stress, caring environment.
Japan-related instruction as a result of study tour to Japan—at U. of Maryland project to introduce other cultures to schools.
Japanese resource center available through Mid-Atlantic Region Japan in Schools.
Has PreK program with approximately 20 students, the larger K class has 2 sections, other grades range from 21–28 with one section.
Several non-U.S. students in each

class, under 10% minority enrollment.
30 out-of-area students.

Curriculum

CTBS Test Scores: G3*
Reading: 80 percentile
Math: 89 percentile
Language: 97 percentile
Science: 73 percentile
CBC curriculum guidelines used.
Math: Merrill text as resource, computer program with up-to-date computer lab.
Japanese program offers cultural enrichment with language, gardening.
Environmental science program; science 2x/wk with teacher hired by PTA; National Geographic science enrichment.
Above level reading and math groups for every class; homeroom teacher and librarian team used.
New approach in K due to increased parent/teacher ratio. Two teachers and one aide team teach in two spaces. One focuses on language arts and small motor skills, while other focuses on math and science and larger motor skills.

*May 1989 results.

Calisthenics, games, ball kicking, throwing in 1x/week PE class.

Special Spots

__x__ Computer room (10 IBM, LOGO)
__x__ Science lab (mobile equip)
_____ Dedicated music room
_____ Music practice room
_____ Gymnasium
__x__ Dedicated art room (Fillmore)
__x__ Ceramic studio (Fillmore)
_____ Auditorium
_____ Tennis court
_____ Pool
__x__ Playing fields
_____ Enrichment rooms
__x__ Library
_____ Language lab
__x__ Dance studio (Fillmore)
_____ Separate lunchroom
__x__ Kitchen
_____ Infirmary
__x__ Conference room
_____ Multipurpose room
__x__ Expansion plans (potential demountables for PreK & K)

Sports News

P.E. Instruction
_____ Swimming

_____ Basketball
_____ Gymnastics
_____ Dance
_____ Softball
_____ Skating
_____ Soccer
_____ Volleyball
__x__ Creative movement

Weekly P.E. class
__1__ Pre-K
_____ Transition
__1__ Kindergarten
__1__ First
__1__ Second
__1__ Third
__1__ Fourth
__1__ Fifth
__1__ Sixth

After-School Activities

Fillmore Arts program with transportation.

Registration/Admissions

April is registration month in DC public schools.
Watch for newspaper notifications or bulletins.
Proof of residency, child's birth certificate, immunization record.
PreK—4 by Dec. 31; K—5 by Dec. 31.
PreK classes fill up quickly and children enrolled on first-come, first-served basis.
Wise to sign up during scheduled registration period.
Anytime parent/teacher ratio goes over 20:1 cannot accept any other out-of-area students. Out-of-area is first-come, first-served handled at Division of Elementary Education. Out-of-state students pay tuition.

Where Next

Hardy Middle School.

Head Profile

Acting principal, taught 20 years, 8 as resource teacher. Head teacher with administrative duties at Hyde. Believes in developmental concept, least restrictive environment, accommodating children with special needs in regular classes.

Faculty Features

__0__ No. male teachers
__11__ No. female teachers
__M__ Turnover
__u__ Typical tenure

- x Art teacher (Fillmore)
- x Vocal music teacher (1x/wk)
- ___ Instrumental music teacher
- x Counselor/psychologist
- ___ Nurse
- x Language teacher (volunteer)
- ___ Math teacher
- ___ Reading teacher
- x P.E. teacher
- ___ Remedial reading teacher
- x Remedial math teacher (part-time computer lab coordinator)
- x Speech therapist (part-time)
- x Full-time science teacher (part-time)
- ___ Enrichment teacher
- x ESL teacher (2x/wk)
- ___ Tutor
- ___ Assistant teachers
- x Librarian

Parents Say

unavailable

Parent Wish List

More P.E., more languages, advanced placement courses.

Parent Involvement

PTA operates extended-day program, pays for K aide, parents help with garden, assist teachers, teach special subjects, and fund raising (Harvest Festival, Family International Night, Book Fair, Christmas Tree Sale, etc.).

Your Notes

Lafayette Elementary School

Northampton Street and Broad Branch Road NW, Washington, DC 20015
202/282-0116
HEAD: Sandra Bond

Basics

Year founded: 1930s
Enrollment: 503
  Boys: 276
  Girls: 227
Grades: PreK–6
Major entry grade: na
Birthdate req.: Dec. 31
Arrival: 9:00 a.m.
Dismissal: 3:00 p.m.
Early dismissal: no
Extended day: 8:00 a.m.–6:00 p.m.
Costs: na
Parent fund raising: $50,000–$100,000
Transportation: no
Lunch: yes
After-school activities: yes
Camp: DC Recreation Dept.
Dress code: none
Neighborhood: Chevy Chase (D.C.)

Special Qualities

Early childhood program has two 4-year-old and four 5-year-old classes.
A lot of spirit and energy in an upbeat environment with high standards.
Musicals, plays.
Principal who fights for the school.
Neighborhood school.
Glee club.
Strong orchestra.

Philosophy and Character

Large, attractive brick building.
Classrooms are open-spaced, allowing for flexibility; however, order and structure are evident and there are clear expectations.

Grade size ranges from 40–80.
Achievement and independence are encouraged, creativity valued.
Each child has a real sense of identity and belonging.
Few out-of-boundary students.

Curriculum

CTBS test scores:	G3*	G6
Reading:	83	86 percentile
Math:	95	95 percentile
Language:	89	90 percentile
Science:	94	91 percentile

Offers PreK program.
K "Writing to Read" Program.
Math and language enrichment for all grades.
Hands-on art and science.
G6 musical production related to studies, i.e., *Oliver*, *My Fair Lady*.
Junior Great Books program.
Strong, basic academic program.
PE concentrates on President's physical fitness and team games.
French and Spanish classes offered before school day begins.

Special Spots

_x_ Computer room
_x_ Science lab
_x_ Dedicated music room
___ Music practice room
_x_ Gymnasium
_x_ Dedicated art room
___ Ceramic studio
_x_ Auditorium
___ Tennis court
___ Pool
_x_ Playing fields
x Enrichment rooms
_x_ Library
___ Language lab
___ Dance studio
___ Separate lunchroom
_x_ Kitchen
_x_ Infirmary
___ Conference room
_x_ Multipurpose room (Cultural Center)
___ Expansion plans

Sports News

P.E. Instruction
___ Swimming
___ Basketball
___ Gymnastics
___ Dance
___ Softball
___ Skating
___ Soccer
___ Volleyball
_x_ Creative movement

*May 1989 results.

Weekly P.E. class:

1	Pre-K
	Transition
1	Kindergarten
1	First
1	Second
1	Third
1	Fourth
1	Fifth
1	Sixth

After-School Activities

D.C. Recreation Dept. runs sports activities on school grounds.

Registration/Admissions

April is registration month in DC public schools.
Watch for newspaper notification or bulletins.
Proof of residency, child's birth certificate, immunization record.
PK: 4 by Dec. 31; K: 5 by Dec. 31.
PreK classes fill up quickly and children enrolled on first-come, first-served basis.
Wise to sign up during scheduled registration period.
Out-of-area is first-come, first-served; handled at Division of Elementary Education.

Where Next

Alice Deal, National Cathedral, Sidwell Friends, Maret, Georgetown Day, Stone Ridge, Edmund Burke.

Head Profile

Principal at Lafayette since 1982. Experience as classroom teacher, assisting principal, and acting principal.

Faculty Features

2	No. male teachers
u	No. female teachers
u	Turnover
u	Typical tenure
x	Art teacher
x	Vocal music teacher
x	Instrumental music teacher
x	Counselor/psychologist
x	Nurse
x	Language teacher
x	Math teacher
x	Reading teacher
x	P.E. teacher
x	Remedial reading teacher
x	Remedial math teacher
	Speech therapist
x	Full-time science teacher
x	Enrichment teacher

_____ ESL teacher
_____ Tutor
__x__ Assistant teachers (PreK, K)

Parents Say

Strong, innovative, authoritarian, and generally accessible. Involved in administrative duties and directing and supervising education program. Works well with parent community.

Parent Wish List

More P.E., art for K, less academic K, more recess time, divided classrooms.

Parent Involvement

Parents extremely involved; opportunities include fall festival, auction, spring fair, library aides, art teacher aide, classroom help.

Parents' fund raisers pay for art and science teachers, nurse, play equipment, supplies.

Your Notes

The Langley School

1411 Balls Hill Road, McLean, VA 22101
703/356-1920
HEAD: Betty J. Brown

Basics

Year founded: 1942
Enrollment: 450
  Boys: 219
  Girls: 231
Grades: N–8
Major entry grade: N, PreK, K, 3
Birthdate req.: 3 yrs. by September 1
Arrival: 8:00 a.m.
Dismissal: 3:20 p.m.
Early dismissal: 3rd Fri. of each month, 12:25 p.m.
Extended day: 3:20 p.m.–6:00 p.m.
Costs: $3675–$6460
Parent fund raising: $100,000
Transportation: bus (northern VA)
Lunch: no
After-school activities: yes
Camp: yes
Dress code: clean, neat
Neighborhood: McLean

Special Qualities

Strong math and reading programs with extra teachers.
Annual foreign language tournament.
Band program best in area—leads to concert program.

Philosophy and Character

Strives to create a supportive, enthusiastic, challenging, and creative environment.
10-acre campus with woods and stream.
Traditional, demanding, but nurturing program.
Campus made available to community groups.
Structured environment, limited class size.
There are 36–44 students per grade with 2 sections per class.

Neighborhood school: 95% VA, 3% DC, 2% MD.
Citizens of other countries represent 5.25%.
10–12% of students use extended day.

Curriculum

Reading: basic communication skills stressed, structured reading and math readiness for K; formal reading for G1–2; ¾ hour G3, 4, 5. Literature and basal readers with students grouped by ability.
Reading lab and reading resource teacher.
Four reading and math teachers G1; 3 for G2–5.
Writing: daily—mechanics and emphasis on creativity.
Math: emphasis on creative thinking and problem solving; labs in room G1–4, plus math lab with teacher G5 and up.
Science: experiential hands-on approach with two labs; animals, reptiles, greenhouse, nature area.
Foreign language: Spanish and French, entirely oral until G4.
Computer in classroom and lab 2x/week.
Social studies: CRAM geography and history.
Music: 2x, one drama production per year for G1–5, Orff instruments and Kodaly method, band G4–8.
Art: 2x, 2 teachers, new art room.
Homework begins G2.

Special Spots

__x__ Computer room
__x__ Science lab (2)
__x__ Dedicated music room
__x__ Gymnasium
__x__ Dedicated music room
_____ Ceramic studio
__x__ Auditorium
_____ Tennis court
_____ Pool
__x__ Playing fields
__x__ Enrichment rooms
__x__ Library (10,000 volumes)
_____ Language lab
_____ Dance studio
_____ Separate lunchroom
_____ Kitchen
_____ Infirmary
__x__ Conference room
_____ Multipurpose room
__x__ Greenhouse
__x__ Expansion plans (new library)

Sports News

P.E. Instruction
_____ Swimming

x Basketball
x Gymnastics
x Dance
x Softball
___ Skating
x Soccer
x Volleyball
___ Creative movement
x Flag football
x Softball, track, cross country

Weekly P.E. class:
___ PreK
___ Transition
___ Kindergarten
2 First
2 Second
2 Third
2 Fourth
2 Fifth
3 Sixth

After-School Activities

Interscholastic sports.

Registration/Admissions

Tim Mathiasen 703/356-1920.
Claire Maxted.
Inquire for materials.
Tour by parents beginning Sept. 1.
Application deadline is Jan. 31.
Parent interview with division head.
Applicant visits classroom.
Kingsbury test results and school recommendations due by Feb. 1.
Financial aid available, apply using Princeton form; $24,000 given 1988–89.

Where Next

25% public; 75% independent—Madeira, Langley, McLean, Yorktown, Landon, Herndon, Gonzaga, St. Agnes, Episcopal.

Head Profile

B.A., Meredith College; M.S.W., University of North Carolina, 1952; M.A. (Ed.Ad.), University of Virginia, 1985. At Langley since 1980. Strong in administration, policy, and curriculum development. Meets with students and advisors weekly, visits classrooms daily. Emphasizes character development and responsible citizenship. Expanded artist-in-residence program, faculty endowment, and professional development. Extensive previous work in child welfare and social work, as teacher, tester, head of preschool, head of summer school.

Faculty Features

6	No. male teachers
37	No. female teachers
N	Turnover (10%)
5	Typical tenure (yrs.)
x	Art teacher
x	Vocal music teacher
x	Instrumental music teacher
x	Counselor/psychologist
	Nurse
x	Language teacher
x	Math teacher
x	Reading teacher
x	P.E. teacher
x	Remedial reading teacher
x	Remedial math teacher
	Speech therapist
x	Full-time science teacher
	Enrichment teacher
	ESL teacher
	Tutor
x	Assistant teachers (in preschool)

Parents Say

Excellent academics in a caring, nurturing environment.

Parent Involvement

Once a co-op, and active parent involvement continues; opportunities include auction, annual fund, fair, square dance, and participation in school programs.

Your Notes

Little Flower School

5601 Massachusetts Avenue, Bethesda, MD 20816
301/320-3273
HEAD: Sister Eva Marie Zlotucha I.H.M.

Basics

Year founded: 1953
Enrollment: 214
Boys: 105
Girls: 109
Grades: PreK–8
Major entry grade: PreK, K
Birthdate req.: 4 yrs. by Dec. 31
Arrival: 8:15 a.m.
Dismissal: 2:45 p.m.
Early dismissal: no
Extended day: 8:00 a.m.–4:00 p.m.
Costs: $1375 (discounts for siblings)
Parent fund raising: none (see Special Qualities)
Transportation: no
Lunch: Wednesdays
After-school activities: yes
Camp: no
Dress code: uniform
Neighborhood: Westbard area of Bethesda

Special Qualities

Small Catholic school located near DC-Bethesda border.
Books and supplies bountiful.
Special needs met.
Dedicated teachers.
Endowment fund ensures no fund raising is necessary.
Family atmosphere.

Philosophy and Character

To provide a loving, supportive environment.
To help each child reach his fullest potential.
To develop strong self-worth, genuine concern and respect for others, spiritual development.
Each child required to do community service prior to Confirmation.
Monthly school masses and

family mass first Sunday of each month.

Classes range in size from 17–28 students.

89% from MD, 10% DC, 1% VA.

7% minority enrollment.

Curriculum

Strong academic and Catholic preparation.

Drill work as well as creative and innovative approaches used.

French and Spanish taught in G1–8.

Computer science instruction begins in K.

Religious instruction daily by certified catechists and weekly sessions with parish priests at all grade levels.

Catholic Youth Organization interscholastic sports programs in G1–8.

Special Spots

x	Computer room
	Science lab
x	Dedicated music room
	Music practice room
x	Gymnasium
	Dedicated art room
	Ceramic studio
x	Auditorium
	Tennis court
	Pool
x	Playing fields
	Enrichment rooms
x	Library (5500 volumes)
	Language lab
	Dance studio
x	Separate lunchroom
x	Kitchen
x	Infirmary
x	Conference room
	Multipurpose room
	Expansion plans

Sports News

P.E. Instruction:

	Swimming
x	Basketball
	Gymnastics
	Dance
x	Softball
	Skating
x	Soccer
	Volleyball
x	Creative movement

Weekly P.E. class:

1	Pre-K
	Transition
1	Kindergarten
1	First
1	Second
1	Third
1	Fourth*
1	Fifth*
1	Sixth*

*Team participation.

2 Seventh
2 Eighth

After-School Activities

Young Astronauts, CYO sports, computer lab, soccer, softball, Irish dance, basketball, art class.

Registration/Admissions

Sister Eva Marie.
Open House-February; Registration-March.
Tour for students and parents.
Must submit previous report cards.
Testing when necessary or upon request by classroom teachers in school.
Financial aid: Archdiocesan form or speak with pastor. Substantial aid and numerous grants given.
All requests met.

Where Next

Gonzaga, Georgetown Prep, Visitation, Stone Ridge, Connelly, St. John's, Good Counsel.

Head Profile

Principal for 20 years, 9 years at Little Flower, 11 years in Oneida, NY, and Bridgeport, CT; taught G2–8, 1957–69, M.A., University of Portland (OR), 1968; administration credits from Lehigh University, Fairfield University.

Faculty Features

1	No. male teachers
10	No. female teachers
M	% turnover
1–20	Typical tenure (yrs.)
	Art teacher
x	Vocal music teacher
x	Instrumental music teacher
	Counselor/psychologist
x	Nurses (2 volunteer)
x	Language teacher (2)
x	Math teacher
x	Reading teacher
x	P.E. teacher
x	Remedial reading teacher
x	Remedial math teacher
	Speech therapist
x	Full-time science teacher
	Enrichment teacher
	ESL teacher
x	Tutor (2)
	Assistant teachers

Parents Say

Head is supportive, honest, friendly, fair, open-minded. Facilities are outstanding; academics are strong and include good programs in music, foreign language, and computer.

Parent Wish List

Stronger art program; more P.E. classes.

Parent Involvement

Parents very involved in developing school policy.

Active Parish Council (similar to PTA); volunteer opportunities include reading mothers, Wednesday workshop, lunchroom, school nurse, playground aide.

Your Notes

The Lowell School

16th and Decatur Streets NW, Washington, DC 20011
202/726-9153
HEAD: Abigail B. Wiebenson

Basics

Year founded: 1965
Enrollment: 171
  Boys: 94
  Girls: 77
Grades: N–3
Major entry grade: N3
Birthdate req.: 3 yrs. by Oct. 1
Arrival: 8:30 a.m.
Dismissal: 12:00 noon, 3:00 p.m. (depending on grade)
Early dismissal: Fri., 12:00 noon
Extended day: 6:00 p.m. (K–3)
Costs: $3400–$6000
Parent fund raising: $80,000
Transportation: no
Lunch: no
After-school activities: yes
Camp: yes
Dress code: none
Neighborhood: Crestwood/ Shepherd Park areas of D.C.

Special Qualities

Integrated curriculum.
Diversity of student body.
Parent support and involvement.
Well-designed P.E. program.
Individual styles met.

Philosophy and Character

Independent school with a new primary school facility at Himmelfarb mansion owned by school; cooperative rather than competitive environment.
Individual styles accommodated.
Developmental learning approach.
"The Lowell Way" is based on respect for children, knowledge of their growth, and development of self-esteem.
Cognitive learning rooted in motor learning and therefore have carefully designed P.E.
N has 78 students in 4 sections; K and G1 have 36 and 28, respectively, with 2 sections; G2–3 have 1 section with fewer than 20 students.

70% students from DC, 30% MD.
30% minority enrollment.
Students have very diverse economic backgrounds.
Religious holidays not celebrated.

Curriculum

Strong skill-based curriculum based on works of Jean Piaget and Haim Ginott.
Emphasis on process skills—how to approach problems, make choices, become effectively articulate.
Teachers are facilitators.
Curriculum is integrated. All disciplines woven together by a central theme—i.e., Olympics, Colonial America.
Math and science integrated and based on data activities—i.e., analysis of names and letter frequency, probability exercises, study of insect life cycles.
Manipulative-based activities encourage collaborative learning.
Students write and publish their own books, write news stories, make class books and maps of projects.
Some teachers teach G1–3 so they know how each child learns and can build on strengths.
Homework begins G1 with ½ hour.
P.E. program can use the Carter Barron field.

Special Spots

____ Computer room
__x__ Science lab
__x__ Dedicated music room
____ Music practice room
____ Gymnasium
__x__ Dedicated art room
____ Ceramic studio
____ Auditorium
____ Tennis court
____ Pool
__x__ Playing fields
____ Enrichment rooms
__x__ Library (1700 volumes)
____ Language lab
____ Dance studio
____ Separate lunchroom
____ Kitchen
____ Infirmary
____ Conference room
____ Multipurpose room
__x__ Expansion plans

Sports News

P.E. Instruction
____ Swimming
____ Basketball

_____ Gymnastics
_x_ Dance
_x_ Softball
_____ Skating
_x_ Soccer
_____ Volleyball
_x_ Creative movement
_x_ Kickball/T-ball

Weekly P.E. class
_2_ Pre-K
_____ Transition
_5_ Kindergarten
_5_ First
_5_ Second
_5_ Third
_____ Fourth
_____ Fifth
_____ Sixth

After-School Activities

Planned for fall, 1989.

Registration/Admissions

Diane Williams 202/726-9153.
Oct.–Feb. brief phone interview with parents, tours scheduled.
Applications due end of Feb.
Jan.–Mar. child visits scheduled.
Tests are low-key, nonstandardized, done by classroom teachers (only for primary applicants).
Mid-March admissions decision made.
Test results are shared in informal phone conferences if requested.
Application fees are waived for previous year's wait list applicants.
Financial aid in 1988–89: $54,000.
All requests have been met.
Princeton SSS used as a guide to determine grant.

Where Next

St. Patrick's, Sheridan, Potomac, Maret, Holton Arms, National Cathedral.

Head Profile

Wiebenson has been at Lowell since 1988. B.A., Smith College, 1963; M.A. George Washington University, 1972. Public and private school experiences in California, Massachusetts, and DC; headed a cooperative nursery, moderated NAIS workshops, served on board of Washington Preschools Inc. Regularly attends AISGW conferences for administrators.

Faculty Features

2	No. male teachers
20	No. female teachers
M	Turnover (0%)
8–10	Typical tenure (yrs.)
	Art teacher
	Vocal music teacher
x	Instrumental music teacher
	Counselor/psychologist
x	Nurse
	Language teacher
	Math teacher
x	Reading teacher
x	P.E. teacher (¾)
	Remedial reading teacher
	Remedial math teacher
	Speech therapist
x	Full-time science teacher
	Enrichment teacher
	ESL teacher
	Tutor
x	Assistant teachers (2)

Parents Say

Communication with parents and faculty is a high priority. Staff is extremely focused on kids; teachers know each child very well; curriculum emphasizes science/math, physical development, and language arts. Director is well liked.

Parent Wish List

Better art program in primary grades.

Parent Involvement

Parents form an essential support system and lead all fund-raising activities

(Bazaar, book fair, auction, annual giving, capital campaign), help in library, drive on field trips, help out with Lowell Primary Press (typing and binding of children's books), organize Parent Pot Luck Supper and Parenting Education lectures/workshops.

Parents hold 8 of 16 board of trustee slots.

Your Notes

Horace Mann Elementary School

Newark and 44th Streets NW, Washington, DC 20016
202/282-0126
HEAD: Patricia Patton

Basics

Year founded: 1931
Enrollment: 192
  Boys: 107
  Girls: 85
Grades: PreK–6
Major entry grade: na
Birthdate req.: 4 yrs. by Dec. 31
Arrival: 8:55 a.m.
Dismissal: 3:00 p.m.
Early dismissal: no
Extended day: no
Costs: na
Parent fund raising: $50,000–$60,000
Transportation: no
Lunch: available
After-school activities: no
Camp: no
Dress code: none
Neighborhood: Wesley Heights/Spring Valley

Special Qualities

Small, family-centered, neighborhood school.
Student council K–6
Teamwork of teachers, parents, and principal.
Adjacent playing fields and community center.
High academic performance.

Philosophy and Character

Mann is part of six-school complex: the complex is an alliance of four elementary schools (Hyde, Key, Stoddert, and Mann), a middle school (Hardy), and an arts center (Fillmore). Each school has its own faculty, PTA, and campus. The complex was formed in 1974.
"Public school that looks private."
Parents feel school teaches children not subjects, emphasizes basic academic skills and that learning is enjoyable.
Students and parents have great pride in school and sense of ownership.

Children involved in decision-making via Student Council for K–6.

Diverse international student body.

Curriculum

CTBS Test Scores:	G3	G6
Reading:	89	89 percentile
Math:	97	88 percentile
Language:	96	94 percentile
Science:	90	82 percentile

DCPS CBC Guide form basis for curriculum.

Children grouped heterogeneously in classroom and then grouped by level of performance and need for teaching purposes.

Homework begins G1.

Classroom aides for PreK–3 for small-group instruction.

Fillmore program for K–6 provides small-group instruction in visual arts, music, dance/movement, and theater.

School-wide annual enrichment theme-based program for 8–10 weeks.

Science classes enriched by PTA-sponsored hands-on program, school science fair for G3–6.

School newspaper produced by G1–6 students.

Computer lab has 10 IBM PC Jrs. with PTA-hired teacher.

Math program moving toward risk, estimating, computers. Math enrichment teacher for G3 up.

Strong language arts program, with emergent literacy program in K; Junior Great Books program.

Presidential Physical Fitness Goals; ball skills; PTA supports 1 class during lunch.

Special Spots

x Computer room
___ Science lab
___ Dedicated music room
___ Music practice room
___ Gymnasium
___ Dedicated art room
___ Ceramic studio
___ Auditorium
___ Tennis court
___ Pool
x Playing fields
x Enrichment rooms
x Library (5000 volumes)
___ Language lab
x Dance studio (Fillmore)
___ Separate lunchroom
___ Kitchen
___ Infirmary
___ Conference room
x Multipurpose room
x Expansion plans (community center)

Sports News

P.E. Instruction

____	Swimming
____	Basketball
x	Gymnastics
x	Dance (Fillmore)
____	Softball
____	Skating
____	Soccer
____	Volleyball
x	Creative movement

After-School Activities

Arts and gymnastics at Fillmore; PE through DC Recreation Dept.

Registration/Admissions

April is registration month in DC public schools.
Watch for newspaper notification or bulletins.
Proof of residency, birth certificate, and immunization record are required.
PreK classes fill up quickly and children enrolled on first-come, first-served basis.
Wise to sign up during scheduled registration period.
Apply for out-of-boundary admission at school; acceptance is limited.
Out-of-state admission requires tuition of $1880–$2727.

Where Next

Sidwell, St. Albans, National Cathedral; Maret, St. Andrew's, St. Stephen's, Hardy Middle School.

Head Profile

B.A. and M.A. from Case Western Reserve; further graduate work at UCLA, University of Maryland, and Trinity. Eight and a half years as principal at Mann and Stoddert, 6 years as director of Hardy Middle. Assistant principal, Connelly, 2 years.

Faculty Features

10	No. Male teachers
8	No. female teachers
Avg.	% turnover
14	Typical tenure (yrs.)
x	Art teacher (Fillmore)
x	Vocal music teacher (Fillmore)
x	Instrumental music teacher (Fillmore)
x	Counselor/psychologist (½)
____	Nurse

_____ Language teacher
__x__ Math teacher (1x/wk)
__x__ Reading teacher (1x/wk)
__x__ P.E. teacher (1x/wk)
_____ Remedial reading teacher
_____ Remedial math teacher
__x__ Speech therapist (1x/wk)
__x__ Full-time science teacher (part-time paid for by PTA)
__x__ Enrichment teacher
__x__ ESL teacher (½ time—Bldg. Res. Teacher)
__x__ Tutor (volunteer)
_____ Assistant teachers
__x__ Aides (6)
__x__ Special education resource teacher (½ time)

Parents Say

Principal is traditional, attentive, friendly, responsive, tuned-in, open, respectful of teachers and parents. Parents have strong voice in affairs of six-school complex.

Parent Wish List

Better math curriculum, science lab, smaller classes, more P.E. and after-school activities.

Parent Involvement

Very active parents volunteer in PTA, classroom activities, and initiating new programs.

Organized Horace Mann press (publishing creative works which led to bookbinding project).

Fund raising includes fall festival, book fair, bake sales, etc., which pay for teachers' aides, arts program, science, computer, and supplies.

Parents teach where qualified and needed.

Your Notes

Maret School

3000 Cathedral Avenue NW, Washington, DC 20008
202/939-8800
HEAD: Carolyn Gold (Lower School K–4)

Basics

Year founded: 1911
Enrollment: 100 (Lower School; 500 for K–12)
Boys: 50
Girls: 50
Grades: K–12
Major entry grade: K, 4, 7, 9
Birthdate req.: 5 yrs. by Oct. 1
Arrival: 8:15 a.m.
Dismissal: 3:10 p.m.
Early dismissal: Wed., 1:00 p.m.
Extended day: no
Costs: $5250–$6050
Parent fund raising: $60,000
Transportation: no
Lunch: yes
After-school activities: no
Camp: yes
Dress code: clean and neat
Neighborhood: Woodley Park

Special Qualities

Very academic with lots of homework, yet classrooms comfortable, relaxed, and inviting.
One-half of teachers are male in overall school.
All grades are located on one campus.
Small class size.
Individualized teaching.
Thematic curriculum.
Warm, sensitive.

Philosophy and Character

Independent, coed, K–12 school located on 7-acre Woodley estate with historic manor house.
Rigorous academic program stresses individual development in an atmosphere of trust, respect, and diversity.
Competition discouraged except in sports.
Field trips use city's rich resources.
Sense of community and respect for differences.

K–3 grades have 16–18 students with 1 section; G4–6 increase to 30 students in 2 classes.
Many World Bank families: 15% diplomatic, 10% minority, also religiously diverse.
Assembly every Fri. featuring authors, storytellers, folk singers, and children's own performances.

Curriculum

Thematic approach unifies curriculum, which is often based on a social studies topic.
Class taught by primary teacher with resource teachers for music, art, science.
Reading: phonics stressed, individualized approach, sustained silent reading program; parents asked to read ½ hour every night to children.
Writing: process writing, lots of dictating, journals, publishing; very strong aspect of curriculum.
Math: new and old methods blended; manipulatives, conceptualization, and drill.
Computer 1x, library 1x, art 2x, gym 5x, foreign language 4x, music 2x/week.
Science observation and experimentation in lab, classes 2x/week.
Music: Kodaly philosophy—music literacy, folk rhymes, song, dance, Orff instruments.
French instruction begins in K, mostly conversational; Spanish also offered.
P.E.: program teaches fundamental skills of movement and coordination.
Detailed narrative reports 2x/yr.

Special Spots

x	Computer room
x	Science lab
x	Dedicated music room
x	Music practice room
x	Gymnasium
x	Dedicated art room
x	Ceramic studio
x	Auditorium
	Tennis court
	Pool
x	Playing fields
x	Enrichment rooms
x	Library
x	Language lab
	Dance studio
x	Separate lunchroom
x	Kitchen
	Infirmary
x	Conference room
	Multipurpose room
	Expansion plans

Sports News

P.E. Instruction

____	Swimming
x	Basketball
____	Gymnastics
____	Dance
x	Softball
____	Skating
x	Soccer
x	Volleyball
____	Creative movement
x	Racquetball and handball

Weekly P.E. Class

____	Pre-K
____	Transition
5	Kindergarten
5	First
5	Second
5	Third
4	Fourth
4	Fifth
4	Sixth

Registration/Admissions

Admissions office: 202/939-8814.
Parent tours Oct.–Feb. 8:45 a.m. by appointment.
Applications due Feb. 1.
Applicant interviews.
Testing by Kingsbury Center or Specific Diagnostics.
Teacher recommendations required.
Notifications sent in March.
Financial aid: request school form, $50,000 in financial aid given in 1988–89.

Where Next

Approximately 8–10 of 16 K students stay through G12.

Head Profile

Has been head of Lower School since 1977. Taught at Maret 6 years prior to that. A.B., Radcliffe; M.A., George Washington University.

Faculty Features

4	No. male teachers
10	No. female teachers
M	% turnover (8%)
8	Typical tenure (yrs.)
x	Art teacher
x	Vocal music teacher
x	Instrumental music teacher
x	Counselor/psychologist
____	Nurse
x	Language teacher
____	Math teacher
____	Reading teacher
x	P.E. teacher

_____ Remedial reading teacher
_____ Remedial math teacher
_____ Speech therapist
__x__ Full-time science teacher
__x__ Enrichment teacher
_____ ESL teacher
_____ Tutor
__x__ Assistant teachers

Parents Say

Student body and faculty are both diverse. Academics are top-notch. Significant homework assigned. School has nurturing but challenging environment.

Parent Wish List

More team sports and after-school activities in lower school; less homework.

Parent Involvement

Parents Association is active.
Parents' influence on policies is not substantial.
Volunteer opportunities include annual auction, fête champêtre, class representative, and bookmaking.

Your Notes

Mater Dei School

Seven Locks Road, Bethesda, MD 20817
301/365-2700
HEAD: Christopher S. Abell

Basics

Year founded: 1960
Enrollment: 200
  Boys: 200
  Girls: 0
Grades: 1–8
Major entry grade: 1, 7
Birthdate req.: unavailable
Arrival: 8:30 a.m.
Dismissal: 3:15 p.m.
Early dismissal: 1st Fri. of each month, 12:00 noon
Extended day: no
Costs: $4350
Parent fund raising: 0
Transportation: no
Lunch: no
After-school activities: no
Camp: yes
Dress code: uniform
Neighborhood: Potomac area

Special Qualities

Close relationship between students and teachers.
Excellent music and art teachers.
Very successful sports program G5–8.
Small, personal.
Emphasis on moral development, strong Catholic education.

Philosophy and Character

Small, private, Catholic school for boys where playing hard, working hard, and being an all-around good guy is the emphasis.
Academic achievement, character development, and understanding religious teachings stressed.
New chapel completed in 1989.
90% of students from MD, 5% VA, 5% DC.
9% minority.
DC week and outdoor education week for older grades—understanding subway, rock climbing, and canoeing.

Curriculum

Fairly fast-paced.
Language arts emphasis.
Reading comprehension taught through G8.
Teach to top ½ of class, starting in G3.
Pull kids to potential—not push.
Computers in lower grade classrooms.
Reading starts with phonetic work, vocabulary development, and comprehension.
Specific skills series used.
Music 2x/week, note reading and basic melody.
Religion study daily.
Science: SCs program emphasizes experiential reasoning and decision making.
Homework begins G1—15 min. increasing to 90 min. in G6.

Special Spots

x Computer room
___ Science lab
___ Dedicated music room
x Music practice room
x Gymnasium
x Dedicated art room
___ Ceramic studio
___ Auditorium
x Tennis court
x Pool
x Playing fields
___ Enrichment rooms
x Library (5000 volumes)
___ Language lab
___ Dance studio
___ Separate lunchroom
___ Kitchen
___ Infirmary
x Conference room
x Multipurpose room
x Expansion plans (improvements of lower school, bookstore, and field)

Sports News

P.E. Instruction
___ Swimming
x Basketball
___ Gymnastics
___ Dance
x Softball
___ Skating
x Soccer
___ Volleyball
___ Creative movement
x Football, baseball, wrestling, lacrosse, intramurals

Weekly P.E. class
___ Pre-K
___ Transition
___ Kindergarten
5 First
5 Second

5 Third
5 Fourth
5 Fifth
5 Sixth

After-School Activities

None

Registration/Admissions

Call for brochure and application.
Application due January or chances are slim.
School confirms receipt and then parent requests appointment with Head.
Head meets with parents.
School records and recommendations required.
Feb. testing of all applicants by teachers.
Decisions mailed March 1; responses due April 1.
Accepted students spend a day at school.
Many come from Stone Ridge Kindergarten.
First-come, first-served acceptance policy provided child is qualified for reasonably fast-track program.
Financial aid is limited; very few grants; contact headmaster.

Where Next

Georgetown Prep, Gonzaga, St. Albans, Episcopal High School, The Episcopal School, Portsmouth Abbey, Landon.

Head Profile

Head at Mater Dei since 1985, teacher and coach for 14 years previously. B.A., history (1970); M.A., history (1974); J.D. (1979). Most time spent on policy development, involvement with students and faculty.

Faculty Features

7 No. male teachers
4 No. female teachers
M Turnover
7 Typical tenure (yrs.)
x Art teacher
x Vocal music teacher
___ Instrumental music teacher
x Counselor/psychologist
___ Nurse
___ Language teacher
___ Math teacher
x Reading teacher
___ P.E. teacher
___ Remedial reading teacher
___ Remedial math teacher

_____ Speech therapist
_____ Full-time science teacher
_____ Enrichment teacher
_____ ESL teacher
_____ Tutor
_____ Assistant teachers

Parents Say

Head is a good communicator, calm, fair, determined, intelligent. Core subjects are grade level ahead. Good students expected; exceptional students need additional challenge out of school.

Parent Wish List

Science lab, bus service, lunch, better library and video equipment, more emphasis on study skills.

Parent Involvement

Many board members are current or previous parents.
No parent-sponsored fund-raising activities.
An annual giving drive funds improvements to buildings, computers, etc.

Your Notes

McLean School of Maryland

8224 Lochinver Lane, Potomac, MD 20854
301/299-8277
HEAD: Alexander Hamilton Bishop III

Basics

Year founded: 1952
Enrollment: 243
  Boys: 137
  Girls: 106
Grades: K–9; Lower school K–6
Major entry grade: K, 7
Birthdate req.: 5 yrs. by Sept.–Oct.
Arrival: 8:55 a.m.
Dismissal: 3:00 p.m.
Early dismissal: Fri., 12:00 noon
Extended day: no
Costs: $5125–$6550 ($7175–$7850 Catch Up*)
Parent fund raising: $170,000
Transportation: yes
Lunch: no
After-school activities: yes
Camp: no
Dress code: uniform
Neighborhood: Tuckerman Lane and Seven Locks Road

Special Qualities

Catch-up and mainstream class structure: school is unique in dual program and in programs for mildly learning-disabled students.
Small classes with individual attention in a supportive environment.

Philosophy and Character

Coed independent school.
Emphasizes full development of academic potential in challenging, comfortable but noncompetitive environment.
Structured academic program with emphasis on the basics.
Maintain a 2:1 ratio between mainstream and catch-up students.

---

*Catch Up tuition refers to cost for mildly learning-disabled students.

Encourages development of each student's personality and maturity.
Class sizes range from 14–16 students in lower grades with one section and 24–30 students in G3–6 with 2 sections.
12% minority enrollment.
65–75% from MD with 10–15% from VA and 15–20% from DC.
School assemblies, plays, etc., 2–3x/month.
Active participation in community service projects.

Curriculum

School offers mainstream sections from G2 on with maximum of 17 pupils with one teacher and a catch-up section for mildly learning-disabled with 12 max and 1.5 teachers.
The CU curriculum is designed to meet the unique learning style of each student.
Reading: K–3, HBJ basal readers, stress phonics, and vocabulary taught in ability groups; literature G4 up, taught in ability groups.
Math: ability groups with emphasis on manipulatives.
K is readiness-oriented, formal math and reading begin G1.
Science by classroom teacher with hands-on approach.
Spanish introduced G6.
Art: art studio with focus on variety of media.
Music: 2 classes/week, with yearly class play and 3 musical productions.
Homework begins G1, letter grades start G3.
Interscholastic sports opportunity begins G5.

Special Spots

__x__ Computer room
__x__ Science lab
__x__ Dedicated music room
_____ Music practice room
_____ Gymnasium
__x__ Dedicated art room
_____ Ceramic studio
_____ Auditorium
_____ Tennis courts
_____ Pool
__x__ Playing fields (2)
_____ Enrichment rooms
__x__ Library (16,600 volumes)
_____ Language lab
_____ Dance studio
_____ Separate lunchroom
_____ Kitchen
_____ Infirmary
_____ Conference room
__x__ Multipurpose room
__x__ Expansion plans (campus acquisition and enrollment expansion under consideration)

Sports News

P.E. Instruction

___	Swimming
x	Basketball
___	Gymnastics
___	Dance
x	Softball
___	Skating
x	Soccer
x	Volleyball
___	Creative movement
x	Field and street hockey, touch football, lacrosse

After-School Activities

Athletics, art, piano lessons.

Registration/Admissions

Linda Handy, Admissions Dean.
Request literature and appointment with Handy.
Rolling admissions process.
School records and recommendations required.
Applicant visits school for a day.
Entrance testing required, for mainstream—WPPSI or Metropolitan Readiness G1–2 and ERB G3–9; for catch-up, informal testing, Woodcock Johnson, WISC-R.
Financial aid available, uses Princeton form; gave $25,000 1988–89 year.
Admissions priority given to siblings.

Where Next

30% public, 70% private; St. Andrew's, Newport Prep., Churchill High School, Bullis, Field, Edmund Burke, Gonzaga, Good Counsel, Holy Child, George School, Christchurch, Gaithersburg.

Head Profile

B.A., history, M.Ed. from Johns Hopkins University. Former head Gilman Lower School (Baltimore) and Belfield School and St. Anne's-Belfield. Headmaster at McLean since 1979. Hopes to see school buy property and expand school to PreK–G12.

Faculty Features

2	No. male teachers
32	No. female teachers
N	Turnover (10–15%)
7	Typical tenure (yrs.)
x	Art teacher
x	Vocal music teacher

_____ Instrumental music teacher
__x__ Counselor/psychologist
_____ Nurse
__x__ Language teacher
__x__ Math teacher
__x__ Reading teacher
__x__ P.E. teacher (2)
_____ Remedial reading teacher
_____ Remedial math teacher
_____ Speech therapist
__x__ Full-time science teacher
_____ Enrichment teacher
_____ ESL teacher
__x__ Tutor
__x__ Assistant teachers

Parents Say

unavailable

Parent Wish List

unavailable

Parent Involvement

Parents' Association raises funds through auction night, Fall Festival, and Book Fair.

School policies set by board of trustees.

Your Notes

Montessori School of McLean

1711 Kirby Road, McLean, VA 22101
703/790-1049
HEAD: Joan Marie Parasine

Basics

Year founded: 1973
Enrollment: 136
  Boys: 66
  Girls: 70
Grades: PreK–6
Major entry grade: PreK
Birthdate req.: 2½ yrs.
Arrival: 8:45 a.m.
Dismissal: 3:00 p.m. (5–12 yrs.); noon (PreK)
Early dismissal: no
Extended day: 12:00 noon–3:00 p.m.
Costs: $2550–$3200
Parent fund raising: $5000
Transportation: yes
Lunch: no
After-school activities: yes
Camp: yes
Dress code: preschool: appropriate for school; elementary: uniforms
Neighborhood: Chesterbrook area of McLean

Special Qualities

Ungraded classrooms.
Montessori education philosophy.
Emphasis on "cultural classes."
Very small student body.

Philosophy and Character

Follows Maria Montessori's principles: respect for child and child's individuality.
Child learns at own pace.
School aims to provide best PreK and elementary Montessori education in northern Virginia.
Preschool classes have mixed age groupings of 2½–5 years. There are approximately 25 students per class and 4 sections per grade.
Transition class for 5-year-olds.
Older grades have 16–20 students per class and one section per grade.
No religious holiday celebrations,

schoolwide gatherings, or community outreach programs.
Large number of students with international background.
All students from VA.

Curriculum

Elementary class is for students aged 6–12.
Program tailored to each child.
Traditional Montessori curriculum with extensive cultural classes (art, music, French, dance).
Reading: starts in PreK with Montessori materials, phonics stressed, SRA reading labs K–6, library use encouraged.
Language arts: focus on composition and daily writing or report.
Math: Montessori materials and approach.
Science: scientific method used, animals and plants in class, many experiments.
French begins K.
Computer: PreK intro, teaches LOGO.
Social studies: focus on the effects of geography and biology on human development with more research after age 6.
Music: music and drama teacher with yearly music program.
Art: local artist teaches, focus on techniques.
Homework begins G1.

Special Spots

__x__ Computer room
__x__ Science lab
__x__ Dedicated music room
_____ Music practice room
_____ Gymnasium
__x__ Dedicated art room
_____ Ceramic studio
_____ Auditorium
_____ Tennis court
_____ Pool
__x__ Playing fields
_____ Enrichment rooms
__x__ Library (4500 volumes)
_____ Language lab
__x__ Dance studio
_____ Separate lunchroom
__x__ Kitchen
_____ Infirmary
_____ Conference room
_____ Multipurpose room
_____ Expansion plans

Sports News

P.E. Instruction:
_____ Swimming
__x__ Basketball
_____ Gymnastics
__x__ Dance

_x_ Softball
____ Skating
_x_ Soccer
_x_ Volleyball
_x_ Creative movement
_x_ Field hockey and cricket
____ Tennis

Weekly P.E. class
_1_ PreK
_1_ Transition
_1_ Kindergarten
_1_ First
_1_ Second
_1_ Third
_1_ Fourth
_1_ Fifth
_1_ Sixth

After-School Activities

Occasional parent-led Camp Fire group.

Registration/Admissions

Dorothy P. Di Dio.
Rolling admissions process.
No entrance testing required.
Waiting list maintained.
PreK entrance based on age and school readiness; others need prior Montessori experience.
No financial aid available.

Where Next

Langley School, Potomac School, Maret, Chesterbrook Elementary, McLean area public schools; evenly divided between public and private schools.

Head Profile

School founder with B.S., education, and Montessori certification. Teaches. Co-head is Dorothy P. Di Dio, who has B.A. in English and French with certificate from Washington Montessori Institute. Teaches transition class. School heads focus on teaching, student and faculty relations, policy, and curriculum development.

Faculty Features

_0_ No. male teachers
_6_ No. female teachers
_M_ Turnover
_3–5_ Typical tenure (yrs.)
_x_ Art teacher
_x_ Vocal music teacher
____ Instrumental music teacher
____ Counselor/psychologist
_x_ Nurse

__x__ Language teacher (French)
_____ Math teacher
_____ Reading teacher
__x__ P.E. teacher
_____ Remedial reading teacher
_____ Remedial math teacher
_____ Speech therapist
_____ Full-time science teacher
_____ Enrichment teacher
_____ ESL teacher
_____ Tutor
__x__ Assistant teachers (6)

Parents Say

unavailable

Parent Wish List

unavailable

Parent Involvement

Parents Association raises funds.
Parents volunteer for various school functions, annual raffle/auction, field trip chaperone, and special class activities.

Your Notes

Murch Elementary School

36th and Davenport Streets NW, Washington, DC 20008
202/282-0130
HEAD: Mary Gill

Basics

Year founded: 1930
Enrollment: 425
  Boys: 209
  Girls: 216
Grades: PreK–6
Major entry grade: na
Birthdate req.: Dec. 31
Arrival: 8:45 a.m.
Dismissal: 3:00 p.m.
Early dismissal: no
Extended day: 7:30 a.m.–6:00 p.m.
Costs: na
Parent fund raising: $70,000
Transportation: no
Lunch: yes
After-school activities: yes
Camp: no
Dress code: none
Neighborhood: Chevy Chase, Forest Hills areas of D.C.

Special Qualities

Neighborhood school with strongly involved parents.
Diverse staff with many talents.
Excellent extended-day program.
Great use of city for various field trips.
Public service programs.
Computer facilities and teacher.

Philosophy and Character

Neighborhood public school with strong community feeling.
Murch's goal is to provide age-appropriate experiences at all levels so student can reach full potential.
Offers small sections in each class and special programs for gifted and remedial.
Grades range in size from mid-60s in K, to 76 in G1 and decline to 32 in G2.
Diverse student population with students from 40 different countries, speaking 18 native languages.
Approximately 10–15% students

from out of boundary but applications not being accepted due to strong neighborhood enrollment.

Curriculum

CTBS test

scores*	G3	G6
Reading:	84	86 percentile
Math:	94	96 percentile
Language:	97	85 percentile
Science:	92	81 percentile

Half-day PreK program.
K has IBM "Writing to Read" program.
Reading and math classes have skill-specific groups limited to 4–6 children.
Great Books program.
Emphasis on social studies.
Embassy Adoption program.
School-wide science fair.
Drama with Peter Barry players.
School sponsors competitions in poetry, math, science, etc.
French instruction starts G2, Chinese offered in G6.

Special Spots

x Computer room
x Science lab
x Dedicated music room
___ Music practice room
___ Gymnasium
x Dedicated art room
___ Ceramic studio
x Auditorium
___ Tennis court
___ Pool
x Playing fields
x Enrichment rooms
x Library
___ Language lab
___ Dance studio
___ Separate lunchroom
x Kitchen
x Infirmary
___ Conference room
___ Multipurpose room
___ Expansion plans

Sports News

P.E. Instruction
___ Swimming
x Basketball
x Gymnastics
___ Dance
x Softball
___ Skating
x Soccer
___ Volleyball
x Creative movement

Weekly P.E. class:
1 PreK
2 Kindergarten

*May 1989 results.

2	First
2	Second
2	Third
2	Fourth
2	Fifth
2	Sixth

After-School Activities

Woodworking, ceramics, tap dance, pillow polo, karate, piano, soccer, basketball activities (run by HSA).

Registration/Admissions

April is registration month in DC public schools.

Watch for newspaper notification or bulletins.

Proof of residency, child's birth certificate, and immunization record are required.

PreK classes fill up quickly, and children enrolled on first-come, first-served basis.

Wise to sign up during scheduled registration period.

Apply for out-of-boundary admission at school; acceptance is limited. Out-of-state admission requires tuition of $1880–$2727.

Where Next

Alice Deal.

Head Profile

Has been principal at Murch since November 1984, with 22 years' teaching experience in D.C. area.

Faculty Features

5	No. male teachers
25	No. female teachers
N	% turnover
10	Typical tenure (yrs.)
x	Art teacher
x	Vocal music teacher
	Instrumental music teacher
x	Counselor/psychologist
x	Nurse (part-time)
x	Language teacher
x	Math teacher
	Reading teacher
x	P.E. Teacher (full-time)
x	Remedial reading teacher
	Remedial math teacher
	Speech therapist
x	Part-time science teacher (hoped in 1990)
x	Enrichment teacher coordinator (HSA employed)
x	ESL teacher

_____ Tutor
__x__ Assistant teachers (HSA employed)
We also have, full-time, librarian, special ed teacher, talented and gifted program teacher, extension teacher

Parents Say

Principal has strong leadership qualities and is fair, child-oriented, friendly, accessible. School is a true neighborhood school; is multicultural and diverse, has involved parent body, but could benefit by improvement of facilities.

Parent Wish List

New gymnasium, additional playing field, better P.E., smaller classrooms, science teacher, more music and art instruction.

Parent Involvement

Murch has an active Home and School Association (HSA).

School has several fund raisers including fall fair, spring auction, and book fair.

Funds raised for extra workbook materials, special purchases for school, after-school activities, and teachers for extra classes.

Parents have active role in molding school programs.

Parents may volunteer for classroom assistance, fund raisers, library, administrative work, field trip chaperone, etc.

Your Notes

National Presbyterian School

4121 Nebraska Avenue NW, Washington, DC 20016
202/537-0922
HEAD: Jane B. Harter

Basics

Year founded: 1969
Enrollment: 200
  Boys: 100
  Girls: 100
Grades: N3–6
Major entry grade: N3
Birthdate req.: 3 yrs. by Sept.
Arrival: 8:10 a.m.
Dismissal: 3:00 p.m.
Early dismissal: Fri., 12:00 noon
Extended day: 5:45 p.m.
Costs: $3960–$5910
Parent fund raising: $80,000
Transportation: no
Lunch: no
After-school activities: yes
Camp: yes
Dress code: neat, clean, simple
Neighborhood: American University Park

Special Qualities

Small coed school.
Open, warm, friendly nature.
Caring faculty.
Community spirit abounds.
Traditional emphasis on secondary school preparation.
Strong academic program.
Excellent "transition class" offered.

Philosophy and Character

Independent school affiliated with the National Presbyterian Church.
Dedicated to educational excellence and meeting individual's needs in Christian setting.
School helps students to reach their potential.
Active pursuit of community involvement by students.
Transition class is small with 10–12 students. Other classes have 20–24 students with two sections per grade. Students primarily from DC (64%), MD

(33%), VA (3%).

14% minority enrollment.

Varying religious affiliations: 24% Presbyterian, 20% Episcopalian, 19% Catholic, 9% Jewish, 28% other.

Plans to expand minority enrollment.

New gymnasium and classroom facilities.

Curriculum

Formal reading program begins G1, using basal readers and literature.

Math taught in classroom, small groups, use manipulatives.

French begins G1 with reading and writing added G4.

Religious studies begin G4, with all students attending weekly chapel.

Homework starts G2.

Formal grading (A–F) starts G4.

Almost daily P.E. classes.

N3–4 classes focus on social, manipulative, and oral skill development.

Transition program combines N4 and developmentally appropriate K curriculum.

K presents number concepts and phonics with music, art, science, social studies, and P.E. classes.

Art: process-oriented; G1 up use Art Studio; major art exhibition each spring.

Music is daily activity N–K; classes 2x/wk for N4–G6; program combines elements of Orff and Kodaly philosophy; chorus, handbell choir; piano and recorder lessons.

Drama available for G1–6.

Computer introduced K, LOGO instruction starting G2; a nongraded, interactive, individualized approach.

Special Spots

x	Computer room (10 Apple IIE, 2 Apple GS)
x	Science lab
x	Dedicated music room
	Music practice room
x	Gymnasium
x	Dedicated art room
x	Ceramic studio
x	Auditorium
	Tennis court
	Pool
	Playing fields
	Enrichment rooms
x	Library (8000 volumes)
	Language lab
	Dance studio
	Separate lunchroom
x	Kitchen
	Infirmary

__x__ Conference room
_____ Multipurpose room
__x__ Expansion plans

Sports News

P.E. Instruction
_____ Swimming
__x__ Basketball
__x__ Gymnastics
__x__ Dance
__x__ Softball
_____ Skating
__x__ Soccer
__x__ Volleyball
__x__ Creative movement

Weekly P.E. class:
_____ PreK
__4__ Transition
__4__ Kindergarten
__4__ First
__4__ Second
__4__ Third
__4__ Fourth
__4__ Fifth
__4__ Sixth

After-School Activities

Art, sports, computer, video making, drama, Brownies, and Scouts.

Registration/Admissions

Katherine Stanton.
Group tour by appointment.
Testing for N4 up at Kingsbury or Specific Diagnostics with results shared after admission decision.
Student school visit required.
Application deadline is March 1.
Recommendations for N4 up required.
Siblings and NPC members given entrance priority.
Financial aid for 1988–89 was $35,000; apply to NPS by April 1.

Where Next

National Cathedral, St. Albans, Holton Arms, Landon, Maret, St. Andrew's, Sidwell Friends.

Head Profile

Head of NPS since 1974. M.Ed., University of Virginia; teaching experience in public and private schools. Involved in school administration, students, future school placements, professional organizations, and community activities. Highly praised by parents.

Faculty Features

2	No. male teachers
16	No. female teacher
M	% turnover
5	Typical tenure (yrs.)
x	Art teacher
x	Vocal music teacher
x	Instrumental music teacher
	Counselor/psychologist
	Nurse
x	Language teacher
	Math teacher
x	Reading teacher
x	P.E. teacher
	Remedial reading teacher
	Remedial math teacher
x	Speech therapist (before and after school)
x	Full-time science teacher
	Enrichment teacher
	ESL teacher
	Tutor
	Assistant teachers

Parents Say

NPS focuses on individual child; school is especially strong in language arts, language instruction, and music.

Parent Wish List

Expand science lab, offer lunch.

Parent Involvement

Volunteering strongly encouraged. Opportunities include fund raisers (Harvest Festival, auction, Breakfast for Books), library, PTA, hospitality work, room parent. Parents feel involved in developing policies, e.g., decision not to require uniform.

Your Notes

The Newport Schools (formerly Town and Country Day School)

11311 Newport Mill Road, Kensington, MD 20895
301/942-4550
HEADS: Nina S. Olin (N–4); Andrew A. Zvara (G5–12)

Basics

Year founded: 1930
Enrollment: 274 (214, N–8)*
  Boys: 161
  Girls: 113
Grades: N–12
Major entry grade: PreK, K, 7, 9
Birthdate req.: 3 yrs. by Dec. 31
Arrival: 8:30 a.m.
Dismissal: 3:45 p.m.
Early dismissal: no
Extended day: 7:00 a.m.–6:00 p.m.
Costs: $3800–$6600 (N–4); $7000–$7500 (G5–8)
Parent fund raising: u
Transportation: independent van service
Lunch: yes
After-school activities: yes
Camp: yes
Dress code: uniform
Neighborhood: Kensington

Special Qualities

Involved but relaxed school atmosphere.
Diverse student body.
Imaginative classroom displays and artwork.
Longevity of staff.
Small classes.
Luxurious amount of space.
Chess club.
School chosen by University of Maryland in 1986 for research project on young children and computers.
Strong academic program.

Philosophy and Character

A nonprofit, independent school located on a leased former public jr. high school facility on 55 acres of parkland.

*Enrollment is fluid and may change each year due to expansion potential.

Family-like, structured environment with program designed to develop a lifestyle of learning with foundation of skills.

"Take children as far as they can go, as fast as they can go."

Geared for average to gifted student.

Self-discipline expected.

Sponsors Brazilian child.

Handbell choir performs at nursing homes, and students take part in food drives, Jump-for-Heart, Trike-a-thon.

Class size ranges from 10–24. There is one section per grade until G5, when there are two sections.

31 nations represented in student body.

25–30% Afro-American, 15% Asian-American, 5% other countries.

Most students come from MD, 5–10% from DC.

Contract bus service available for fee.

15–20% use after-school service.

Curriculum

N–K students take home "My Day Note," daily checklist of information and activities.

Two-teacher classrooms (both with degrees).

Classes grouped by ability.

Hands-on science.

Spanish begins PreK.

Art: use of many forms to develop visual literacy.

Computer education K–8 since early '60s; LOGO problem solving begins in K.

Homework begins G1.

G1–6 participate in a production every year; N–K do separate productions.

Handbell choir, vocal choir.

Special Spots

_x_ Computer room (2)
_x_ Science lab (1 Lower School)
_x_ Dedicated music room
___ Music practice room
_x_ Gymnasium
_x_ Dedicated art room (2)
___ Ceramic studio
_x_ Auditorium
_x_ Tennis court
___ Pool
_x_ Playing fields
___ Enrichment rooms
_x_ Library
___ Language lab
___ Dance studio
_x_ Separate lunchroom
_x_ Kitchen
_x_ Infirmary
_x_ Conference rooms
_x_ Expansion plans (enrollment)

Sports News

P.E. Instruction

	Swimming
x	Basketball (school strength)
x	Gymnastics
	Dance
x	Softball
	Skating
x	Soccer

Weekly P.E. class

2	PreK
2	Transition
2	Kindergarten
2	First
2	Second
2	Third
3–5	Fourth
5	Fifth
5	Sixth

After-school Activities

Chess—largest club in MD—begins in G1.

Sports, drama, gymnastics, dance, handbell choir, choir.

Registration/Admissions

Joyce Zier.

Rolling admissions but no commitment required until March 15.

Individual parent tour given.

Student visit/interview required.

Admission testing done by admissions staff (results shared within a week). ERB given for G2 up.

Students should test average or above average and show interest in learning, be able to succeed in structured environment.

Rarely accept special needs.

Priority given to siblings.

$600 deposit required.

Apply to Princeton for financial aid.

Aid based on need; $136,343 given in 1988–89.

Where Next

Students stay through G12.

Head Profile

Nina S. Olin (George Washington University, B.A., 1953; University of Maryland, M.A., 1976), headmistress; Andrew A. Zvara (Oberlin College, A.B., 1963; University of Maryland, M.A. 1974). Both are responsible for curriculum development and administration of school, also very involved with students.

Faculty Features

- 6 No. male teachers
- 35 No. female teachers
- M % turnover
- 10 Typical tenure (yrs.)
- x Art teacher
- x Vocal music teacher
- ___ Instrumental music teacher
- ___ Counselor/psychologist
- x Nurse
- x Language teacher (Spanish)
- x Math teacher
- x Reading teacher
- x P.E. teacher
- ___ Remedial reading teacher
- ___ Remedial math teacher
- ___ Speech therapist
- x Full-time science teacher
- ___ Enrichment teacher
- ___ ESL teacher
- ___ Tutor

Parents Say

School provides a warm, friendly environment where concern for students' well-being and academic performance is evident. Student body is diverse. Highly regarded principals.

Parent Wish List

None

Parent Involvement

Newport Schools Community Association provides parent volunteers. Parents encouraged to share expertise in classrooms and participate on committees.

Your Notes

Norwood School

8821 River Road, Bethesda, MD 20817
301/365-2595
HEAD: Richard T. Ewing, Jr.

Basics

Year founded: 1952
Enrollment: 250
  Boys: 122
  Girls: 128
Grades: K–6
Major entry grade: K
Birthdate req.: age appropriate
Arrival: 8:10 a.m.
Dismissal: 2:30 p.m. (K–2); 3:30 p.m. (G3–6)
Early dismissal: Fri., 12:30
Extended day: no
Costs: $6400–$6600
Parent fund raising: na
Transportation: no
Lunch: no
After-school activities: yes
Camp: yes
Dress code: simple
Neighborhood: River Road/ Bradley Boulevard areas of Bethesda

Special Qualities

Arts center.
"Norwood musicals" developed under grant from NEH in 1978.
25-acre campus with expansive facilities.
Daily nondenominational chapel gathering.
Academic program.

Philosophy and Character

Independent co-ed school stressing reading, writing, and mathematical skills.
Objective is to help each child grow intellectually, morally, physically, and socially.
School gathers for a weekly 15-min. nondenominational chapel and/or daily chapel service.

Each class chooses a community outreach project.
Grade size ranges between 36–39 with one section per class.
Homogeneous student body with no minority enrollment.
3% World Bank or IMF family students.
93% students from MD.

Curriculum

Large classes with small-group instruction.
Homework begins G3 with graded reports G3 up.
No foreign language instruction.
Reading: small-group instruction, grouped according to ability, use Houghton-Mifflin basals and teachers' supplements.
Math and computer begin in K, small-group teaching.
Daily social studies, art, music, outdoor activity.
Science and PE begin G1; campus has pond, marsh, trails.
Numerous "living history" musical and play productions each year.
Chapel time used for values teaching.

Special Spots

x Computer room
x Science lab
x Dedicated music room
x Music practice room
x Gymnasium
x Dedicated art room
___ Ceramic studio
x Auditorium
___ Tennis court
___ Pool
x Playing fields
___ Enrichment rooms
x Library
___ Language lab
___ Dance studio
___ Separate lunchroom
x Kitchen
___ Infirmary
___ Conference room
___ Multipurpose room
x Expansion plans (increase enrollment to 290, renovation and new construction)

Sports News

P.E. Instruction:
___ Swimming
x Basketball
x Gymnastics
x Dance
x Softball
___ Skating
x Soccer
x Volleyball
___ Creative movement

Weekly P.E. class:

____	Pre-K
____	Transition
4	Kindergarten
4	First
4	Second
4	Third
4	Fourth
4	Fifth
4	Sixth

After-School Activities

French and Spanish classes, Girl Scouts and Brownies, basketball team, soccer.

Registration/Admissions

Mrs. Block.

Applications accepted September–Thanksgiving.

Required parental visit and discussion.

School administers WIPPS test but will accept others.

Results shared with parents with decision letter.

Applicants visit school for evaluation.

Siblings and legacies given admission priority.

Financial aid available using Princeton form, $54,800 given in 1988–89.

Where Next

Landon, St. Andrew's, Holton-Arms, St. Albans, National Cathedral, Potomac.

Head Profile

B.A., Yale; M.Ed., University of Virginia; Ed.D., Harvard. Head of Norwood since 1983. Previously taught G6 at Norwood and was Administrative Director. Greets students daily, teaches, leads chapel services, and actively involved in graduating class placement. Mrs. Miriam Fulton Block acts as head of PK–3.

Faculty Features

6	No. male teachers
30	No. female teachers
M	% turnover (5%)
8	Typical tenure (yrs.)
x	Art teacher
x	Vocal music teacher
____	Instrumental music teacher
x	Counselor/psychologist
____	Nurse
____	Language teacher
x	Math teacher
x	Reading teacher
x	P.E. teacher

_____ Remedial reading teacher
_____ Remedial math teacher
_____ Speech therapist
__x__ Full-time science teacher
_____ Enrichment teacher
_____ ESL teacher
_____ Tutor
_____ Assistant teachers

Parents Say

Wonderful art and music programs. Very structured, family-oriented school. Rigorous academic program. Very favorable opinion of head. School tries to "keep children children." Not enough field trips. Teachers know each student.

Parent Wish List

Transportation.
Language instruction during school day.
Pool, hot lunch.
More day-to-day parent involvement.

Parent Involvement

Parents Association sponsors book fair, school picnic, and silent auction.
Parents can participate on board-designated committees, in library, as class parents, or as field trip chaperone.
Parents influence beginning to increase.

Your Notes

James F. Oyster Bilingual Elementary School

29th and Calvert Streets NW, Washington DC 20008
202/673-7297
HEAD: Elena Izquierdo

Basics

Year founded: 1971
Enrollment: 296
Boys: 142
Girls: 154
Grades: PreK–6
Major entry grade: PreK
Birthdate req.: Dec. 31
Arrival: 8:45 a.m.
Dismissal: 3:00 p.m.
Early dismissal: no
Extended day: 7:30 a.m.–6:30 p.m.
Costs: na
Parent fund raising: $30,000
Transportation: no
Lunch: yes
After-school activities: yes
Camp: yes
Dress code: none
Neighborhood: Woodley Park

Special Qualities

Model bilingual program with world- and country-wide visitors.
Dynamic and innovative principal.
Diverse student body.
Good facilities.
Innovative approaches to teaching.
Involved in many DC programs, competitions, field trips.
Well staffed.

Philosophy and Character

Bilingual public school offering English-Spanish instruction.
Native English-speaking children benefit from exposure to other cultures and non-native speakers benefit from instruction in their language.
Provides children with an enriched program to be well prepared academically.
Remains a neighborhood school.
Very diversified student body: 67% Hispanic and number of nationalities, many white and black children.

Significant number apply from out of boundary.
Grades have 2 sections and range in sizes from 26–49; PreK program has 26 with one section.

Curriculum

CTBS scores*	G3	G6
Reading:	65	73 percentile
Math:	84	94 percentile
Language:	88	91 percentile
Science:	59	71 percentile

CBC curriculum with many modifications as desired and necessary for bilingual program.
Resource teachers in math, ESL, and computer.
Language: each subject taught in English or Spanish, remedial help is given if experiencing problem; PreK has language immersion program.
Math: taught by homeroom teacher, enrichment by math resource and computer teachers.
Computer: introduction PreK–2 with LOGO training for G3–6, lab open during recess; 5 Apple computers and unique bilingual program software.
Science: taught in homeroom with many supplemental materials provided by Community Council, science club.
Reading and Writing: focus on writing, examples everywhere, formal program begins G1 with basal readers and literature; one trip to library per week.
Art: one class/week of 1¼ to 1½ hours, tries to complement studies when possible, theme- and project-oriented.
Music: piano and percussion instruments taught, teacher programs complement assemblies and other productions/events.
1–2 field trips per month.

Special Spots

x	Computer room (10 IBM, 5 Apple)
	Science lab
	Dedicated music room
	Gymnasium
x	Dedicated art room
	Ceramic studio
	Auditorium
	Tennis court
	Pool
x	Playing fields
x	Enrichment rooms
x	Library

*May 1989 results.

____	Language lab
____	Dance studio
____	Separate lunchroom
____	Kitchen
____	Infirmary
____	Conference room
x	Multipurpose room
____	Expansion plans
	Uses demountables for PreK and K classes.

Sports News

P.E. Instruction

____	Swimming
x	Basketball
x	Gymnastics
____	Dance
x	Softball
____	Skating
x	Soccer
x	Volleyball
____	Creative movement

Weekly P.E. class

1	Pre-K
____	Transition
1	Kindergarten
1	First
1	Second
1	Third
1	Fourth
1	Fifth
1	Sixth

After-School Activities

Creative activities program. Gymnastics, recorder, piano lessons, swimming, crafts, Levine School of Music program, adult classes in English or Spanish.

Registration/Admission

April is registration month in D.C. public schools.

Watch for newspaper notifications or bulletins.

Proof of residency, child's birth certificate, and immunization record are required.

PreK classes fill up quickly and children enrolled on first-come, first-served basis.

Wise to sign up during scheduled registration period.

Apply for out-of-boundary admission at school; acceptance is limited. Out-of-state admission requires tuition of $1880–$2727.

Where Next

Deal, National Cathedral, St. Albans, Sidwell Friends.

Head Profile

New at Oyster. From El Paso, Texas. M.A., applied linguistics, and Ph.D. (pending), bilingual education, Georgetown University. Taught in DC public schools, St. Albans, Georgetown Day School. Wants school to focus on developmentally appropriate teaching methods, cooperative learning, and child-centered curriculum. (Administrative Intern Gloria Henderson)

Faculty Features

4	No. male teachers
22	No. female teachers
M	% turnover
15	Typical tenure (yrs.)
x	Art teacher
x	Vocal music teacher
x	Instrumental music teacher
x	Counselor/psychologist
x	Nurse (1 day)
x	Language teacher (each class has both English and Spanish speaking teachers)
x	Math teacher
	Reading teacher
x	P.E. teacher (3 days)
	Remedial reading teacher
	Remedial math teacher
x	Speech therapist
	Full-time science teacher
x	Enrichment teacher
x	ESL teacher (SSL teacher)
x	Tutor (GWU students, volunteers)
x	Assistant teachers

Parents Say

Principal is intelligent, warm, challenging, and strong in curriculum development, policy, and new program implementation.

Parent Wish List

Modernize building.

Parent Involvement

Community Council very active in school support and fund raising for purchase of books, additional teachers, staff development, school materials.

Your Notes

Paint Branch Montessori School

3215 Powder Mill Road, Adelphi, MD 20783
301/937-2244
HEAD: Patricia Barshay

Basics

Year founded: 1975
Enrollment: 100
Boys: 50
Girls: 50
Grades: N–6
Major entry grade: PreK
Birthdate req.: 3 yrs. by Dec. 31
Arrival: 8:45 a.m.
Dismissal: 11:45 a.m. (PreK); 3:00 p.m. (K–6)
Early dismissal: 1st Friday of each month, 12:00 noon
Extended day: 8:00 a.m.–5:00 p.m.
Costs: $2364–$3445
Parent fund raising: $1000–$3000
Transportation: no
Lunch: no
After-school activities: yes
Camp: no
Dress code: none
Neighborhood: Prince George's County

Special Qualities

Classroom views of wooded campus.
Mixed age groups of students.
Montessori philosophy.

Philosophy and Character

Montessori educational philosophy.
Students progress at own pace within environment prepared for their needs.
Mixed age grouping for 3–6, 6–9, 9–12-year-old students.
Academically challenging school will work with learning disabled students.
N and PreK grades have 16–18 students with 3 sections, K has 26 with 3 sections, G1–3 have 10 and 2 sections while G4–6 have 6 in 1 section.

Upper elementary students work at food distribution center and perform at nursing homes.
Families are lower- to upper-middle-class.
20% minority enrollment.
All students from MD, primarily Prince George's County.

Curriculum

Montessori language arts and math programs use specially designed manipulative materials.
Cooperative learning approach.
Homework begins in G1 level.
P.E. taught at P.G. Gymnastics Club.
Recorder taught G3 up.
Computers are in elementary classrooms.
Literature-based reading program G4–6.

Special Spots

_____ Computer room
_____ Science lab
_____ Dedicated music room
_____ Music practice room
_____ Gymnasium
_____ Dedicated art room
_____ Ceramic studio
_____ Auditorium
_____ Tennis court
_____ Pool
_____ Playing fields
_____ Enrichment rooms
__x__ Library
_____ Language lab
_____ Dance studio
_____ Separate lunchroom
__x__ Kitchen
_____ Infirmary
_____ Conference room
__x__ Multipurpose room
_____ Expansion plans

Sports News

P.E. Instruction
_____ Swimming
_____ Basketball
__x__ Gymnastics
_____ Dance
_____ Softball
_____ Skating
_____ Soccer
_____ Volleyball
_____ Creative movement

Weekly P.E. class
__1__ PreK
_____ Transition
__1__ Kindergarten
__1__ First
__1__ Second
__1__ Third
__1__ Fourth
__1__ Fifth
__1__ Sixth

After-School Activities

Offerings on rotating bases: drama, cooking, tie-dying.

Registration/Admissions

Sandra Thomas 301-937-2244.
School visit by appointment.
Meet with administrator.
Students interviewed by teacher.
Applications accepted Feb. for current families, March for others.
No testing required.
Priority given to siblings, teachers' children, previous applicants.
No financial aid.

Where Next

P.G. County Magnet schools for talented and gifted, Green Acres, Sidwell Friends, Sandy Springs, White Oak Jr. High, Martin Luther King Jr. Middle School Academic Center.

Head Profile

Educational director since 1976; B.A., Pennsylvania State University, Montessori teacher training. Involved with faculty, students, parents, programs, and curriculum development, among other responsibilities.

Faculty Features

0	No. male teachers
10	No. female teachers
M	% turnover
5	Typical tenure (yrs.)
	Art teacher
x	Vocal music teacher
x	Instrumental music teacher
	Counselor/psychologist
	Nurse
	Language teacher
	Math teacher
	Reading teacher
	P.E. teacher
	Remedial reading teacher
	Speech therapist
	Full-time science teacher
	ESL teacher
	Tutor
	Assistant teachers

Parents Say

Outstanding outdoor environment with facilities that meet the needs of school. Director is viewed favorably and is easily accessible.

Parent Wish List

Foreign language instruction, swimming lessons, ice skating lessons.
Expand to include G7–8.

Parent Involvement

Volunteering encouraged: field trips, annual book fair.

Your Notes

The Potomac School

1301 Potomac School Road, Box 430, McLean, VA 22101
703/356-4101
HEAD: Camille M. Passarella (Lower School)

Basics

Year founded: 1904
Enrollment: 230 (PreK–6); 428 (PreK–12)
  Boys: 109 (PreK–3); 89 (G4–6)
  Girls: 120 (PreK–3); 111 (G4–6)
Grades: PreK–3 (Lower School); 4–6 Middle School)
Major entry grade: PreK, K, 4
Birthdate req.: 4 yrs. by Sept. 1
Arrival: 8:20 a.m.
Dismissal: 3:10 p.m. (12:00 noon PreK)
Early dismissal: Wed., Jan.–Mar., K and G1
Extended day: no
Costs: $4450–$6800
Parent fund raising: $160,000
Transportation: yes
Lunch: no
After-school activities: no
Camp: yes
Dress code: uniform G4 up
Neighborhood: McLean

Special Qualities

Strong sense of community.
Art, drama, music, library programs are excellent.
Focus on development of "whole" child.
Respect for individual success.
Weekly assemblies where parents are welcome.
Transportation provided from many parts of metropolitan area.
Large, secluded campus.

Philosophy and Character

70-acre campus with rambling modern buildings and spacious feeling.
Lower school celebrates childhood and emphasizes love of learning in creative and friendly environment, seeks to develop self-confident,

responsible children who can excel to their highest potential academically, creatively, and athletically.

Middle School has strong and respected traditions, few rules but high expectations.

All sections have between 14–18 students. Grades range in size from 48 in K, 54 in G1–3, and 64 in G4–6.

55% students from VA with wide geographic diversity of student body.

Curriculum

Reading: basals until G3, literature based G4–6, outstanding libraries with Lower School library and 15,000 volumes in Intermediate Middle School library, 2 library periods per week PreK–G3.

Math: traditional curriculum with emphasis on problem solving, support, and enrichment provided.

Computers: lab program, computers in classroom.

Music: Orff method, PreK–G1, 2x/week, G2–3, 3x/week, strong and varied choral and instrumental programs G4–6.

Art: K–G3 provides exposure to all media and G4–6 studio art with variety of media and approaches within structured art lessons.

Science: creative, lab animals and garden; PreK–G3, 2x/week; G4–5 lab science 2x/week and G6, 4x/week.

Sports program emphasizes large motor skills and coordination PreK–G3 and skill building and sportsmanship G4–6.

Small PreK class of 14 students.

Special Spots

x	Computer room
x	Science lab
x	Dedicated music room
x	Music practice room
x	Gymnasium (LS activities room and Chester Gym)
x	Dedicated art room
	Ceramic studio
x	Auditorium
x	Tennis court
x	Pool (camp)
x	Playing fields
x	Library
	Language lab
	Dance studio
x	Separate lunchroom
x	Kitchen
x	Infirmary
x	Conference room
x	Expansion plans
x	Multipurpose room

Sports News

P.E. Instruction

___	Swimming
x	Basketball
x	Gymnastics
___	Dance
x	Softball
___	Skating
x	Soccer
x	Volleyball
x	Creative movement

Weekly P.E. class:

2	PreK
___	Transition
2	Kindergarten
2	First
2	Second
2	Third
2	Fourth
2	Fifth
2	Sixth

After-School Activities

None

Registration/Admissions

Charlotte Nelsen, Director.
School visits begin mid-Sept.; applications due by Jan. 15.
Children visit Jan.–March.
Tests: achievement level test given by Potomac for G2 and up, McCarthy for K.
Teacher recommendations required.
March 25 decisions sent out.
Financial aid is available by submitting forms to SSS in Princeton.
Siblings given admissions preference if possible.

Where Next

Potomac's Intermediate and Upper School.

Head Profile

Three years as head of Potomac Lower School, 3 years as assistant director, 5 years in admissions positions, 9 years as primary grades teacher. Goals (shared with head of middle school, Cynthia Ivorian-Jones): directly involved with academic programs in all classrooms and involved with students, teachers, parents through assembly programs and plays. Foster joy of learning, build success and self-confidence, while helping children take risks. Seek racial and cultural diversity in faculty and student body. Expect balance of new ideas and wisdom with experienced and new teachers.

Faculty Features

8	No. male teachers
28	No. female teachers
M	% turnover
10	Typical tenure (yrs.)
x	Art teacher
x	Vocal music teacher
x	Instrumental music teacher
	Counselor/psychologist
x	Nurse
	Language teacher
x	Math teacher
x	Reading teacher
x	P.E. teacher
	Remedial reading teacher
	Remedial math teacher
	Speech therapist
x	Full-time science teacher
x	Enrichment teacher
	ESL teacher
x	Tutor
x	Assistant teachers

Parents Say

School offers diverse range of opportunities and develops individual strengths.

Parent Wish List

Foreign language instruction in lower grades.

Parent Involvement

Involvement is appreciated.

Opportunities to participate in development office, libraries, as class reps, assisting with social functions and publications.

Parents help with Fall Frolics, raising $150,000 for scholarships and book fair, raising $7000 for library.

Your Notes

The Primary Day School

7300 River Road, Bethesda, MD 20817
301/365-4355
HEAD: Carter-Anne Nadonley

Basics

Year founded: 1944
Enrollment: 172
  Boys: 85
  Girls: 87
Grades: PreK–2
Major entry grade: PreK, K
Birthdate req.: 4 yrs. turning 5 yrs.
Arrival: 8:45 a.m.
Dismissal: 12:45 p.m.; 2:00 p.m. (G2)
Early dismissal: Fri., 12:45 p.m.
Extended day: no
Costs: $3000–$3800
Parent fund raising: not significant
Transportation: no
Lunch: no
After-school activities: yes
Camp: no
Dress code: none
Neighborhood: just inside Beltway exit for Potomac

Special Qualities

Phonovisual method of teaching reading.
Low budget, efficient school.
Children develop self-confidence through Friday assembly performances and with "Beak," the school mascot.

Philosophy and Character

Traditional, specialized, academic, disciplined school.
Situated at present location since 1955.
Focuses on learning to read and loving it, including strong foundation for reading, writing, spelling, math.
Success in mastering skills through drill and motivational games.
Develop security and independence.

Good attitude and work habits stressed for high achievement.
All grades have 2 sections with 42–44 students.
Friday assemblies where classes perform.
A new wing completed 1989 to accommodate two PreK classes, an art room, and science lab.
Most children from Potomac, Chevy Chase, Bethesda, northern VA, Gaithersburg.
Birthdays and Halloween are especially celebrated.

Curriculum

Demonstration school for phonovisual method: a kinesthetic approach to reading using auditory and visual discrimination (pictorial charts arranged with phonetic foundation).
Sight reading also taught simultaneously, starts in PreK on individual basis, many students are reading by end of K. Formally taught in G1.
Tape recorder and earphones develop auditory discrimination in PreK.
Variety of basal readers used to develop large vocabularies.
Librarian directs individualized program, visit several times a week.
Music: 1x/week with music teacher; ear training and games, original songs, also in class.
Science: observe, classify, experiment.
Math: "Stern structural math" in K and G1 and self-directed activities, problem solving, large number blocks, and counting rods.
"Fitness Fun" program in P.E. class.
French is taught in G2.

Special Spots

__x__ Computer room (Apple IIC, Apple GS)
__x__ Science lab
_____ Dedicated music room
_____ Music practice room
_____ Gymnasium
__x__ Dedicated art room
_____ Ceramic studio
__x__ Auditorium
_____ Tennis court
_____ Pool
__x__ Playing fields
__x__ Enrichment rooms
__x__ Library (5000 volumes)
_____ Language lab
_____ Dance studio
_____ Separate lunchroom

_____ Kitchen
_____ Infirmary
__x__ Conference room
__x__ Multipurpose room
_____ Expansion plans

Sports News

P.E. Instruction
_____ Swimming
_____ Basketball
_____ Gymnastics
_____ Dance
_____ Softball
_____ Skating
_____ Soccer
_____ Volleyball
__x__ Creative movement

Weekly P.E. class:
_____ Pre-K
_____ Transition
_____ Kindergarten
_____ First
__2__ Second
_____ Third
_____ Fourth
_____ Fifth
_____ Sixth

After-School Activities

K and G1: art, music, dance, computer, Fitness Fun.

Registration/Admissions

Open house Tues. after Thanksgiving.
Very informative demonstration of phono-visual method.
Apply by Jan. with $40 fee.
Individual interview with informal or standardized tests for each applicant.
Criteria for admission: age, maturity, average intelligence.
Schoolfield Scholarship Program available.

Where Next

Holton, Landon, Norwood, Sidwell Friends.

Head Profile

At Primary Day since 1970; assistant head 6 years; director since 1987. Phonovisual specialist, still teaches. Graduate of Immaculata College, some graduate work at George Washington University and Virginia Polytechnic Institute.

Faculty Features

__0__ No. male teachers
__18__ No. female teachers

_____ Turnover
_____ Typical tenure
__x__ Art teacher
__x__ Vocal music teacher
_____ Instrumental music teacher
_____ Counselor/psychologist
_____ Nurse
__x__ Language teacher (French G2)
__x__ Math teacher
__x__ Reading teacher (resource)
_____ P.E. teacher
_____ Remedial reading teacher
_____ Remedial math teacher
_____ Speech therapist
_____ Full-time science teacher
__x__ Enrichment teacher
_____ ESL teacher
__x__ Tutor
_____ Assistant teachers

Parents Say

Headmistress is strong in curriculum development, thorough, gentle, concerned, and candid.

Parent Wish List

More organized P.E. activities.
More after-school activities.
More class field trips.

Parent Involvement

There are no PTA and no specific volunteer programs but parents have organized class parties, helped with plays, volunteered to develop after-school activities.

Parents recently organized fund raising for new wing.

Your Notes

The Rock Creek School

5307 Connecticut Avenue NW, Washington, DC 20015
202/363-2111
HEAD: J. Daniel Hollinger, Ph.D.

Basics

Year founded: 1988
Enrollment: 50
Boys: 25
Girls: 25
Grades: N–1
Major entry grade: N
Birthdate req.: 2½ yrs. by Sept.
Arrival: 9:00 a.m.
Dismissal: 3:00 p.m.
Early dismissal: no
Extended day: 8:00 a.m.–6:00 p.m.
Costs: $3800–$5700
Parent fund raising: none
Transportation: available from downtown
After-school activities: yes
Camp: yes
Dress code: none
Neighborhood: Chevy Chase (DC)

Special Qualities

Language programs in French, Spanish, Japanese.
Small classes, individual attention.
New school.
Highly qualified staff.
Day care provided during school vacations.

Philosophy and Character

Emphasis on commonality of peoples and cultures around the world, while celebrating the differences.
Help children develop a positive attitude toward learning and develop at their own pace.
Continuous assessment of each child's needs.
Cognitive physical, emotional, and social development of each child nurtured.
Semi-monthly field trips.
This expanding school has projected capacity for 6 in 2-year class, 16 in 3-year, and 20 in 4-year classes, with 15 and 20 in K and G1, respectively.

Culturally diverse student body.
70% from DC, 25% MD, 5% VA.
50% use extended day.

Curriculum

Extensive exposure to foreign culture and language.
Complete curriculum in two languages.
Reading: phonics-based, ability grouping.
Writing daily, creativity stressed.
Library daily, public library monthly.
Math: basic skills applied practically.
Science: hands-on using materials from nature.
French, Spanish, Japanese programs from N on.
Computer skills taught in K.
Social studies stresses international understanding.
Music-drama, creative movement by classroom teacher.
Art: individual creative expression.
Grading: mastery, emerging, introductory.

Special Spots

_____ Computer room
_____ Science lab
_____ Dedicated music room
_____ Music practice room
_____ Gymnasium
_____ Dedicated art room
_____ Ceramic studio
_____ Auditorium
_____ Tennis court
_____ Pool
_____ Playing fields
_____ Enrichment rooms
_____ Library
_____ Language lab
_____ Dance studio
_____ Separate lunchroom
_____ Kitchen
_____ Infirmary
_____ Conference room
_____ Multipurpose room
__x__ Expansion plans (one grade to be added each year through high school)

Sports News

P.E. Instruction
_____ Swimming
_____ Basketball
_____ Gymnastics
__x__ Dance
_____ Softball
_____ Skating
_____ Soccer
_____ Volleyball
__x__ Creative movement

Weekly P.E. class
__10__ Pre-K
_____ Transition

10 Kindergarten
5 First
___ Second
___ Third
___ Fourth
___ Fifth
___ Sixth

After-School Activities

Music-Kindermusik, Great Vibrations; creative movement and dance, art, academic enrichment, second language.

Registration/Admissions

J. Daniel Hollinger.
Parents visit school.
Application filed with $50 fee.
Child and parents meet with director.
Admissions decision made by director within one week of meeting.
Rolling admissions.
Parent must be committed to philosophy of program.
"Special needs" children considered if able to be successful in mainstream program.
Financial aid available.

Where Next

Not applicable: too new to know.

Head Profile

Founded school in Fall, 1988. Ph.D., education, University of Virginia, 1987. M.Ed., 1983. Experience in private and public classroom; as resource teacher; and as headmaster, university professor, and educational consultant. Goal: to develop international school from nursery through high school.

Faculty Features

0 No. male teachers
3 No. female teachers
3 Assistant teachers
na % turnover
na Typical tenure
x Art teacher
x Vocal music teacher
x Instrumental music teacher
___ Counselor/psychologist
___ Nurse
x Language teacher
___ Math teacher
___ Reading teacher
___ P.E. teacher
x Remedial reading teacher
x Remedial math teacher
x Speech therapist
___ Full-time science teacher
x Enrichment teacher
x ESL teacher
x Tutor

Parents Say

The language program is very strong. Indoor facilities are excellent. Very pleased with school head.

Your Notes

Parent Wish List

Larger play space.

Parent Involvement

Parents meet monthly.
Volunteers used as field trip chaperones.

Rosemary Hills Elementary School

2111 Porter Road, Silver Spring, MD 20910
301/650-6400
HEAD: Dr. Linda Weber

Basics

Year founded: 1956
Enrollment: 547
  Boys: unavailable
  Girls: unavailable
Grades: K–2
Major entry grade: na
Birthdate req.: 5 yrs. by Dec. 31
Arrival: 8:50 a.m.
Dismissal: 2:50 p.m.
Early dismissal: no
Extended day: no*
Costs: na
Parent fund raising: $10,000+
Transportation: yes
Lunch: yes
After-school activities: yes
Camp: yes
Dress code: none
Neighborhood: Silver Spring

Special Qualities

Desegregation magnet school program.
Media center.
Diverse student body.
High quality teaching staff.
Magnet school for math, science, computer, gifted and talented students.
Small class section (relative to other MCPS).

Philosophy and Character

Parents say school fosters each child's educational growth and personal development.
School is working on developing a specific science.
Known as a "reading school."
Class enrollment ranges from 160–185 with a small Head-Start program.
Approximately 49% minority enrollment.
Chosen for participation in Montgomery County's

*Bus service to day care centers provided.

Flexibility Pilot Project concerning local school autonomy and management.
School was renovated in 1988.

Curriculum

Full-day K program.
Head-Start program.
Homework begins G1.
Art and music class 1x/wk with special teachers, more provided by homeroom teacher.
Computer class 1x/week with Apple computers in class and lab.
Classrooms balanced by race and gender.
Formal reading begins K, with expectation to read by end of K.
No more than 20 per section in K with teacher and aide.
Section size in G1–2 is 25 with teacher and aide.

Special Spots

__x__ Computer room
_____ Science lab
__x__ Dedicated music room
_____ Music practice room
__x__ Gymnasium
__x__ Dedicated art room
_____ Ceramic studio
_____ Auditorium
_____ Tennis court
_____ Pool
__x__ Playing fields
__x__ Enrichment rooms
__x__ Library
_____ Language lab
_____ Dance studio
_____ Separate lunchroom
__x__ Kitchen (satellite)
__x__ Infirmary
__x__ Conference room
__x__ Multipurpose room
_____ Expansion plans

Sports News

P.E. Instruction
_____ Swimming
_____ Basketball
__x__ Gymnastics
_____ Dance
_____ Softball
_____ Skating
__x__ Soccer
_____ Volleyball
__x__ Creative movement

Weekly P.E. class
_____ Pre-K
_____ Transition
__1__ Kindergarten
__2__ First
__2__ Second
_____ Third

_____ Fourth
_____ Fifth
_____ Sixth

After-School Activities

Hands-on science, sports, Spanish instruction, Brownies.

Registration/Admissions

Registration at school throughout school year.
Documents required: birth certificate, immunization record, transcript if appropriate.
Non-U.S. citizens enroll through International Students Admissions Office, 301/230-2843.
May request transfer to out-of-boundary school at home school from Jan. 1–April 30.

Where Next

Chevy Chase Elementary, North Chevy Chase Elementary, Westland Intermediate.

Head Profile

Principal since 1988. Has taught at Burning Tree Elementary. Collegial decision-making style. Progressive educational philosophy. Playground aide on daily basis.

Faculty Features

5 No. male teachers
36 No. female teachers
M % turnover
5–15 Typical tenure (yrs.)
x Art teacher
x Vocal music teacher
_____ Instrumental music teacher
x Counselor/psychologist
x Nurse
_____ Language teacher
_____ Math teacher
x Reading teacher (1.5)
x P.E. teacher
_____ Remedial reading teacher
_____ Remedial math teacher
x Speech therapist
_____ Full-time science teacher
x Enrichment teacher (for gifted and talented)
x ESL teacher (2)
_____ Tutor
x Assistant teachers (24 aides)
x Resource room teacher
x Disadvantaged teacher
x Resource room teacher
x Media specialist

Parents Say

Very favorable view of principal. Facilities are outstanding. Some concerns by Chevy Chase parents over change from attending neighborhood school to long bus ride to Rosemary Hills.

Parent Wish List

More hands-on science after school.
More modern equipment for school staff use.

Parent Involvement

Active PTA which sponsors Fall fund raiser, Book Fair, Spring Fair. Money goes toward cultural arts program, books, science lab equipment, and discretionary funds for teachers.

Volunteer opportunities in classrooms, media center, library, as field trip chaperone. Established a Parent Assembly as part of flexibility pilot in school-based governance/administration.

Your Notes

St. Agnes School

400 Fontaine Street, Alexandria, VA 22302
703/549-3542
HEAD: Joan Ogilvy Holden

Basics

Year founded: 1924
Enrollment: 264 (K–6)
 Boys: 58 (K–4)
 Girls: 206
Grades: K–12 (Lower School K–5)
Major entry grade: K, 1
Birthdate req.: 5 yrs. by Oct. 1
Arrival: 8:15 a.m.
Dismissal: 3:10 p.m.
Early dismissal: no
Extended day: 7:30 a.m.–6:00 p.m.
Costs: $6650–$7150
Parent fund raising: $50,000/year
Transportation: yes
Lunch: yes
After-school activities: yes
Camp: yes
Dress code: neat, clean, some restrictions
Neighborhood: Jefferson Park area of Alexandria

Special Qualities

Strong academics in warm environment.
Leadership and involvement of headmistress.
Interaction among students, faculty, school, and parents.
Low pupil-teacher ratio.
Goes on to be a college-preparatory all-girls school.

Philosophy and Character

College preparatory church school of Virginia Episcopal Diocese.
High academic standards with strengths in science, humanities, and arts programs.
Provides Christian environment.
Respects individual's needs and style.
Offers weekly chapel services, studies in religion and ethics.

Community involvement in RIF, Toys for Tots, March of Dimes, collections for homeless.

Coed K–5; all girls G6–12.

School aims to give elementary students strong academic start and foster personal and spiritual development.

There are 30–40 students per grade with 2 class sections for each.

Majority families middle- and upper-middle-class with 13% on financial aid.

42% Episcopalian, 48% Christian, and 10% Jewish, Moslem, Hindu; 15% minority enrollment; 94% students from VA, 4% MD, 2% DC.

Curriculum

Full-day K program.

French from G4, 2x/week.

Religion 1x/week K–5.

Music 2x/week.

Art 2x/week, K–5.

Science 2x/week, K–3; 5x/week, G4–5; activity-oriented lab; school has science fair.

Library for reading enrichment and skills.

Computer: intro to LOGO with computers in classrooms.

Social studies integrated into curriculum.

Reading: K–3 phonetic approach using Scribner series, adding literature G3–5, Great Books Program G3–6, reading groups begin G1.

Heterogeneous grouping of class sections.

Math uses textbooks, workbooks, computers and manipulatives; stresses understanding of concepts and skills.

Homework begins G3.

Special Spots

x	Computer room
x	Science lab
x	Dedicated music room
x	Music practice room
x	Gymnasium
x	Dedicated art room
	Ceramic studio
	Auditorium
x	Tennis court
	Pool
x	Playing fields
	Enrichment rooms
x	Library (6000 volumes)
x	Language lab
	Dance studio
x	Separate lunchroom
x	Kitchen
x	Infirmary
x	Conference room
x	Multipurpose room
	Expansion plans

Sports News

P.E. Instruction

	Swimming
x	Basketball
x	Gymnastics
x	Dance
x	Softball
	Skating
x	Soccer
x	Volleyball
x	Creative movement

Weekly P.E. class

	PreK
	Transition
2	Kindergarten
3	First
3	Second
3	Second
3	Third
4	Fourth
4	Fifth
3	Sixth

After-School Activities

Art, Brownies/Girl Scouts, Cubs/Boy Scouts, gymnastics, violin, science, piano and instrument lessons, private art lessons.

Registration/Admissions

Diane Dunning 703/836-2199.
Individual tours and interviews given Oct. through March, with an Open House on Sunday before Thanksgiving.
Application deadline is January 1.
January testing at St. Agnes: K–1 readiness test and play day; G2–11 aptitude and achievement test; results shared upon request.
Financial aid—$156,000 in 1988–89 and $210,000 for 1989–90; apply through SSS in Princeton by March 1.
Entrance priority given to qualified siblings and alumnae children.
Requires previous school record, test, letter of recommendation, interview.

Where Next

Girls continue through G12.

Head Profile

At St. Agnes since 1984. B.A., Tufts; M.Ed., Harvard. Teaching and administrative experience at Groton School. Objective is to run school of highest possible quality in an environment conducive to care of each individual student. Striving for regulation-size gym, auditorium, upgraded upper school libary. Has open-door policy for students and teachers. Knows each student, reads to kindergartners, and invites all students to home.

Faculty Features

1	No. male teachers
24	No. female teachers
M	% turnover (6–11%)
7	Typical tenure (yrs.)
x	Art teacher
x	Vocal music teacher
x	Instrumental music teacher
x	Counselor/psychologist
x	Nurse
x	Language teacher
x	Math teacher
x	Reading teacher
x	P.E. teacher
x	Remedial reading teacher
	Remedial math teacher
x	Speech therapist
x	Full-time science teacher
	Enrichment teacher
	ESL teacher
x	Tutor
	Assistant teachers

Parents Say

Very favorable opinion of headmistress. Feel she has an "open door policy." Facilities excellent. Teachers care.

Parent Wish List

Improve gymnasium.
Transportation to wider geographic areas.

Parent Involvement

Parents involved in fund raising, magazine drive, spring festival/gala.
Volunteers in library, classroom, art class, field trips, admissions, after-school activities.
95% participation in PTO.
Board of governors determines policies.

Your Notes

St. Jane Frances de Chantal School

9525 Old Georgetown Road, Bethesda, MD 20814
301/530-1221
HEAD: Elizabeth Hamilton

Basics

Year founded: 1953
Enrollment: 355
  Boys: 175
  Girls: 180
Grades: K–8
Major entry grade: K
Birthdate req.: 5 yrs. by Dec. 31
Arrival: 8:00 a.m.
Dismissal: 2:50 p.m.
Early dismissal: Fri., 12:30 p.m.
Extended day: 7:00 a.m.–6:00 p.m.
Costs: $1200–$3300
Funds raised: $30,000
Transportation: yes, Gaithersburg area
Lunch: no
After-school activities: yes
Camp: no
Dress code: uniform
Neighborhood: Wyngate, Ashburton, Alta Vista

Special Qualities

Academic excellence.
Committed faculty.
Religious programs.

Philosophy and Character

Christ-centered educational community transmitting gospel message to students of varying abilities and personalities.
Received "Excellence in Education" award from U.S. Dept. of Education.
All grades have 2 sections with size ranging from 66–50 per grade.
New enrichment program 1 hr./week involves a parent-taught class featuring talents from cricket to puppetry.

10% minority enrollment.
Students mostly from MD with 1% each from DC and VA.
Families from low to above average income levels.

Curriculum

Follows Diocesan curriculum.
Homework begins G1 (½ hour).
Computer education begins K using Apple II and Atari computers.
Three R's are stressed.
Catholic Youth Organization of the Archdiocese of Washington sports program.
All classes participate in music with one musical in spring. Band program for G4 up.
Artwork is displayed in Spring.

Special Spots

x	Computer room
	Science lab
x	Dedicated music room
	Music practice room
	Gymnasium
	Dedicated art room
	Ceramic studio
x	Auditorium
	Tennis court
	Pool
	Playing fields
	Enrichment rooms
x	Library
	Language lab
	Dance studio
	Separate lunchroom
	Kitchen
	Infirmary
	Conference room
	Multipurpose room
	Expansion plans

Sports News

P.E. Instruction*

	Swimming
	Basketball
	Gymnastics
	Dance
	Softball
	Skating
	Soccer
	Volleyball
	Creative movement

Weekly P.E. class

1	Pre-K
1	Transition
1	Kindergarten
1	First
1	Second
1	Third
1	Fourth
1	Fifth
1	Sixth

*P.E. instruction is dependent on Catholic Youth Organization program.

After-School Activities

Scouts, sports.

Registration/Admissions

Registration begins 1st week of March.

Parents tour school at November Open House.

Applicants are interviewed and tested by school psychologist using Stanford test during scheduled times in May.

Decision made when tests are evaluated.

Most children accepted when registered unless testing shows learning disability that the school is not equipped to handle to child's benefit.

Limited financial aid available; Rectory handles.

Apply using Princeton forms.

Siblings, Catholics given admission priority.

Where Next

Gonzaga, St. John's, Good Counsel, Immaculata, Holy Cross, Visitation.

Head Profile

Principal of de Chantal since 1989; teacher 5 years previous to that. Graduate of St. Francis College, Loretto, PA; master's in counseling from Catholic University.

Faculty Features

1	No. male teachers
26	No. female teachers
M	% turnover
10	Typical tenure (yrs.)
____	Art teacher
x	Vocal music teacher
x	Instrumental music teacher
x	Counselor/psychologist
____	Nurse
____	Language teacher
x	Math teacher
____	Reading teacher
____	P.E. teacher
____	Remedial reading teacher
____	Remedial math teacher
____	Speech therapist
x	Full-time science teacher
____	Enrichment teacher
____	Tutor
____	Assistant teachers

Parents Say

Happy environment. Rigorous academic program. Good communication between school and parents.

Your Notes

Parent Wish List

More foreign language instruction.
Better history and geography instruction.

Parent Involvement

Volunteer opportunities: class parent, teacher's aide, expert lecturer.
Home School Association is active in fund raising.
High level of parent commitment to school.

St. Mary's School of Piscataway

13407 Piscataway Road, Clinton, MD 20735
301/292-2522
HEAD: Margaret Ellinger

Basics

Year founded: 1962
Enrollment: 237
  Boys: 121
  Girls: 116
Grades: K–8
Major entry grade: K
Birthdate req.: 5 yrs. by Dec. 31
Arrival: 8:15 a.m.
Dismissal: 2:45 p.m.
Early dismissal: 1st Fri. of month, 12:30 p.m.
Extended day: 7:00 a.m.–6:00 p.m.
Costs: $1100–$1490
Parent fund raising: $5,000
Transportation: yes
Lunch: no
After-school activities: no
Camp: no
Dress code: uniform G1–8
Neighborhood: Clinton

Special Qualities

Emphasis on Christian values.
Active parent support system.
Friendly and challenging school.
Teachers give individual attention.

Philosophy and Character

School aims to offer an excellent curriculum incorporating religious values.
Emphasis on development of whole person and positive self-image.
Students involved in some local nursing home activities.
All grades have one section and range in size from 23–30.
Mostly middle-income families.
80% students are Catholic.
Neighborhood school.
26% minority enrollment.
All students from MD.

Curriculum

Priority placed on religion and basic skills.

Daily instruction of math, reading, language, social studies, science.
Art, music, Spanish, computers, and P.E. 1 or 2x/week.
Reading program uses Houghton-Mifflin and Open Court series with phonics G1–3 and more literature G4 up.
Computer uses CES Compu-Tech, Inc., program in K–8.
Religion required.
Math focuses on skills and their application.
Science is hands-on K–G2, G4 up uses Heath Series.
Spanish instruction begins in K.

Special Spots

x	Computer room
x	Science lab
	Dedicated music room
x	Music practice room
	Gymnasium
	Dedicated art room
	Ceramic studio
x	Auditorium
	Tennis court
	Pool
x	Playing fields
	Enrichment rooms
x	Library
	Language lab
	Dance studio
x	Separate lunchroom
x	Kitchen
x	Infirmary
	Conference room
	Multipurpose room
	Expansion plans

Sports News

P.E. Instruction

	Swimming
x	Basketball
x	Gymnastics
	Dance
x	Softball
	Skating
x	Soccer
x	Volleyball
x	Creative movement

Weekly P.E. class

	Pre-K
	Transition
1	Kindergarten
1	First
1	Second
1	Third
1	Fourth
1	Fifth
1	Sixth

After-School Activities

Activities in extended day include arts and crafts, computer, athletics, drama and puppetry, piano and instrumental music.

Registration/Admissions

Admission granted in sequence (1) Catholic member of St. Mary's parish; (2) Catholic child in another parish; (3) non-Catholic child.
Priority given to siblings.
Entrance testing by school for K and G1.
Financial aid available from Archdiocese of Washington.
Registration is last week of January.

Where Next

Bishop McNamara, La Reine, St. Mary's Academy, Gwynn Park, Oxon Hill, Friendly, Bishop Ireton.

Head Profile

Although in her first year at St. Mary's, Mrs. Ellinger has been a school administrator for 20 years. M.Ed. in administration and supervision; varied experiences in education. Works closely with children, teachers, and parents and is directly involved in instructional program. Believes good self-concept paramount to success and happiness.

Faculty Features

3	No. male teachers
11	No. female teachers
N	% turnover (10%)
13	Typical tenure (yrs.)
	Art teacher
	Vocal music teacher
x	Instrumental music teacher
	Counselor/psychologist
x	Nurse/Health Aide
x	Language teacher
x	Math teacher
x	Reading teacher
x	P.E. teacher
	Remedial reading teacher
	Remedial math teacher
	Speech therapist
x	Full-time science teacher
	Enrichment teacher
	ESL teacher
x	Tutor
x	Assistant teachers (K)

Parents Say

unavailable

Parent Wish List

Expanded P.E. program.

Your Notes

Parent Involvement

St. Mary's Home and School Association, $5 dues.

Room parents.

Volunteers encouraged in classroom, library, learning centers, health room, typing, school yard.

St. Patrick's Episcopal Day School

4700 Whitehaven Parkway NW, Washington, DC 20007
202/342-2805
HEAD: Robert Ross Peterson

Basics

Year founded: 1956
Enrollment: 365
  Boys: 183
  Girls: 182
Grades: N–6
Major entry grade: N, K, 3, 4
Birthdate req.: 3 yrs. by Sept. 1
Arrival: 8:10 a.m. (9:00 a.m. N)
Dismissal: 3:00 p.m. (12:00 noon N)
Early dismissal: Fri., 12:30 p.m.
Extended day: 7:45 a.m.–6:00 p.m.
Costs: $4400–$6930
Parent fund raising: $180,000–$200,000
Transportation: no
Lunch: no
After-school activities: yes
Camp: yes
Dress code: neat
Neighborhood: Palisades

Special Qualities

Friendly, personal, supportive environment.
Strong science and art programs.
Variety of enrichment and after-school programs.
Diverse student body.

Philosophy and Character

Family-oriented, low pressure, very nurturing and supportive Episcopal parish school.
Concerned with child's total development through rich variety of learning experiences.
Stress on academics with resource teachers.
Enrollment for each grade ranges from 30–40 students with 2 sections per class. Nursery classes have an extra small section; K, which is very

large with an enrollment of 60, has 3 sections.
Spiritual development stressed.
Housed in new brick building with 2 acres of playing fields.
Children encouraged to participate in the Senior Citizens Center, Grate Patrol, and other community outreach programs; school sponsors another school in Haiti.
Primarily a neighborhood school, 80% of students from DC, 15% MD, 5% VA.; Episcopalians 40%, Catholics 20%, Afro-Americans 13%, Hispanic-Americans 2%, Asian-Americans 1%, citizens of other countries 15%.
10% of children regularly use extended day.

Curriculum

Reading: Open Court basals K–1; Houghton-Mifflin in G2–3; literature-based G4–6, extensive use of novels.
Graves writing program K–6, daily writing, creative and expository writing for G4–6, research papers G4–6.
Math: concepts, manipulatives, abstract, rote.
Science: 1x/week for N–K, 2x/week for G1–6.
French in K, Latin G5–6.
Computer: LOGO problem-solving K–3.
Religion: 1x/week, Old, New Testament, comparative religions, chapel 1x/week.
Music: 2x/week by specialist.
Drama production 2x/year (schoolwide class).
Homework: K—¼ hour; G1–2—½ hour; G3—¾ hour; G4—1 hour; G5—1¼ hours; G6—1¼–2 hours.
Grading: effort grades given G1–3 and letter grades for G4–6.

Special Spots

__x__ Computer room
__x__ Science lab (2)
__x__ Dedicated music room
_____ Music practice room
__x__ Gymnasium
__x__ Dedicated art room
_____ Ceramic studio
__x__ Auditorium
_____ Tennis court
_____ Pool
__x__ Playing fields
_____ Enrichment rooms
__x__ Library (10,000 volumes)
__x__ Language lab
_____ Dance studio
_____ Separate lunchroom
_____ Kitchen
__x__ Infirmary

__x__ Conference room
__x__ Darkroom
_____ Multipurpose room
_____ Expansion plans

Sports News

P.E. Instruction:
_____ Swimming
__x__ Basketball
__x__ Gymnastics
__x__ Dance
__x__ Softball
_____ Skating
__x__ Soccer
__x__ Volleyball
_____ Creative movement
__x__ Football and field hockey

Weekly P.E. class
__2__ PreK
_____ Transition
__2__ Kindergarten
__2__ First
__2__ Second
__4__ Third
__4__ Fourth
__4__ Fifth
__4__ Sixth

After-School Activities

Gymnastics, soccer, stitchery, cooking, computer, tutoring.

Registration/Admissions

Nursery school: Pat Spector.
Parents: visit in groups on Wed.
Apply by Jan. 31.
Elementary School: Mardy O'Neil; G4–6: Rob Peterson.
Individual interviews and tour apply by Feb. 1.
Test: McCarthy—K, WPPSI—G1, WISD—G2–6.
Test results shared in a letter.
Students: visit, recommendations, transcript.
Financial aid given: $181,000 in 1988–89.
Complete SSS forms by Feb. 15.
Special needs: mildly learning disabled.
Notification: March 3–15.

Where Next

National Cathedral, St. Albans, St. Andrew's Episcopal, Holton Arms, Landon, Maret.

Head Profile

Williams College, B.A.; Fairfield University, M.Ed. Fourteen years at Brunswick School in Greenwich, CT, teaching history, math, and English; administration, admissions director, development director, and head of Lower School. At St. Patrick's since 1986. Job focuses on administration, faculty relations, and communicating with students and parents.

Faculty Features

4	No. male teacher
35	No. female teachers
N	Turnover (15%)
5	Typical tenure (yrs.)
x	Art teacher
	Vocal music teacher
	Instrumental music teacher
x	Counselor/psychologist
	Nurse
x	Language teacher
	Math teacher
	Reading teacher
x	P.E. teacher
	Remedial reading teacher
	Remedial math teacher
x	Speech therapist
x	Full-time science teacher
	Enrichment teacher
	ESL teacher
	Tutor
	Assistant teachers

Parents Say

Peterson interested in children—goes on field trips to get to know students better. Facilities are excellent. Diversity of student body and availability of extra help are appreciated by parents.

Parent Wish List

Spring vacations to coincide with other schools.
More academic and character diversity.
More stress on athletic and academic achievement.
Lunch, bus service, computers in classrooms.

Parent Involvement

Strong parent association with volunteers in classroom, library, as reading mother, field trips, sports, publishing students' work, class reps.
Fund raisers include casino-auction (for scholarships), book fair, plant sale, spring fair, Christmas Classics.

Your Notes

St. Peter's Interparish School

422 Third Street SE, Washington, DC 20003
202/544-1618
HEAD: Mary Randolph

Basics

Year founded: 1880
Enrollment: 255
Boys: 127
Girls: 128
Grades: PreK–8
Major entry grade: PreK, K
Birthdate req.: 4 yrs. by Oct. 1
Arrival: 8:30 a.m.
Dismissal: 3:00 p.m.
Early dismissal: Wed., 12:30 p.m.
Extended day: 7:15 a.m.–6:00 p.m.
Costs: $1490 parishioners, $1850 other
Parent fund raising: $25,000–$30,000
Transportation: no
Lunch: no
After-school activities: yes
Camp: yes
Dress code: uniform
Neighborhood: Capitol Hill

Special Qualities

New reading resource teacher.
High but reasonable standards.
Children behave and respect school and teachers.
Nurturing, loving, no-nonsense, cohesive, friendly school.
Disciplined but not rigid.
Low-cost parish school on Capitol Hill.
Diverse student body.

Philosophy and Character

Integration of Christian perspective in a friendly, safe, challenging environment.
Emphasis on community spirit.
Respect for self and others.
Involve families in development of their children.
The PreK class has 15 students

and K–G6 range from 24–28, all with 1 section.
Economic diversity includes extremely poor to extremely wealthy.
Generally a neighborhood school serving Catholic community (89% DC, 10% MD, 1% VA).
25% use extended day.
Very active community service projects.
Monthly assemblies.

Curriculum

Strong basic education, moral values stressed.
French instruction G6–8.
Extensive use of community—i.e., Folger Library, Smithsonian.
Very strong instrumental music and band, won Archdiocese award.
Spectacular library and librarian, who has been at school 15 years.
Opportunities for public performances before parents and school community.
Computer education lab—hands-on; math basics stressed.
Schoolwide emphasis to write well.
Religion classes daily.
Homework introduced G1, 10 min. to 1 hr. in G6.

Special Spots

__x__ Computer room
__x__ Science lab
_____ Dedicated music room
_____ Music practice room
_____ Gymnasium
_____ Dedicated art room
_____ Ceramic studio
_____ Auditorium
_____ Tennis court
_____ Pool
_____ Playing fields
_____ Enrichment rooms
__x__ Library
_____ Language lab
_____ Dance studio
_____ Separate lunchroom
_____ Kitchen
_____ Infirmary
_____ Conference room
__x__ Multipurpose room
_____ Expansion plans

Sports News

P.E. Instruction
_____ Swimming
__x__ Basketball
_____ Gymnastics
_____ Dance
_____ Softball
_____ Skating
_____ Soccer
_____ Volleyball
_____ Creative movement

Weekly P.E. class

1	Pre-K
	Transition
1	Kindergarten
1	First
1	Second
1	Third
1	Fourth
1	Fifth
1	Sixth

After-School Activities

Basketball, drama, art, madrigals, cooperation with Capitol Hill Arts Workshop.

Registration/Admissions

Mary Randolph.
Deadline for application is February 28.
Open House: 1st Sunday in March.
Interview required.
No testing.
Catholics have priority.
Notification by phone and letter.
No provisions for ESL or handicapped students.
Financial aid: all requests are met, substantial grants given (based on need)—$15,000 in 1988–89.

Where Next

Gonzaga, Archbishop Carroll, Georgetown Visitation, Bishop O'Connell, St. John's, Elizabeth Seton, St. Anselm's.

Head Profile

At St. Peter's since 1984; administrative internship, Fairfax County, 1985; 10 years public school teacher. B.S., elementary education, 1975; M.Ed., administration and supervision, 1980. Very involved with students and parents.

Faculty Features

2	No. male teachers
14	No. female teachers
M	% turnover (5%)
5	Typical tenure (yrs.)
x	Art teacher
x	Vocal music teacher
x	Instrumental music teacher
x	Counselor/psychologist (part-time)
	Nurse
x	Language teacher
x	Math teacher
	Reading teacher
x	P.E. teacher
x	Remedial reading teacher (enrichment)

_____ Remedial math teacher
__x__ Speech therapist
_____ Full-time science teacher
__x__ Enrichment teacher
_____ ESL teacher
__x__ Tutor (volunteers)
_____ Assistant teachers
__x__ Social worker

Parents Say

Principal is firm and at same time loving; has sound educational philosophy, is organized, goal-oriented, very accessible.

Parent Wish List

Gymnasium, cafeteria, better science lab, more computer time, more language opportunities, 50% more parent involvement, growth in endowment, lunch.

Parent Involvement

Parent views sought and considered.
Routine informal coffees to share thoughts.
Volunteering in library, chaperoning field trips, classroom activities and fund raising (auction, yard sale, etc.).
Money raised funds scholarships, teacher bonuses, language instruction, computers, library, art, playground equipment.

Your Notes

St. Stephen's School

4401 West Braddock Road, Alexandria, VA 22304
703/379-6050
HEAD: Barbara Logan (Lower School)

Basics

Year founded: 1944
Enrollment: 171 (K–12 600)
  Boys: 130
  Girls: 41
Grades: K–5 (Lower School)
Major entry grade: K, 3, 6
Birthdate req.: 5 yrs. by Sept. 1
Arrival: 8:35 a.m.
Dismissal: 3:00 p.m.
Early dismissal: no
Extended day: 6:00 p.m.
Costs: $6700–$7500
Parent fund raising: $300,000 (for K–12)
Transportation: yes
Lunch: yes
After-school activities: yes
Camp: yes
Dress code: no blue jeans or T-shirts; neat
Neighborhood: St. Stephens Road/Seminary Road

Special Qualities

Individual attention in structured school based on Christian love as community ideal.
Learning Center for students with special needs (enrichment or remedial).
Newly renovated facility with separate Lower School campus.
Strong school spirit.

Philosophy and Character

Founded as church school in Virginia Episcopal Diocese; as of May 1989 governed by independent board of governors.
Offers liberal arts program; religion of reason and faith; individual given appropriate development of mind, spirit, and body.

Help children learn to live balanced lives.
Children involved in many community service projects, such as ALIVE, Carpenters Shelter, Red Cross, animal shelter.
95% students from VA with 48% from Fairfax, 36% from Alexandria, and 9% from Arlington; 7% minority enrollment.

Curriculum

Developmentally appropriate curriculum aimed at forming well-rounded student.
Classes take monthly field trip.
Weekly chapel service, theology class.
Homework begins G1.
K stresses learning through play activities.
Reading: phonics-based, use Scribners series.
Math Their Way program with weekly math lab, which has games and manipulatives.
Hands-on work in science and computer labs.
Weekly art and music class with private music lessons, spring musical production.
Language arts stresses process writing approach and study skills.

Special Spots

__x__ Computer room
__x__ Science lab
__x__ Dedicated music room
__x__ Music practice room
__x__ Gymnasium
__x__ Dedicated art room
_____ Ceramic studio
_____ Auditorium
__x__ Tennis court
_____ Pool
__x__ Playing fields
__x__ Enrichment rooms
__x__ Library (6000 volumes)
_____ Language lab
_____ Dance studio
__x__ Separate lunchroom
__x__ Kitchen
__x__ Infirmary
__x__ Conference room
__x__ Multipurpose room
__x__ Expansion plans (1988–89 Lower School new building, add K–2, coed K–12)

Sports News

P.E. Instruction:
_____ Swimming
__x__ Basketball
__x__ Gymnastics
_____ Dance
__x__ Softball
_____ Skating

_x_ Soccer
____ Volleyball
____ Creative movement

Weekly P.E. class:
____ PreK
____ Transition
_3_ Kindergarten
_3_ First
_5_ Second
_5_ Third
_5_ Fourth
_5_ Fifth
____ Sixth

After-School Activities

Daisies, Brownies, Tiger Cubs, Cub Scouts, Science Encounters, French club, Spanish club, choir, band.

Registration/Admissions

John T. Kennedy 703/751-0056 or 703/845-9462.
Obtain admissions package in fall.
Attend Open House or personal tour.
Submit application, 2 teacher recommendations, transcript.
Testing for K–2 by GWU Reading Center at St. Stephen's (developmental and math and reading achievement test), ERB test for G3 up; results shared with parents by request.
Sibling and legacies given admission priority.
Early Decision: Feb. 1; rolling admissions subsequently.
Financial aid available; $335,000 given in 1988–89.

Where Next

St. Stephen's Middle School.

Head Profile

Lower School director since 1984. B.A., history and education; M.Ed., elementary curriculum and instruction. Taught in public and private schools. Focuses on programs, faculty relations, parent relations, and curriculum development. Occasional classroom teaching.

Faculty Features

_3_ No. male teachers
_22_ No. female teachers
_M_ % turnover
_5+_ Typical tenure (yrs.)
_x_ Art teacher

_x_ Vocal music teacher
_x_ Instrumental music teacher
___ Counselor/psychologist
___ Nurse
___ Language teacher
_x_ Math teacher
_x_ Reading teacher
_x_ P.E. teacher
_x_ Remedial reading teacher
_x_ Remedial math teacher
___ Speech therapist
_x_ Full-time science teacher (part-time)
_x_ Enrichment teacher
___ ESL teacher
_x_ Tutor
___ Assistant teachers

Parents Say

Outstanding lower school facility. Excellent family life program for K–12.

Parent Wish List

Improve instrumental music program.

Parent Involvement

Mothers' Club and Dads' Club sponsor dinner dance/auction to raise funds for equipment, computers, etc.

Headmaster's Parents Committee for parent input.

Parents can volunteer in library, as field trip chaperone, room parent, and choir assistant.

Your Notes

Sheridan School

4400 36th Street NW, Washington, DC 20008
202/362-7900
HEAD: Hugh C. Riddleberger III

Basics

Year founded: 1927
Enrollment: 202
  Boys: 105
  Girls: 97
Grades: K–8
Major entry grade: K
Birthdate req.: 5 yrs. by Sept. 1
Arrival: 8:30 a.m.
Dismissal: 1:45 p.m. K/3:30 p.m. G1–8
Early dismissal: Wed., 2:40 p.m.
Extended day: 7:30 a.m.–6:00 p.m.
Costs: $6600–$8195
Parent fund raising: $185,000
Transportation: no
Lunch: yes
After-school activities: yes
Camp: yes (computer and science)
Dress code: K–3 plain, simple; G4 up uniform on Fri.
Neighborhood: North Cleveland Park

Special Qualities

Emphasis on academic excellence, discipline, and moral values.
Mountain campus—130 acres in Shenandoah Valley.
Small, traditional, structured grammar-style school.

Philosophy and Character

Small, family school emphasizing academic excellence and attention to the individual.
School stresses values such as honesty, courtesy, and respect for others.
Has "buddy grades" system and family-style meals at lunch.
Routine visits to Lisner Home and Friendship Terrace.
Class size averages 24–25 students with one section per grade.
Sheridan seeks diverse multi-

racial, and international student body (15%); 17% minority enrollment; 70% students from DC, 5% VA, 25% MD.

Curriculum

Occasional homework assigned G1–2, formally begins G3.
K–3 classes each have two teachers and special teachers for art, music, science, computer, P.E.
G4 up has homeroom teacher for "central subject" (English, history, geography) with departmental teachers for math, science, French, art, music, P.E.
French instruction starts G4.
Reading: phonics stressed, using phonovisual method, ability grouping.
Math: drills support concept learning, manipulatives used, Math Their Way.
Computer: 1x/week, small groups, LOGO and BASIC instruction, word processing by G5.
Science: problem solving, 1x/week in K, 2x/week thereafter, pond at mountain campus.
Art: 1x/week in art studio.
Music: Friday music assemblies, recorder ensemble, choral groups, use Orff-Schulwerk instruments, 2x/week all grades.
Interscholastic sports team competition G4 up.
Letter grading begins G4.
Learning specialist on staff.

Special Spots

__x__ Computer room
__x__ Science lab
__x__ Dedicated music room
_____ Music practice room
__x__ Gymnasium
__x__ Dedicated art room
_____ Ceramic studio
__x__ Auditorium
_____ Tennis court
_____ Pool
__x__ Playing fields
_____ Enrichment rooms
__x__ Library (8000 volumes)
_____ Language lab
_____ Dance studio
_____ Separate lunchroom
__x__ Kitchen
_____ Infirmary
_____ Conference room
_____ Multipurpose room
_____ Expansion plans

Sports News

P.E. Instruction:
_____ Swimming
__x__ Basketball

_____ Gymnastics
_____ Dance
__x__ Softball
_____ Skating
__x__ Soccer
_____ Volleyball
_____ Creative movement

Weekly P.E. class:
_____ PreK
_____ Transition
__5__ Kindergarten
__5__ First
__5__ Second
__5__ Third
__4__ Fourth
__4__ Fifth
__4__ Sixth

After-School Activities

Basketball, science club, guitar, computer club, newspaper, computer, orchestra.

Registration/Admissions

Martha Gerson.
Request brochure.
Appointment for tour and parent interview Oct.–Feb.
Submit application between Oct. 1–March 1.
Teacher recommendation and transcripts required.
K applicants visit school in Jan.; parent meets with headmaster.
K–3 applicants tested at Kingsbury or Specific Diagnostics, using McCarthy test, G4–8 during school visit.
Siblings given admissions preference.
Financial aid available—$75,000 given 1988–89.
Apply for aid using Princeton form.

Where Next

St. Albans, Sidwell Friends, Georgetown Day, Maret, National Cathedral.

Head Profile

Headmaster since 1987. B.A., University of Michigan; Ed.M., Harvard. Previously head of Metairie Park Country Day School, New Orleans. Greets each child in morning and teaches some classes. Focuses on curriculum review, improving faculty development, and graduates' school placement, less so on admissions.

Faculty Features

__6__ No. male teachers
__18__ No. female teachers

N	% turnover
12–15	Typical tenure (yrs.)
x	Art teacher
x	Vocal music teacher (1½)
x	Instrumental music teacher
x	Counselor/psychologist (consultant)
	Nurse
x	Language teacher
x	Math teacher
	Reading teacher
x	P.E. teacher
	Remedial reading teacher
	Remedial math teacher
	Speech therapist
x	Full-time science teacher (2)
	Enrichment teacher
	ESL teacher
	Tutor
	Assistant teachers

Parents Say

School has friendly, family atmosphere. Small school where all students and staff know each other. Excellent music and art programs. Facilities need improvement.

Parent Wish List

More foreign language instruction in lower elementary grades.

Bus service.

More space and better athletic facilities.

Parent Involvement

Active Parents Association.

Involvement in school life strongly encouraged.

Opportunities: fund raising (auction, spring fair), library, grounds management, field trip chaperone, reading assistant.

Funds raised augment operating budget.

Long-range planning committee has board, faculty, and parent members.

Your Notes

The Sidwell Friends School (PreK–4)

5100 Edgemoor Lane, Bethesda, MD 20814
301/656-4081 (mail to: 3825 Wisconsin Avenue NW, Washington, DC 20016)
HEAD: Richard Lodish

Basics

Year founded: 1883
Enrollment: 280
  Boys: 140
  Girls: 140
Grades: Lower School PreK–4
Major entry grade: PreK, K, 3
Birthdate req.: 4 yrs. by Oct. 1
Arrival: 8:30 a.m.
Dismissal: 3:00 p.m.
Early dismissal: Tues., 2:00 p.m.
Extended day: 6:00 p.m. at Wisconsin Avenue campus
Costs: $6960–$7630
Parent fund raising: $150,000 (for PreK–12)
Transportation: yes
Lunch: yes
After-school activities: no
Camp: yes
Dress code: none
Neighborhood: Edgemoor (Lower School)

Special Qualities

Quaker philosophy.
Weekly silent meeting for worship.
Separate lower, middle, and upper school campuses.
Writer-in-residence program.
"Staff Review of a Child" program to diagnose and help students experiencing difficulty.
Active community involvement by students.
Warm, caring, nurturing climate.
Diverse student body.

Philosophy and Character

Independent, Quaker school.
Dedicated to educating child's mind, body, and spirit with special emphasis on Quaker principles of dignity, self-worth, and reverence for life.

High academic expectations with awareness of others.

Develop sense of world and need to perform service to others.

Understand equal importance of speaking up for beliefs and quiet reflection.

Weekly community service integral part of school life—i.e., Wednesday Soup Day.

Learning in a relaxed, creative, caring environment.

School directed by independent board of trustees, majority of whom are Quakers/parents.

Class size ranges from 28–56 students per grade with 2–4 sections.

50% students DC; 40% MD; 10% VA; 10% students are Quaker; 20% siblings; 28% minority enrollment.

Curriculum

Thematic approach.

Both single- and multi-age sections in each grade.

Uses different teaching styles.

Teachers have broad responsibility to plan curriculum, order materials, choose teaching methods.

Language arts emphasizes reading, writing, and speaking skills with writer-in-residence program.

Field trips and outdoor education activities.

Math stresses computational skills and conceptual understanding; uses manipulatives, concrete materials, and other developmentally appropriate techniques; math coordinator starting 1989–90.

Social studies focuses on life in and beyond child's community, forms core of thematic approach.

Science: PreK–1 in homeroom, G2–4 in science room with hands-on projects.

Art materials in classroom and in studio 1x/week for G1–4.

Orff-Schulwerk and Kodaly choral methods for teaching music-drama with weekly assemblies.

Computers: LOGO, used as an aide to thinking, not teaching tool; word processing for older students; computer room and computers in classrooms.

Full-time resource room/special instruction teacher to help students.

Homework begins G2, increasing to 1–1½ hours by G3 and 4.

Full-day PreK and K programs.

Special Spots

__x__ Computer room
__x__ Science lab
__x__ Dedicated music room
_____ Music practice room
__x__ Gymnasium

__x__ Dedicated art room
_____ Ceramic studio
__x__ Auditorium
_____ Tennis court
_____ Pool
__x__ Playing fields
_____ Enrichment rooms
__x__ Library
_____ Language lab
_____ Dance studio
_____ Separate lunchroom
__x__ Kitchen
__x__ Infirmary
_____ Conference room
__x__ Multipurpose room
__x__ Expansion plans (3-story science, music, and art building by summer 1990)

Sports News

P.E. Instruction
_____ Swimming
__x__ Basketball
__x__ Gymnastics
__x__ Dance
__x__ Softball
_____ Skating
__x__ Soccer
__x__ Volleyball
__x__ Creative movement

Weekly P.E. class
__3–4__ PreK
_____ Transition
__3–4__ Kindergarten
__4__ First
__4__ Second
__4__ Third
__4__ Fourth
_____ Fifth
_____ Sixth

After-School Activities

None at Lower School.

Registration/Admissions

Diane Wilson, 202/537-8111.
Optional pre-application tours and/or open houses.
Applications accepted Sept. 1–Jan. 15.
Applicant takes McCarthy Scales or WISC-R, with results given to parents.
Current school sends records and evaluations.
Parent submits history of child.
Applicant attends a group session.
Admission priority to Quakers; former students; siblings; children of alumni, staff, trustees.
Financial aid form to SSS in Princeton by Feb. 8.
Sidwell Friends school loan available; apply by May 1.
Emphasis on recruiting minority students.
18% student body receives financial aid.
$150,000 given for Lower School scholarships in 1988–89.

Where Next

Lower School students attend Middle School.

Head Profile

Lower School principal since 1976. Doctorate in education from Harvard. Taught in Cleveland public schools. Believes schools should be concerned with matters of the heart as well as the head.

Faculty Features

3	No. male teachers
33	No. female teachers
M	% turnover (5%)
u	Typical tenure (yrs.)
x	Art teacher
x	Vocal music teacher
x	Instrumental music teacher
x	Counselor/psychologist
x	Nurse
x	Language teacher
x	Math teacher
x	Reading teacher
x	P.E. teacher
x	Remedial reading teacher
	Remedial math teacher
x	Speech therapist
x	Full-time science teacher
x	Enrichment teacher
	ESL teacher
x	Tutor
	Assistant teachers

Parents Say

Quaker atmosphere. Facilities are somewhat limited but are being improved. Teachers care about each student. Good bus service. Strong social studies program. Parent input sought and encouraged on school related-social issues.

Parent Wish List

Improvement of facilities.
Instrumental music lessons during school day.
Foreign language instruction.
Indoor swimming pool.
After-school activities.
Separate lunch and gym facilities.

Parent Involvement

Many programs for parents: "Education for Parenting," and parent peer groups.
Volunteers sought and encouraged: room parents, chaperone field trips, teaching assistants, resource people, newsletter, library, and event planning.
Parents work with their children on community service.
Fair share annual giving.

Your Notes

Somerset Elementary School

5811 Warwick Place, Chevy Chase, MD 20815
301/657-4985
HEAD: Sally Veres

Basics

Year founded: 1928
Enrollment: 351
  Boys: unavailable
  Girls: unavailable
Grades: K–6
Major entry grades: na
Birthdate req.: 5 yrs. by Dec. 31
Arrival: 9:00 a.m.
Dismissal: 3:00 p.m.
Early dismissal: no
Extended day: 7:30 a.m.–6:00 p.m.
Costs: na
Parent fund raising: $10,000–$15,000
Transportation: yes
Lunch: yes
After-school activities: yes
Camp: yes
Dress code: none
Neighborhood: Somerset and West Chevy Chase

Special Qualities

Magnet school program.
International student body.
Parent involvement.
Small size.
Neighborhood school.

Philosophy and Character

School chosen to participate in Flexibility Pilot Program.
School is located on 3.5 acre grounds.
Friendly and warm school climate.
Total capacity is 341, with grades ranging in size from 30–63.
Approximately 20% minority enrollment (Hispanic, black, Asian).

Curriculum

Full-day K program.
Excellent music and art programs.
Homework begins in K.
Have Apple and Commodore computers in lab and classrooms.

Special Spots

x	Computer room
	Science lab
x	Dedicated music room
	Music practice room
	Gymnasium
	Dedicated art room
	Ceramic studio
	Auditorium
	Tennis court
	Pool
x	Playing fields
x	Enrichment rooms
x	Library
	Language lab
	Dance studio
	Separate lunchroom
x	Kitchen
x	Infirmary
	Conference room
x	Multipurpose room
	Expansion plans

Sports News*

P.E. Instruction

	Swimming
	Basketball
	Gymnastics
	Dance
	Softball
	Skating
	Soccer
	Volleyball
	Creative Movement

Weekly P.E. class

	Pre-K
	Transition
1	Kindergarten
1	First
1	Second
1	Third
1	Fourth
1	Fifth
1	Sixth

After-School Activities

Large selection which changes every semester; selections have included soccer, art, drama, chess, hands-on science.
Programs run by MCPS and the PTA.

*Unavailable.

Head Profile

unavailable

Faculty Features

2	No. male teachers
29	No. female teachers
M	% turnover
15	Typical tenure (yrs.)
x	Art teacher
x	Vocal music teacher
x	Instrumental music teacher
x	Counselor/psychologist
	Nurse
	Language teacher
	Math teacher
x	Reading teacher
x	P.E. teacher
	Remedial reading teacher
	Remedial math teacher
x	Speech therapist
	Full-time science teacher
	Enrichment teacher
x	ESL teacher
	Tutor
	Assistant teachers
x	Resource room teacher
x	Media specialist

Parents Say

Facilities need improvement; principal accessible. Excellent music and art program.

Parent Wish List

Decrease competitiveness.
More sports programs.
Language instruction.

Parent Involvement

Very active PTA. Parents participate as classroom aides, in fund raising. Funds raised for playground equipment, teacher classroom spending money, and computers.

Your Notes

Stoddert Elementary School

39th and Calvert Streets NW, Washington, DC 20007
202/282-0143
HEAD: Patricia Patton

Basics

Year founded: 1932
Enrollment: 170
  Boys: unavailable
  Girls: unavailable
Grades: PreK–4
Major entry grade: na
Birthdate req.: 4 yrs. by Dec. 31
Arrival: 9:00 a.m.
Dismissal: 3:00 p.m. (PreK 12:30 p.m.)
Early dismissal: no
Extended day: 8:00 a.m.–9:00 a.m./3:00 p.m.–6:00 p.m.
Costs: na
Parent fund raising: $25,000
Transportation: no
Lunch: yes
After-school activities: yes
Camp: yes
Dress code: none
Neighborhood: Glover Park

Special Qualities

Model primary school of 6-school complex.
Each class plants and harvests own garden.
Small size of school.
Dedicated staff.
Lots of land and play space for a city school.
Diverse student body.
PTA fund raising supplements many areas of school activities.

Philosophy and Character

Stoddert is part of a six-school complex: the complex is an alliance of four elementary schools (Hyde, Key, Stoddert, and Mann); a middle school (Hardy); and an arts center (Fillmore). Each school has its own faculty, PTA, and campus. The complex was formed in 1974.
Parents feel school stresses academic achievement based on individual needs in a small, friendly community environment.

Student body is ethnically, economically, and culturally diverse, with Asians, Hispanics, blacks, whites, and students with special needs.
Dedicated, creative staff.
Out of boundary: only siblings.
Stoddert has some students from Mann district.

Curriculum

CTBS Test Scores (G3)
Reading: 89 percentile
Math: 97 percentile
Language: 88 percentile
Science: 82 percentile
Reading taught G1 on.
Students from K–6 attend Fillmore Arts Center: K–6 Fridays half-day for art, music, drama, dance instruction; PreK does activities at Stoddert.
Computer and hands-on science enrichment programs enhanced by PTA.
Computer program for G1–4 supports and enhances classroom skills.
Science: varied and creative experiments.
Student-produced newspaper.
Math: use of manipulatives in early years; students excel in tests later.
Presidential goals for physical fitness.
Homework begins G1.
Junior Great Books.

Special Spots

__x__ Computer room (3 Apple, 10 IBM)
_____ Science lab
__x__ Dedicated music room (Fillmore)
_____ Music practice room
__x__ Gymnasium (use church)
__x__ Dedicated art room (Fillmore)
__x__ Ceramic studio (Fillmore)
__x__ Auditorium (use church)
_____ Tennis court
_____ Pool
__x__ Playing fields (Parkland Recreation Department)
_____ Enrichment rooms
__x__ Library (3000 volumes)
_____ Language lab
__x__ Dance studio (Fillmore)
_____ Separate lunchroom
_____ Kitchen
_____ Infirmary
_____ Conference room
_____ Multipurpose room
_____ Expansion plans

Sports News

P.E. Instruction
_____ Swimming
_____ Basketball
__x__ Gymnastics

x	Dance
	Softball
	Skating
	Soccer
	Volleyball
x	Creative movement
	Tennis

Weekly P.E. class:

1	PreK
1	Kindergarten
1	First
1	Second
1	Third
1	Fourth

After-School Activities

Activities located at Fillmore Arts Center—art, music, gymnastics.
Extended day provides computer program.
Soccer at D.C. Recreation Department next door.

Registration/Admissions

April is registration month in DC public schools.
Watch for newspaper notifications or bulletins.
Proof of residency, child's birth certificate, and immunization record are required.
PreK classes fill up quickly and children enrolled on first-come, first-served basis.
Wise to sign up during scheduled registration period.
Apply for out-of-boundary admission at school; acceptance is limited. Out-of-state admission requires tuition of \$1880–\$2727.

Where Next

Large percentage of G4 go to Hardy Middle School, Potomac, Holy Trinity, Annunciation, Sidwell Friends.

Head Profile

B.A. and M.A. from Case Western Reserve; further graduate work at UCLA, University of Maryland, and Trinity. Also principal of Horace Mann, 8½ years as principal at Mann and Stoddert; 6 years as director of Hardy Middle; assistant principal, Connelly, 2 years.

Faculty Features

2	No. male teachers
6	No. female teachers
M	% turnover (minimal)
8–10	Typical tenure (yrs.)

- x Art teacher (Fillmore)
- x Vocal music teacher (½ day)
- ___ Instrumental music teacher
- x Counselor/psychologist (½ day)
- ___ Nurse
- ___ Language teacher
- ___ Math teacher
- x Reading teacher (2 days)
- x P.E. teacher (1 day) (Fillmore)
- ___ Remedial reading teacher
- ___ Remedial math teacher
- x Speech therapist (1 day)
- x Full-time science teacher (3 days; PTA hired)
- x Enrichment teacher (building resource teacher—50% Mann)
- x ESL teacher (50%)
- x Tutor (volunteers)
- x Educational aides (2)
- x Computer teacher (PTA hired)
- x Special education resource teacher (50%)

Parents Say

Principal is traditional, attentive, friendly, responsive, tuned-in, open, respectful of teachers and parents. Parents have strong voice in affairs of six-school complex.

Parent Wish List

Six-school complex math/science center.
Science lab.
Gym-auditorium.
Foreign language instruction.
Lunchroom, indoor multipurpose room, better library.

Parent Involvement

High overall level of parent involvement.
Fund raisers include Fall Festival and Spring Fair.
Opportunities for volunteering: recess supervision, Book Fair, Clean Up Day, Bulb Planting Day, Christmas Tree Sale, teaching, fund raising. Proceeds pay for professional classroom aides, science teachers, computer aides, ceiling fans, outdoor play, etc.

Your Notes

Stone Ridge Country Day School of the Sacred Heart

9101 Rockville Pike, Bethesda, MD 20814
301/657-4322
HEAD: Anne Dyer, RSCJ

Basics

Year founded: 1923
Enrollment: 175 (PreK–4); 166 (G4–8)
  Boys: 16
  Girls: 306 (PreK–8)
Grades: PreK–4, Lower School; G5–8, Middle School
Major entry grade: PreK, K
Birthdate req.: Sept. 1 (PreK)
Arrival: 8:00 a.m.
Dismissal: 3:00 p.m./3:30 p.m.
Early dismissal: no
Extended day: 6:00 p.m.
Costs: $3550–$6100
Parent fund raising: $85,000
Transportation: no
Lunch: no
After-school activities: yes
Camp: yes
Dress code: uniform
Neighborhood: Locust Hill/NIH Medical Center subway stop

Special Qualities

Designated as Exemplary Secondary School in 1986–87 by U.S. Department of Education.
Communications lab in Middle School.
Learning style strategies.

Philosophy and Character

Independent Roman Catholic day school for girls PreK–12 and boys PreK–K.
Based on faith, intellectual values, social awareness, building community, personal growth.
Marked by concern for individual's total development, emphasis on serious study, teaching social responsibility, laying foundation of strong faith.

All grades have 2 sections and range in size from 22 at PreK level to 38 by G6.

75% students from MD, 20% DC, and 5% VA; 25% minority enrollment.

Children of many faiths attend.

Curriculum

Administrator is certified Meyers Briggs specialist who annually trains faculty teaching strategies for developing lessons to meet varied learning styles.

Focus on fundamental skills.

Reading taught daily with Lippincott basals K–2 and Houghton-Mifflin G1–4; also use literature and experience stories taught by librarian 2x/wk.

Language arts daily with stress on creative writing and lots of journal work.

Math by classroom teacher PreK–4, all taught with manipulatives.

Music teacher focuses on vocal with Ward method (sight reading).

Art PreK–K with special teacher G1–4.

Homework begins G1.

Friday afternoon awards assembly called "Primes" acknowledges accomplishments. Every child commended at some point in year.

Monthly worship and religion classes.

Computer: begins in K, Apple IIE computers used, instruction curriculum gradually expands to include word processing, data base, and spread sheet work.

Foreign language: begins G5.

Communications lab in Middle School specializes in teaching communications skills and group dynamics to prepare for later work on teams—i.e., surgical team, engineering, etc.

Special Spots (Lower School)

__x__ Computer room
_____ Science lab
__x__ Dedicated music room
_____ Music practice room
__x__ Gymnasium
__x__ Dedicated art room
_____ Ceramic studio
__x__ Auditorium
__x__ Tennis court
_____ Pool
__x__ Playing fields
_____ Enrichment rooms
__x__ Library (7,000 volumes)
_____ Language lab
_____ Dance studio
_____ Separate lunchroom

__x__ Kitchen
__x__ Infirmary
__x__ Conference room
__x__ Multipurpose room
__x__ Expansion plans (considerations for long-range plan)

Sports News

P.E. Instruction (Lower School)
_____ Swimming
_____ Basketball
__x__ Gymnastics
_____ Dance
_____ Softball
_____ Skating
_____ Soccer
_____ Volleyball
__x__ Creative movement

Weekly P.E. class
__2__ Pre-K
_____ Transition
__2__ Kindergarten
__2__ First
__2__ Second
__2__ Third
__2__ Fourth
__5__ Fifth (Middle School)
__5__ Sixth (Middle School)

After-School Activities

Brownies, Jr. Chorus (L.S.).

Registration/Admissions

Sandy Dubinsky.
Request application and brochure.
Tours available—fall Open House.
Application preferred by February 1.
Recommendations, transcript, and test required.
Student and parent interview with student visit.
Decision by March 1 and acceptance within 2 weeks.
Financial aid available, use Princeton form; $296,500 given Aug. 8, 1989; applications due Feb. 15.

Where Next

Most students continue through G12.

Head Profile

Twenty-two years at Stone Ridge, head since 1968. B.A., Wheaton College; M.A. Manhattanville; M.S.A., Notre Dame. Twenty-five years teaching experience. Interests in arts and athletics.

Faculty Features

- 3 No. male teachers
- 30 No. female teachers
- M % turnover
- 11 Typical tenure (yrs.)
- x Art teacher
- x Vocal music teacher
- ___ Instrumental music teacher
- x Counselor/psychologist
- x Nurse
- x Language teacher
- ___ Math teacher
- ___ Reading teacher
- x P.E. teacher
- x Remedial reading teacher
- ___ Remedial math teacher
- ___ Speech therapist
- ___ Full-time science teacher
- ___ Enrichment teacher
- ___ ESL teacher
- x Tutor
- ___ Assistant teacher

Parents Say

Morale is high; parents very pleased. Caring community where traditional education takes place in an untraditional way.

Parent Wish List

Swimming pool, easier access for arrivals & dismissals.

Parent Involvement

Parents involved in fund-raising activities such as auction, used book sale.

They give tours of school, work as aides in offices, help with coaching after-school athletics, serve hot dog lunches, run school shop, involved with alumnae department, drive on field trips, serve as room mothers, develop roster of people to give talks.

Your Notes

Washington Episcopal School

5161 River Road, (P.O. Box 39182), Washington, DC 20016
301/652-7878
HEAD: Isabelle S. Schuessler

Basics

Year founded: 1986
Enrollment: 191–195
Boys: 103
Girls: 88
Grades: N3–6
Major entry grade: N3, N4, K
Birthdate req.: Sept. 1
Arrival: 8:15 a.m.
Dismissal: 3:15 p.m. (N–12:00 noon)
Early dismissal: Fri., 12:30 p.m.
Extended day: 8:00 a.m.–6:00 p.m.; N–afternoon option
Costs: $4000–$6800
Parent fund raising: $200,000
Transportation: independent van service
Lunch: no
After-school activities: yes
Camp: yes
Dress code: uniform G1–6
Neighborhood: Kenwood area of Chevy Chase

Special Qualities

Seasoned, dedicated teachers.
Strong academic program.
Small school with small classes, giving individual attention.
Traditional educational philosophy.
Early language introduction.
Honor Code and emphasis on considerate behavior.
Weekly chapel.
Well-developed curriculum.

Philosophy and Character

Independent Episcopal school not affiliated with a parish.
Emphasizes high academic expectations, development up to potential, building self-esteem, instilling sense of God's love in each child.
Focuses on moral values and ecumenical religious teaching.
Traditional structured environment.

Nursery enrollment includes 10 children with one section. Transition has 26 with 2 sections. K–2 has 32–34 students with 2 sections. G3–6 averages 15 students per class with just one section.
Students from economically diverse backgrounds.
Majority students from MD and DC, 5% VA.
Students involved in many community activities.

Curriculum

Provides enriched, accelerated academic program.
Reading readiness PreK; phonics and beginning reading in K; Open Court reading program starts G1; Junior Great Books program (G2–6).
Math in homeroom using manipulatives and textbook.
Science instructor G2 up.
French begins PreK with Latin G5–6.
Art, music, drama emphasized.
Homework begins G1.
Enrichment and remedial teachers used extensively.

Special Spots

__x__ Computer room
__x__ Science lab
__x__ Dedicated music room
_____ Music practice room
__x__ Gymnasium (large P.E. room)
__x__ Dedicated art rooms
_____ Ceramic studio
__x__ Auditorium (multipurpose with stage)
_____ Tennis court
__x__ Pool (St. Albans)
__x__ Playing fields (public park)
_____ Enrichment room
__x__ Library (4000 volumes)
__x__ Language lab
_____ Dance studio
_____ Separate lunchroom
_____ Kitchen
__x__ Infirmary
__x__ Conference room
__x__ Multipurpose room
__x__ Expansion plans (permanent site, increase enrollment, add G7–12)

Sports News

P.E. Instruction
__x__ Swimming
__x__ Basketball
__x__ Gymnastics
__x__ Dance
__x__ Softball
_____ Skating
__x__ Soccer
__x__ Volleyball
__x__ Creative movement
__x__ Floor hockey
_____ Tennis

Weekly P.E. class
- 1 PreK
- 2 Transition
- 2 Kindergarten
- 2 First
- 2 Second
- 2 Third
- 2 Fourth
- 2 Fifth
- 2 Sixth

After-School Activities

Sports and gymnastics; art, music, photography, drama, science.
Study hall (supervised); Junior Achievement Club.
Journalism class, computer lab open, social skills (K–2).

Registration/Admissions

Admissions Director, Susan S. Lewis.
Request brochure, attend group meeting, file application.
Request recommendations and transcripts.
Applicant visits school.
Testing at school available.
Applicant given McCarthy test K–6 or WISC-R with results sent to parents within two weeks.
Application deadline: Feb. 1.
Notification mid-March with acceptance early April.
Princeton form used; $40,000 financial aid given 1988–89.

Where Next

St. Albans, National Cathedral, St. Andrew's, Holton Arms, Landon.

Head Profile

Schuessler started WES in 1986 after 24 years at St. Patrick's School. A.B., George Washington University. Strong in administration, policy implementation, faculty supervision, parent relations. Known for getting things done.

Faculty Features

- 0 No. male teachers
- 17 No. female teachers
- na Typical tenure
- na Turnover
- x Art teacher (2)
- x Vocal music teacher
- x Instrumental music teacher
- x Counselor/psychologist
- ___ Nurse
- x Language teacher

_____ Math teacher
_____ Reading teacher
__x__ P.E. teacher
__x__ Remedial reading teacher (G1–2)
__x__ Remedial math teacher (G1–2)
__x__ Speech therapist
__x__ Full-time science teacher
__x__ Enrichment teacher
_____ ESL teacher
_____ Tutor

Parents Say

Teaching faculty is outstanding and curriculum is well thought out and stimulating. School is highly academic with significant amount of homework assigned regularly. School head is conservative. School is looking for an expanded, permanent site.

Parent Wish List

Permanent site.
Expand after-school activity choices, greater integration of computer into curriculum, more athletics, gymnasium, all of which are planned for 1989–90.

Parent Involvement

High level of parent participation. Opportunities include board, working in library, art center, fund raising, as room parent.
Parents influence long-term planning, less so academic and administrative matters.

Your Notes

Washington International School

3100 Macomb Street NW, Washington, DC 20008 (G4–12); 2735 Olive Street, NW, Washington, DC 20007 (N–3)
202/364-1800
HEAD: Tina Thuermen (Lower School)

Basics

Year founded: 1966
Enrollment: 220 (N–3) (585 N–12)
  Boys: unavailable
  Girls: unavailable
Grades: N–3 (Lower School)
Major entry grade: N, K, 4, 7
Birthdate req.: 4 yrs. by Sept. 1
Arrival: 8:45 a.m.
Dismissal: 3:00 p.m.
Early dismissal: no
Extended day: 8:00 a.m.–6:00 p.m.
Costs: $2700–$6700
Parent fund raising: $155,000
Transportation: limited
Lunch: no
After-school activities: yes
Camp: yes
Dress code: none
Neighborhood: Georgetown (N–3)

Special Qualities

Bilingual education—total language immersion.
Children learn to read in two languages.
Advanced drama productions.
Small classes.
Culturally diverse student body.

Philosophy and Character

Independent school offering rigorous bilingual curriculum.
Strong traditional values.
Foster appreciation and understanding of all cultures (60 countries represented).
To prepare for best American and European universities.
To feel successful and comfortable anywhere in the world.
A local perspective of teaching

history, geography, literature to understand interrelations between historical periods, cultural and literary trends.

All grades have 45 students and 3 sections.

Other campus for G4–12 located in Cleveland Park.

Casual, reassuring, but challenging atmosphere.

40% American 40% foreign, 20% dual; ⅓ IMF or World Bank families.

Curriculum

G1–3: ½ day is in English; ½ day in French or Spanish; N, PreK, K total immersion.

Formal reading begins in both languages G1.

Library: 1x/wk, interactive reading and checking out books.

Process writing in both languages.

Math manipulatives, use Open Court series and Rathtike.

Computer science: 1x/wk LOGO and Bank Street writer familiarity.

Social studies emphasized; folk legends, geographical areas and emphasis in select group of countries.

Music, computer, art, sports, science taught by specialists.

Grading is descriptive (G1–3); letter grades (G4–6).

General games and fitness to develop motor skills and enthusiasm for physical activity.

Use Jelleff Sports Club for P.E. program.

Special Spots

_x_ Computer room
_x_ Science lab
_x_ Dedicated music room
___ Music practice room
___ Gymnasium
_x_ Dedicated art room
___ Ceramic studio
_x_ Auditorium
___ Tennis court
___ Pool
_x_ Playing fields
___ Enrichment rooms
_x_ Library (7000 volumes)
___ Language lab
___ Dance studio
___ Separate lunchroom
___ Kitchen
___ Infirmary
___ Conference room
___ Multipurpose room
_x_ Expansion plans (gymnasium, theater)

Sports News

P.E. Instruction
___ Swimming
_x_ Basketball

x	Gymnastics
	Dance
	Softball
	Skating
x	Soccer
x	Volleyball
	Creative movement

Weekly P.E. class

2	Pre-K
	Transition
2	Kindergarten
2	First
2	Second
2	Third
2	Fourth
2	Fifth
2	Sixth

After-School Activities

Soccer, music lessons, choral group.

Registration/Admissions

Dorrie Fuchs 202/364-1815.
One-hour tours fall through early winter.
Applications by Jan. 31.
Applicants visit school.
Parents interviewed.
Developmental assessment for Lower School applicants.
Recommendations, grades, testing must indicate child's ability to handle demanding curriculum.
Financial aid available based on need.
Substantial grants given: $420,000 includes faculty reductions.

Where Next

Most stay through G12.

Head Profile

Lower School head since 1987. Working on Ed.D. Previous experience as admissions director and teacher. Primarily involved with students, faculty relations, parent relations, and policy and curriculum development. Takes playground duty and reads to children in class.

Faculty Features

3	No. male teachers
27	No. female teachers
10	% turnover
6–8	Typical tenure (yrs.)
x	Art teacher
x	Vocal music teacher
x	Instrumental music teacher

_____ Counselor/psychologist
_____ Nurse
__x__ Language teacher
__x__ Math teacher
_____ Reading teacher
__x__ P.E. teacher
_____ Remedial reading teacher
_____ Remedial math teacher
_____ Speech therapist
_____ Full-time science teacher
_____ Enrichment teacher
__x__ ESL teacher
_____ Tutor
_____ Assistant teachers
__x__ Part-time teachers

Parents Say

Rigorous international school with diverse student body and sense of camaraderie at the school.

Parent Wish List

Improved sports program and facilities.
Larger art and science facilities.
Less rigorous music curriculum.

Parent Involvement

Many volunteer possibilities: parent association, class parent, reading assistant, clubs, fund raising, which includes Annual Giving Campaign (phone-a-thon), auction, international events; monies fund new equipment and programs, scholarships.

Your Notes

Washington Waldorf School

4800 Sangamore Road, Bethesda, MD 20816
301/229-6107
HEAD: Ann S. Finucane

Basics

Year founded: 1969
Enrollment: 237 (PreK–8)
  Boys: 100
  Girls: 137
Grades: N–12 (Lower School PreK–8)
Major entry grades: PreK, 1, 4, 7, 9
Birthdate req.: 3½ yrs. (PreK); 6 yrs. by May 30 (G1)
Arrival: 8:30 a.m.
Dismissal: 3:00 p.m.
Early dismissal: no
Extended day: no
Costs: $5000
Parent fund raising: $25,000+
Transportation: yes
Lunch: yes
After-school activities: yes
Camp: no
Dress code: neat, clean
Neighborhood: Glen Echo, Ft. Sumner

Special Qualities

Block system approach.
Children's Garden Center with focus on healthy physical development.
School faculty collectively oversees administration.
Class teacher remains with students for 8 years, teaching main academic subject.
Greater emphasis on music, art, and handwork skills than many other schools.

Philosophy and Character

One of 500 Rudolf Steiner schools worldwide.
Based on precept that each child has own biography/destiny and school's function is to remove obstacles so destiny can be found in freedom as an adult.
Teaches to head, hand, and heart.

Nonsectarian, but embraces Christian values and principles, celebrates Christian holidays.

PreK and K program has 40 students in 2 sections; G1–8 range from 14–30 with 1 section.

50% students from MD, 25% each from DC and VA.

Very diverse economic backgrounds of students with 10% international population.

Curriculum

Curriculum based on developmental levels of children.

Subject matter taught with an artistic approach.

Day begins with recitation or song, two-hour main lesson for 3-week periods (block system), recess, shorter lessons, and handwork/P.E. in afternoon.

PreK and K (Garden Center) placed in mixed-age section of 20 with 2 teachers; emphasis on artistic and practical (not academic) activities.

Formal reading program deferred to G2, begins with oral approach, no textbooks.

Writing program begins with self-made main lesson books.

Math gradually presented starting with recitation, movement, games.

Foreign language (French and German) introduced G1 with grammar by G4.

Music begins in K, recorder taught, imitation approach, string or wind instrument G3/4, orchestra G5/6.

Games, sports in afternoon, team sports G3 up.

Art integrated throughout studies, in classroom PreK–6.

Homework begins G3, no grades, written reports and parent-teacher conferences.

Long lunch and recess with organized P.E. class 2x/week (1½ hours) G4 up.

Special Spots

__x__ Computer room
__x__ Science lab
__x__ Dedicated music room
__x__ Music practice room
_____ Gymnasium
__x__ Dedicated art room
_____ Ceramic studio
_____ Auditorium
__x__ Tennis court
_____ Pool
__x__ Playing fields
_____ Enrichment rooms
__x__ Library
_____ Language lab

x Dance studio ("Eurythmy Room")
Separate lunchroom
Kitchen
x Infirmary
x Conference room
x Multipurpose room
x Expansion plans (hopes to purchase land and new facility)

Sports News

P.E. Instruction
Swimming
x Basketball
x Gymnastics
Dance
x Softball
Skating
x Soccer
Volleyball
x Eurythmy

Weekly P.E. class
5 Pre-K
5 Kindergarten
2 First
2 Second
2 Third
2 Fourth
2 Fifth
2 Sixth

After-School Activities

Private music lessons, photo club, sports.

Registration/Admissions

Ann Finucane/Barbara Buchmann.
Request literature.
Attend information evening and observation morning tour.
Appointment with class teacher.
Applicant visits with class (except Children's Garden).
Parents provide transcripts.
No testing required.
Acceptance based on right fit for child and parents' support of Waldorf's approach.
Financial aid available, $72,000 in 1988–89.
Rolling admission.

Where Next

Many continue through G12.
Bethesda-Chevy Chase H.S., Field School, Walt Whitman H.S., Wilson H.S., Gonzaga.

Head Profile

Faculty-run school; Finucane is "administrator-secretary." With school since 1974, serves as "glue of the school"; involved with meeting parents' and students' needs, public relations, administration. Aims to improve the methods for "faculty-run" school.

Faculty Features

11	No. male teachers
18	No. female teachers
M	% turnover
4–15	Typical tenure (yrs.)
	Art teacher
x	Vocal music teacher
x	Instrumental music teacher
	Counselor/psychologist
	Nurse
x	Language teacher
	Math teacher
	Reading teacher
x	P.E. teacher
	Remedial reading teacher
	Remedial math teacher
	Speech therapist
	Full-time science teacher
	Enrichment teacher
	ESL teacher
x	Tutor
	Assistant teachers

Parents Say

School has a consensus approach to decision making; school described as supportive, artistic, and spiritual.

Parent Wish List

More parent involvement, auditorium/gymnasium, formal after-school programs.

Parent Involvement

Volunteers are welcome.

Opportunities include field trips, study groups, school store, bazaar, fund raising, development, socials, newsletter.

Your Notes

Westbrook Elementary School

5110 Allan Terrace, Bethesda, MD 20816
301/320-6506
HEAD: Dr. Mary Holly Allison

Basics

Year founded: 1939
Enrollment: 242
  Boys: unavailable
  Girls: unavailable
Grades: K–6
Major entry grades: na
Birthdate req.: 5 yrs. by Dec. 31
Arrival: 8:45 a.m.
Dismissal: 2:45 p.m.
Early dismissal: no
Extended day: yes
Costs: na
Parent fund raising: $16,000
Transportation: yes
Lunch: yes
After-school activities: yes
Camp: no
Dress code: none
Neighborhood: Westmoreland Hills

Special Qualities

Small, neighborhood school.
Day care program adds to school diversity.
G6 has 1 week "outdoor education" trip and Shakespeare production.
Strong academic program.
Newly renovated facility opening Fall 1990.

Philosophy and Character

Parents say school provides sound academic curriculum in personalized setting.
Magnet program.
Adjacent to 10.7-acre parklands.
Approximately 17% minority enrollment.
Total school capacity is 345 with grade size ranging from 20–38.

Curriculum

Full-day K program.
Homework in K, 2x/week.
Reading specialist for advanced students and those needing remedial help.
Computers in each classroom.
Twice yearly parent-teacher conferences.

Special Spots

_____ Computer room
_____ Science lab
_____ Dedicated music room
_____ Music practice room
_____ Gymnasium
_____ Dedicated art room
_____ Ceramic studio
_____ Auditorium
_____ Tennis court
_____ Pool
_____ Playing fields
_____ Enrichment rooms
_____ Library
_____ Language lab
_____ Dance studio
_____ Separate lunchroom
_____ Kitchen
_____ Infirmary
_____ Conference room
_____ Multipurpose room
__x__ Expansion plans (Westbrook facility closed for $3 million renovation 1989–90)

Sports News*

P.E. Instruction
_____ Swimming
_____ Basketball
_____ Gymnastics
_____ Dance
_____ Softball
_____ Skating
_____ Soccer
_____ Volleyball
_____ Creative movement

Weekly P.E. class
_____ Pre-K
_____ Transition
__1__ Kindergarten
__1__ First
__1__ Second
__1__ Third
__1__ Fourth
__1__ Fifth
__1__ Sixth

After-School Activities

Girl/Boy Scouts, ballet, soccer, aerobics.

*Unavailable.

Registration/Admissions

Registration at school throughout school year.
Documents required: birth certificate, immunization record, transcript if appropriate.
Non-U.S. citizens enroll through International Students Admissions Office, 301/230-2843.
May request out-of-boundary school at home school from Jan. 1–April 30.

Where Next

Westland Intermediate.

Head Profile

unavailable

Faculty Features

3	No. male teachers
22	No. female teachers
N	% turnover
5–15	Typical tenure (yrs.)
x	Art teacher
x	Vocal music teacher
x	Instrumental music teacher
x	Counselor/psychologist
	Nurse
	Language teacher
	Math teacher
x	Reading teacher
x	P.E. teacher
	Remedial reading teacher
	Remedial math teacher
x	Speech therapist
	Full-time science teacher
	Enrichment teacher
x	ESL teacher
	Tutor
	Assistant teachers
x	Resource room teacher
x	Special education
x	Media specialist

Parents Say

Appropriate to too much homework. Not enough field trips. Very supportive, up-to-date principal.

Parent Wish List

More art and music instruction in curriculum.

Parent Involvement

Parents are very active in classrooms as assistants, in media center and lunchroom, and as science, math, and reading aides.

Raised $16,000 in 1988–89 with Spring Carnival, Book Fair, Balloon Launch. PTA funds given for cultural arts program, school equipment, extra principal and teacher spending.

Your Notes

Wood Acres Elementary School

5800 Cromwell Drive, Bethesda MD 20816
301/320-6502
HEAD: Kathleen Lasinski

Basics

Year founded: 1952
Enrollment: 436
  Boys: unavailable
  Girls: unavailable
Grades: K–5
Major entry grades: na
Birthdate req.: 5 yrs. by Dec. 31
Arrival: 8:45 a.m.
Dismissal: 2:45 p.m.
Early dismissal: no
Extended day: 6:00 p.m.
Costs: na
Funds raised: $20,000
Transportation: yes
Lunch: yes
After-school activities: yes
Camp: no
Dress code: none
Neighborhood: Wood Acres

Special Qualities

Well-developed curriculum in basic subjects.
Planetarium.
High level of parent involvement.
Neighborhood school.
Stable teaching staff.

Philosophy and Character

Prepare children for junior and senior high school with emphasis on discipline in study and behavior.
School has good communications with parents.
School has hard-working and cheerful climate.
Students participate in canned good drives and disaster relief fund collections.
Total school capacity is 488 with grades ranging from 57–90 students.
Approximately 12% minority enrollment (Asian and Hispanic students).

Curriculum

Half-day K program.
Computer class 1x/week, small group instruction with parent volunteers.
Homework begins K.
P.E.: 1x/week for ½ hour.
Math instruction to small groups based on ability level
Individual music lessons free of charge.

Special Spots*

_____ Computer room
_____ Science lab
_____ Dedicated music room
_____ Music practice room
_____ Gymnasium
_____ Dedicated art room
_____ Ceramic studio
_____ Auditorium
_____ Tennis court
_____ Pool
_____ Playing fields
_____ Enrichment rooms
_____ Library
_____ Language lab
_____ Dance studio
_____ Separate lunchroom
_____ Kitchen
_____ Infirmary
_____ Conference room
_____ Multipurpose room
_____ Expansion plans

Sports News*

P.E. Instruction
_____ Swimming
_____ Basketball
_____ Gymnastics
_____ Dance
_____ Softball
_____ Skating
_____ Soccer
_____ Volleyball
_____ Creative movement

Weekly P.E. class
_____ Pre-K
_____ Transition
__1__ Kindergarten
__1__ First
__1__ Second
__1__ Third
__1__ Fourth
__1__ Fifth
__1__ Sixth

After-School Activities

Brownies/Scouts, music, hands-on science, sports, aerobics, French and Spanish.

*Unavailable.

Registration/Admissions

Registration at school throughout school year.
Documents required: birth certificate, immunization record, transcript if appropriate.
Non-U.S. citizens enroll through International Students Admissions Office, 301/230-2843.
May request transfer to out-of-boundary school at home school from Jan. 1–April 30.

Where Next

Pyle Intermediate.

Head Profile

unavailable

Faculty Features

6	No. male teachers
25	No. female teachers
M	% turnover
15	Typical tenure (yrs.)
x	Art teacher
x	Vocal music teacher
x	Instrumental music teacher
x	Counselor/psychologist
	Nurse
	Language teacher
	Math teacher
x	Reading teacher
x	P.E. teacher
	Remedial reading teacher
	Remedial math teacher
x	Speech therapist
	Full-time science teacher
	Enrichment teacher
x	ESL teacher
	Tutor
	Assistant teachers
x	Resource room teacher
x	Media specialist
x	Special education teacher

Parents Say

Principal is responsive to parents, keeps tight control of school, easily accessible. Facilities meet needs adequately.

Parent Wish List

More music and art classes.
More computer time.
More P.E. instruction/class time.
Sixth graders to stay at Wood Acres (they currently go to Pyle Intermediate because of lack of space).

Parent Involvement

Volunteers strongly encouraged. Parents on PTA board, in classroom, library, cafeteria and provide assistance in hands-on science, computer class. Run major fund-raising event every other year.

Your Notes

The Woods Academy, Our Lady of the Woods

6801 Greentree Road, Bethesda, MD 20817
301/365-3080
HEAD: Madeleine S. Octman

Basics

Year founded: 1975
Enrollment: 180
  Boys: 105
  Girls: 75
Grades: PreK–8
Major entry grade: PreK, 1
Birthdate req.: 2 yrs., 10 months
Arrival: 8:30 a.m.
Dismissal: 3:00 p.m.
Early dismissal: 1st Fri. of each month, 12:00 noon
Extended day: 7:00 a.m.–6:00 p.m.
Costs: $2975–$4575
Parent fund raising: $25,000
Transportation: yes
Lunch: no
After-school activities: yes
Camp: no
Dress code: uniform
Neighborhood: Wyngate, Burning Tree, Bannockburn

Special Qualities

Parents elect board of trustees.
French instruction emphasized.
Spacious campus.
Montessori preschool.
Sports programs.
Year-long extended day care program.
Small classes.

Philosophy and Character

Independent, Catholic, coed school located in a large parklike campus with spacious facilities.
Developing self-reliant and responsible students, striving to reach full potential in Christian environment.
Grade sizes range between 15–20 with 2 sections in nursery through K and 1 section in G1 up.

International student enrollment approximately 30%; 96% students are from MD with 2% each from VA and DC.

Curriculum

Montessori primary program with transition in G1–2 to traditional classroom.
Religion taught.
French begins on daily basis in K, school holds annual French Festival; Spanish is optional.
Belongs to Capital Athletic Conference, has intramural competitions.
Curriculum also includes reading, math, social studies, science, language arts, spelling, art, computer, music, and P.E.
Homework begins G1 and ranges from 1½–2 hours in G5–6.
Guidance department provides sex ed, life skills classes, and family guidance.

Special Spots

x Computer room
x Science lab
x Dedicated music room
___ Music practice room
x Gymnasium
x Dedicated art room
___ Ceramic studio
x Auditorium
x Tennis court
___ Pool
x Playing fields
___ Enrichment rooms
x Library
___ Language lab
___ Dance studio
x Separate lunchroom
x Kitchen
x Infirmary
___ Conference room
x Multipurpose room
___ Expansion plans

Sports News

P.E. Instruction
___ Swimming
x Basketball
x Gymnastics
___ Dance
x Softball
___ Skating
x Soccer
x Volleyball
___ Creative movement
___ Tennis

Weekly P.E. class
___ PreK
___ Transition
2 Kindergarten
2 First
2 Second

2 Third
2 Fourth
2 Fifth
2 Sixth

After-School Activities

Competitive sports.
Spanish for native speakers, stamp club, pottery club.

Registration/Admissions

Barbara Snyder.
Rolling admissions policy.
Parent visit; child spends day at school.
Stanford Achievement entrance test.
Two recommendations and transcripts required.
Financial aid up to 50% tuition is available for G–8, apply to SSS in Princeton by March 15; $20,000 in financial aid given in 1988–89.

Where Next

Gonzaga, Georgetown Visitation, Stone Ridge, Georgetown Prep, Holy Cross, Good Counsel.

Head Profile

Received M.A. in education administration; taught for 6 years and has 18 years administrative experience. At Woods Academy since 1981. Goals include strong academic program, Christian environment with caring faculty. Has open-door policy for students and frequent interaction with teachers.

Faculty Features

4 No. male teachers
14 No. female teachers
M Turnover (10%)
4–5 Typical tenure (yrs.)
x Art teacher
x Vocal music teacher
x Instrumental music teacher
x Counselor/psychologist
___ Nurse
x Language teacher
x Math teacher
x Reading teacher
x P.E. teacher
___ Remedial reading teacher
___ Remedial math teacher
___ Speech therapist
x Full-time science teacher
___ Enrichment teacher
___ ESL teacher
___ Tutor
x Assistant teachers (4)

Parents Say

Students work hard but have fun at same time. Art teacher is one of the best in Montgomery County. Students are prepared academically and socially to enter the high school of their choice with self-confidence and strong self-image.

Parent Wish List

After-school sports for G3–4.
More male teachers in upper grades.

Parent Involvement

Parent-owned school—parents elect board of trustees.
Active parents' organization.
Volunteer opportunities include: fund raising, field trip chaperones, helping with school functions.

Your Notes

Wyngate Elementary School

9300 Wadsworth Drive, Bethesda, MD 20816
301/571-6979
HEAD: Barbara J. Leister

Basics

Year founded: 1952
Enrollment: 504
  Boys: unavailable
  Girls: unavailable
Grades: K–6
Major entry grade: na
Birthdate req.: 5 yrs. by Dec. 31
Arrival: 9:05 a.m.
Dismissal: 3:05 p.m.
Early dismissal: no
Extended day: no
Costs: na
Parent fund raising: $15,000
Transportation: no
Lunch: yes
After-school activities: yes
Camp: yes
Dress code: none
Neighborhood: Alta Vista, Wyngate, Henry Estates

Special Qualities

Traditional warm school, which stresses academics.
Family feeling at school.

Philosophy and Character

Traditional, warm school where academics and students' well-being both stressed.
Students collect toys at Christmas, participate in food drives, and take collections to send disadvantaged children to camp.
Grade size ranges between 60–80 with 3 sections per class until G5, when there are 2 sections.
MCPS provides paid classroom aide when enrollment per section reaches 30.
Students and PTA sponsor Kiwanis summer camp.
Walter Johnson cluster.

Curriculum

Half-day K program.
Computer, music, art, and sports 1x/week for 50 minutes.
French and Spanish start G3.

Math and reading emphasized; individualized reading program with ability grouping.
Some computer exposure in K and G1.
School will have Montgomery County Public Schools' Interrelated Arts Team 1989–90 and 1990–91.

Special Spots

____	Computer room
____	Science lab
x	Dedicated music room
____	Music practice room
x	Gymnasium
x	Dedicated art room
____	Ceramic studio
____	Auditorium
____	Tennis court
____	Pool
x	Playing fields
x	Enrichment rooms
x	Library
____	Language lab
____	Dance studio
____	Separate lunchroom
x	Kitchen
x	Infirmary
____	Conference room
x	Multipurpose room
____	Expansion plans

Sports News

P.E. Instruction

____	Swimming
x	Basketball
____	Gymnastics
____	Dance
____	Softball
____	Skating
____	Soccer
____	Volleyball
____	Creative movement
x	Games

Weekly P.E. class

____	PreK
____	Transition
1	Kindergarten
1	First
1	Second
1	Third
1	Fourth
1	Fifth
1	Sixth

After-School Activities

Science (hands-on program), ballet, music, foreign language, gymnastics.

Head Profile

Long-time experience as principal. Last assignment was at Singapore American School as principal of PreK–8 school (an international private school). At Wyngate since 1987.

Faculty Features

1	No. male teacher
29	No. female teachers
N	Turnover
16	Typical tenure (yrs.)
x	Art teacher
x	Vocal music teacher
x	Instrumental music teacher
x	Counselor/psychologist
	Nurse
	Language teacher
	Math teacher
x	Reading teacher
x	P.E. teacher
	Remedial reading teacher
	Remedial math teacher
x	Speech therapist
	Full-time science teacher
x	Enrichment teacher
x	ESL teacher
	Tutor
	Assistant teachers
x	Curriculum specialist
x	Special education (Learning Disabled/Gifted and Talented)
x	Resource room teacher
x	Media specialist teacher

Parents Say

Facilities better than adequate. School is warm, progressive, competitive. Pleased with school head. Arts not stressed.

Parent Wish List

More computer centers.
Smaller classes.
More P.E. classes each week.
Extended day at school.

Parent Involvement

Very active PTA with parents in classroom, library and special activities, science fair.

Money raised for principal's wish list, teachers' extras, computer program updating.

Your Notes

Part Three

A Comparative Look at Schools

School	Type	Enroll-ment	Grades	Extended Day	Cost Range	Trans-portation	Loca-tion	Foreign Language	Financial Aid	Dead-line	Uniform	P/T Ratio	Religious Affiliation	Early Dismissal
The Alexandria Country Day School	I	104	PreK–8	yes	$2500–$4650	no	VA	yes	yes	rolling	no	5:1	none	no
The Barrie School (Lower School)	I	356 478	N–6 N–12	yes	$3200–$5275	yes	MD	yes	yes	Oct.–Apr.	no	13:1	none	no
Beauvoir	I/RA	355–358	PreK–3	yes	$6430	limited	DC	no	yes	end Jan.	no	10:1	Episcopalian	Fri.
Brown Academy	I	265	PreK–8	yes	$4400–$5150	yes	VA	yes	yes	rolling	no	9:1	none	no
Burgundy Farm Country Day School	I	250	PreK–8	yes	$5650–$6250	yes	VA	yes	yes	Feb. 1	no	8:1	none	no
Capitol Hill Cluster	Pub	223 (Peabody) 447 (Watkins)	PreK–K (Peabody) 1–4 (Watkins)	yes	na	limited	DC	yes	na	year-round	no	25:1	none	no
Capitol Day School	I	213	PreK–8	yes	$4800–$5900	yes	DC	yes	yes	Feb. 28	no	9.3:1	none	Wed.
Capitol Hill Montessori School	I	75	N–4	yes	$2600–$4500	yes	DC	yes	yes	March 1	no	5:1	none	1st Fri. each month
Charles E. Smith Jewish Day School (Lower School)	I/RA	582	K–6	no	$4655	yes	MD	yes	yes	rolling	no	20:1	Jewish	Fri.
Chevy Chase Elementary School	Pub	325	3–6	yes	na	yes	MD	no	na	year-round	no	13:1	none	no
Concord Hill School	I	90	N–3	no	$3565–$4715	no	MD	no	no	rolling	no	8:1	none	Fri.
Congressional School of Virginia	I	330	N–8	yes	$4000–$5200	yes	VA	yes	no	rolling	yes	10:1	none	no
John Eaton Elementary School	Pub	403	PreK–6	yes	na	no	DC	yes	na	year-round	no	u	none	no
Georgetown Day School (Lower School)	I	971 413	PreK–12 PreK–6	yes	$7632–$8436	no	DC	yes (begins G5)	yes	Feb. 15	no	7.5:1	none	no
Grace Episcopal Church Day School	I/RA	91	N–3	yes	$850–$4600	no	VA	no	yes	Jan. 15	no	12:1	Episcopal Church	no

School	Type	Enroll-ment	Grades	Extended Day	Cost Range	Trans-portation	Loca-tion	Foreign Language	Financial Aid	Dead-line	Uniform	P/T Ratio	Religious Affiliation	Early Dismissal
Grace Episcopal Day School	I/RA	180	N–6	yes	$2000–$4000	no	MD	yes	yes	Feb. 15	yes	9:1	Episcopal Church	no
Green Acres School	I	290	N–8	no	$2775–$5550	yes	MD	yes (begins G5)	yes	Feb. 1	no	11:1	none	Wed.
Green Hedges School	I	200	PreK–8	no	$3850–$5850	no	VA	yes	yes	Oct.-Jan.	no	9:1	none	no
The Harbor School	I	150	N–2/3	yes	$2525–$4915	no	MD	yes	yes	FCFS	no	8:1	none	Fri.
Hearst Elementary School	Pub	158	PreK–6	yes	na	no	DC	no	na	year-round	no	u	none	no
Holy Trinity School	Par	325	N–8	yes	N–K $3500 G1–8 $2200–$2600	no	DC	yes	yes	u	yes (G1 up)	u	Catholic	1st, 3rd Thurs.
Hyde Elementary School	Pub	150	PreK–5	yes	na	no	DC	no	na	year-round	no	u	none	no
Janney Elementary School	Pub	285	PreK–6	yes	na	no	DC	yes	na	year-round	no	u	none	no
Key Elementary School	Pub	171	PreK–5	yes	na	no	DC	yes	na	year-round	no	u	none	no
Lafayette Elementary School	Pub	503	PreK–6	yes	na	no	DC	yes (before school)	na	year-round	no	20:1	none	no
The Langley School	I	450	N–8	yes	$3675–$6460	yes	VA	yes	yes	Jan. 31	no	9:1	none	3rd Fri. each month
Little Flower School	Par	214	PreK–8	yes	$1375	no	MD	yes	yes	March	yes	1:13	Catholic	no
The Lowell School	I	171	N–3	yes	$3400–$6000	no	DC	no	yes	Feb. 28	no	12:1	none	Fri.
Horace Mann Elementary School	Pub	192	PreK–6	no	na	no	DC	no	na	year-round	no	u	none	no
Maret School (Lower School)	I	100 500	K–4 K–12	no	$5250–$6050	no	DC	yes	yes	Feb. 1	no	16:1	none	Wed.

School	Type	Enroll-ment	Grades	Extended Day	Cost Range	Trans-portation	Loca-tion	Foreign Language	Financial Aid	Dead-line	Uniform	P/T Ratio	Religious Affiliation	Early Dismissal
Mater Dei School	I/RA	200	1–8	no	$4350	no	MD	no	limited	Jan.	yes	18:1	Catholic	1st Fri. each month
McLean School of MD	I	243	K–9	no	$5125–$6550	yes	MD	no	yes	rolling	yes	7.5:1 (6:1 CU)	none	Fri.
Montessori School of Mc-Lean	I	136	PreK–6	yes (PreK only)	$2550–$3200	yes	VA	yes	no	rolling	yes (not in PreK)	15:1	none	no
Murch Elementary School	Pub	425	PreK–6	yes	na	no	DC	yes (starts G2)	na	year-round	no	u	none	no
National Presbyterian School	I/RA	200	N–6	yes	$3960–$5910	no	DC	yes	yes	March 1	no	8:1	Presbyterian Church	Fri.
The Newport Schools	I	214 274	N–8 N–12	yes	$3800–$7500	yes	MD	yes	yes	rolling	yes	12:1	none	no
Norwood School	I	250	K–6	no	$6400 $6600	no	MD	no	yes	Sept.–Thanksgiving	no	13:1.6	none	Fri.
James F. Oyster Bilingual Elementary School	Pub	296	PreK–6	yes	na	no	DC	yes	na	year-round	no	15:1	none	no
Paint Branch Montessori School	I	100	N–6	yes	$2364–$3445	no	MD	no	no	Feb.; Mar. (new applicants)	no	16:1	none	1st Fri. each month
The Potomac School (Lower and Middle Schools)	I	230 428	PreK–6 PreK–12	no	$4450–$6800	yes	VA	no	yes	Jan. 15	yes (G4 up)	10:1	none	see profile
The Primary Day School	I	172	PreK–2	no	$3000–3800	no	MD	G2	yes	Jan.	no	8.5:1	none	Fri.
The Rock Creek School	I	50	N–1 +	yes	$3800–$5700	limited	DC	yes	yes	rolling	no	12:1	none	no
Rosemary Hills Elemen-tary School	Pub	547	K–2	see profile	na	yes	MD	no	na	year-round	no	18:1	none	no
St. Agnes School (Lower School)	I/RA	264 500	K–6 K–12	yes	$6650–$7150	yes	VA	yes (begins G4)	yes	Jan. 1	no	13:1 (K–5) 11:1(6)	Episcopal Diocese	no
St. Jane Frances de Chan-tal School	Par	355	K–8	yes	$1200–$3300	yes	MD	no	limited	March	yes	20:1	Catholic Church	Fri.

School	Type	Enroll-ment	Grades	Extended Day	Cost Range	Trans-portation	Loca-tion	Foreign Language	Financial Aid	Dead-line	Uniform	P/T Ratio	Religious Affiliation	Early Dismissal
St. Mary's School of Piscataway	Par	237	K–8	yes	$1100–$1490	yes	MD	yes	yes	late Jan.	yes (G1–8)	u	Catholic Archdiocese	1st Fri. of month
St. Patrick's Episcopal Day School	I/RA	365	N–6	yes	$4400–$6930	no	DC	yes	yes	Jan. 31	no	9:1	Episcopal Church	Fri.
St. Peter's Interparish School	Par	255	PreK–8	yes	$1490–$1850	no	DC	yes (G6–8)	yes	Feb. 28	yes	25:1	Catholic	Wed.
St. Stephen's School (Lower School)	I/RA	171 600	K–5 K–12	yes	$6700–$7500	yes	VA	no	yes	Feb. 1 (early); rolling	no	13:1	Episcopalian	no
Sheridan School	I	202	K–8	yes	$6600–$8195	no	DC	yes (begins G4)	yes	Oct. 1–Mar. 1	Fri. only (G4 up)	8:1	none	Wed.
The Sidwell Friends School (Lower School)	I	280 1000	PreK–4 PreK–12	yes	$6960–$7630	yes	MD	no	yes	Sept. 1–Jan. 15	no	10:1	Quaker	Tues.
Somerset Elementary School	Pub	351	K–6	yes	na	yes	MD	no	na	year-round	no	25:1	none	no
Stoddert Elementary School	Pub	170	PreK–4	yes	na	no	DC	no	na	year-round	no	u	none	no
Stone Ridge Country Day School of the Sacred Heart	I/RA	175 341	PreK–4 PreK–8	yes	$3550–$6100	no	MD	yes (begins G5)	yes	Feb. 1	yes	9:1	Catholic (Sacred Heart order)	no
Washington Episcopal School	I/RA	195	N–6	yes	$4000–$6800	yes	MD	yes	yes	Feb. 1	yes (G1–6)	9:1	Episcopal	Fri.
Washington International School (Lower School)	I	220 585	N–3 N–12	yes	$2700–$6700	limited	DC	yes	yes	Jan. 31	no	8:1	none	no
Washington Waldorf School (Lower School)	I	237	PreK–8	no	$5000	yes	MD	yes (begins G1)	yes	rolling	no	22:1	none	no
Westbrook Elementary School	Pub	242	K–6	yes	na	yes	MD	no	na	year-round	no	13.4:1	none	no
Wood Acres Elementary School	Pub	436	K–5	yes	na	yes	MD	no	na	year-round	no	17:1	none	no
The Woods Academy, Our Lady of the Woods	I/RA	180	PreK–8	yes	$2975–$4575	yes	MD	yes	yes	rolling	yes	10:1	Catholic	1st Fri. each month

School	Type	Enroll-ment	Grades	Extended Day	Cost Range	Trans-portation	Loca-tion	Foreign Language	Financial Aid	Dead-line	Uniform	P/T Ratio	Religious Affiliation	Early Dismissal
Wyngate Elementary School	Pub	504	K–6	no	na	no	MD	yes (begin G3)	na	year-round	no	25:1	none	no

Key to Abbreviations

I = Independent school

Pub = Public school

I/RA = Independent school with religious affiliation

Par = Catholic Parish school

N = Class for 3-year-olds

PreK = Class for 4-year-olds

Rolling = Rolling admissions process in a nonpublic school

na = not applicable

u = unavailable

FCFS = First-come, first-served

CU = Catch Up program

Part Four

Lists and Resources

Schools by Geographic Location

Alexandria

The Alexandria Country Day School
Browne Academy
Burgundy Farm Country Day School
Grace Episcopal Church Day School
St. Agnes School
St. Stephen's School

Prince George's County

Paint Branch Montessori School
St. Mary's School of Piscataway

Georgetown/Burleith/Glover Park

Georgetown Day School (High School)
Holy Trinity School
Hyde Elementary School
Stoddert Elementary School
Washington International School (N–3)

Capitol Hill

Capitol Hill Cluster
Capitol Hill Day School
Capitol Hill Montessori School
St. Peter's Interparish School

McLean/Vienna

Green Hedges School
The Langley School
Montessori School of McLean
The Potomac School

Falls Church

Congressional School of Virginia

Upper Northwest/Cleveland Park

Beauvoir
John Eaton Elementary School
Georgetown Day School (PreK–8)
Hearst Elementary School
Janney Elementary School
Key Elementary School
Lafayette Elementary School
The Lowell School
Horace Mann Elementary School
Maret School
Murch Elementary School
National Presbyterian School
Oyster Bilingual Elementary School
The Rock Creek School
St. Patrick's Episcopal Day School
Sheridan School
Washington International School (G4–12)

Potomac area

Mater Dei School
McLean School of Maryland
Norwood School

Kensington/Silver Spring/ Rockville

The Barrie School
Charles E. Smith Jewish Day School
Grace Episcopal Day School
Green Acres School
The Newport Schools
Rosemary Hills Elementary School

Bethesda/Chevy Chase

Chevy Chase Elementary School
Concord Hill School
The Harbor School
Little Flower School
The Primary Day School
St. Jane Frances de Chantal School
The Sidwell Friends School
Somerset Elementary School
Stone Ridge Country Day School of the Sacred Heart
Washington Episcopal School
Washington Waldorf School
Westbrook Elementary School
Wood Acres Elementary School
The Woods Academy, Our Lady of the Woods
Wyngate Elementary School

Schools with a Diverse Student Body*

The Barrie School
Beauvoir
Burgundy Farm Country Day School
Capitol Hill Cluster
Capitol Hill Day School
Congressional School of Virginia
Georgetown Day School
Holy Trinity School
Hyde Elementary School
Janney Elementary School
Lafayette Elementary School
The Lowell School
Maret School
Murch Elementary School
The Newport Schools
Oyster Bilingual Elementary School
Paint Branch Montessori School
The Rock Creek School
Rosemary Hills Elementary School

*Diversity of a student body is the subjective judgment of the authors, based on a school's meeting one or more of the following criteria: approximately 20 percent minority enrollment, international student body, or range of socioeconomic backgrounds.

St. Mary's School of Piscataway
St. Patrick's Episcopal Day School
St. Peter's Interparish School
Sheridan School
The Sidwell Friends School
Stoddert Elementary School
Stone Ridge Country Day School of the Sacred Heart
Washington International School
Washington Waldorf School
The Woods Academy, Our Lady of the Woods

Schools with a Large Campus and/or Superior Facilities

The Barrie School
Beauvoir
Burgundy Farm Country Day School
Congressional School of Virginia
Georgetown Day School
Green Acres School
The Langley School
Maret School
The National Presbyterian School
The Newport Schools
Norwood School
The Potomac School
St. Agnes School
St. Patrick's Episcopal Day School
St. Stephen's School (Lower School)
Sheridan School (mountain campus)
The Sidwell Friends School
Stone Ridge Country Day School of the Sacred Heart
Westbrook Elementary School

Schools by Cost*

Under $3000

Holy Trinity School
Little Flower School
St. Mary's School of Piscataway
St. Peter's Interparish School

$3000–$4500

Capitol Hill Montessori School
Grace Episcopal Church Day School
Grace Episcopal Day School

*Cost based on most expensive elementary grade tuition.

Mater Dei School
Montessori School of McLean
Paint Branch Montessori School
The Primary Day School
St. Jane Frances de Chantal School
The Woods Academy, Our Lady of the Woods

$4500–$6000

The Alexandria Country Day School
The Barrie School
Browne Academy
Capitol Hill Day School
Charles E. Smith Jewish Day School
Concord Hill School
Congressional School of Virginia
Green Acres School
Green Hedges School
The Harbor School
The Lowell School
National Presbyterian School
The Potomac School
The Rock Creek School
Washington Waldorf School

Over $6000

Beauvoir
Burgundy Farm Country Day School
Georgetown Day School
The Langley School
Maret School
McLean School of Maryland
The Newport Schools
Norwood School
St. Agnes School
St. Patrick's Episcopal Day School
St. Stephen's School (Lower School)
Sheridan School
The Sidwell Friends School
Stone Ridge Country Day School of the Sacred Heart
Washington Episcopal School
Washington International School

Schools That Do Not Offer Foreign Language Instruction

Beauvoir
Chevy Chase Elementary School
Concord Hill School
Grace Episcopal Church Day School
Hearst Elementary School
Hyde Elementary School
The Lowell School
Horace Mann Elementary School
Mater Dei School
McLean School of Maryland
Norwood School
Paint Branch Montessori School
The Potomac School

Rosemary Hills Elementary School
St. Jane Frances de Chantal School
St. Stephen's School (Lower School)
The Sidwell Friends School (Lower School)
Somerset Elementary School
Stoddert Elementary School
Stone Ridge Country Day School of the Sacred Heart (G5 up)
Westbrook Elementary School
Wood Acres Elementary School

Schools with a Religious Orientation

Catholic

Holy Trinity School
Little Flower School
Mater Dei School
St. Jane Frances de Chantal School
St. Mary's School of Piscataway
St. Peter's Interparish School
Stone Ridge Country Day School of the Sacred Heart
The Woods Academy, Our Lady of the Woods

Episcopalian

Beauvoir
Grace Episcopal Church Day School
Grace Episcopal Day School
St. Agnes School
St. Patrick's Episcopal Day School
St. Stephen's School
Washington Episcopal School

Jewish

Charles E. Smith Jewish Day School

Presbyterian

National Presbyterian School

Quaker

The Sidwell Friends School

Schools with Nursery, PreKindergarten, and/or Transition Classes

Nursery Program

The Barrie School
Capitol Hill Montessori School
Concord Hill School
Congressional School of Virginia

Grace Episcopal Church Day School
Grace Episcopal Day School
Green Acres School
The Harbor School
Holy Trinity School
The Langley School
The Lowell School
National Presbyterian School
The Newport Schools
Paint Branch Montessori School
The Rock Creek School
St. Patrick's Episcopal Day School
Washington Episcopal School
Washington International School

Transition Program

Alexandria Country Day School
Burgundy Farm Country Day School
National Presbyterian School

Prekindergarten Program

The Alexandria Country Day School
Beauvoir
Browne Academy
Burgundy Farm Country Day School
Capitol Hill Cluster
Capitol Hill Day School
John Eaton Elementary School
Georgetown Day School
Green Hedges School
Hearst Elementary School
Hyde Elementary School
Janney Elementary School
Key Elementary School
Lafayette Elementary School
Little Flower School
Horace Mann Elementary School
Montessori School of McLean
Murch Elementary School
Oyster Bilingual Elementary School
The Potomac School
The Primary Day School
St. Peter's Interparish School
The Sidwell Friends School
Stoddert Elementary School
Stone Ridge Country Day School of the Sacred Heart
Washington Waldorf School
The Woods Academy, Our Lady of the Woods

Schools by End Grade

Schools up to G3

Beauvoir
Concord Hill School
Grace Episcopal Church Day School

The Harbor School (G2/3)
The Lowell School
The Primary Day School (G2)
The Rock Creek School
Rosemary Hills Elementary School (G2)

Schools up to G4, G5

Capitol Hill Montessori School (G4)
Hyde Elementary School (G5)
Key Elementary School (G5)
Stoddert Elementary School (G4)
Wood Acres Elementary School (G5)

Schools up to G6

Chevy Chase Elementary School
John Eaton Elementary School
Grace Episcopal Day School
Hearst Elementary School
Janney Elementary School
Lafayette Elementary School
Horace Mann Elementary School
Montessori School of McLean
Murch Elementary School
National Presbyterian School
Norwood School
Oyster Bilingual Elementary School
Paint Branch Montessori School
St. Patrick's Episcopal Day School
Somerset Elementary School
Washington Episcopal School
Westbrook Elementary School
Wyngate Elementary School

Schools up to G8

The Alexandria Country Day School
Browne Academy
Burgundy Farm Country Day School
Capitol Hill Cluster
Capitol Hill Day School
Congressional School of Virginia
Green Acres School
Green Hedges School
Holy Trinity School
The Langley School
Little Flower School
Mater Dei School
McLean School of Maryland (G9)
St. Jane Frances de Chantal School
St. Mary's School of Piscataway
St. Peter's Interparish School
Sheridan School
The Woods Academy, Our Lady of the Woods

Schools up to G12

The Barrie School
Charles E. Smith Jewish Day School
Georgetown Day School
Maret School
The Newport Schools
The Potomac School
St. Agnes School
St. Stephen's School
The Sidwell Friends School
Stone Ridge Country Day School of the Sacred Heart
Washington International School
Washington Waldorf School

Schools Not Offering Extended Day Care

Charles E. Smith Jewish Day School
Concord Hill School
Green Acres School
Green Hedges School
McLean School of Maryland
Horace Mann Elementary School
Mater Dei School
Maret School
Montessori School of McLean*
Norwood School
The Potomac School
The Primary Day School
Rosemary Hills Elementary School**
Washington Waldorf School
Wyngate Elementary School

Schools Requiring Uniforms

Congressional School of Virginia
Grace Episcopal Day School
Holy Trinity (G1 up)
Little Flower School
Mater Dei School
McLean School of Maryland
Montessori School of McLean (except PreK)
The Newport Schools
The Potomac School (G4 up)
St. Jane Frances de Chantal School
St. Mary's School of Piscataway (G1–8)
St. Peter's Interparish School
Sheridan School (Friday only, G4 up)
Stone Ridge Country Day School of the Sacred Heart
Washington Episcopal School (G1–6)
The Woods Academy, Our Lady of the Woods

Schools Offering Transportation

The Barrie School
Beauvoir (limited)
Browne Academy
Burgundy Farm Country Day School
Capitol Hill Cluster (limited)

---

*Extended day care offered for prekindergarten only.
**See profile.

Capitol Hill Day School
Capitol Hill Montessori School
Charles E. Smith Jewish Day School
Chevy Chase Elementary School
Congressional School of Virginia
Green Acres School
The Langley School
McLean School of Maryland
Montessori School of McLean
The Newport Schools
The Potomac School
The Rock Creek School (limited)
Rosemary Hills Elementary School
St. Agnes School
St. Jane Frances de Chantal School
St. Mary's School of Piscataway
St. Stephen's School (Lower School)
The Sidwell Friends School
Somerset Elementary School
Washington Episcopal School
Washington International School (limited)
Washington Waldorf School
Westbrook Elementary School
Wood Acres Elementary School
The Woods Academy, Our Lady of the Woods

Schools by Size of Enrollment*

Under 175

The Alexandria Country Day School
Capitol Hill Montessori School
Concord Hill School
Grace Episcopal Church Day School
The Harbor School
Hearst Elementary School
Hyde Elementary School
Key Elementary School
The Lowell School
Maret School
Montessori School of McLean
Paint Branch Montessori School
The Primary Day School
The Rock Creek School
St. Stephen's School (Lower School)
Stoddert Elementary School

175–250

Burgundy Farm Country Day School
Capitol Hill Cluster (Peabody)
Capitol Hill Day School
Grace Episcopal Day School

*Schools are categorized based upon enrollment in elementary grades. Some schools will fall into different categories if all grades are considered.

Green Hedges School
Little Flower School
Horace Mann Elementary School
Mater Dei School
McLean School of Maryland
National Presbyterian School
The Newport Schools
Norwood School
The Potomac School
St. Mary's School of Piscataway
St. Stephen's School
Sheridan School
Stone Ridge Country Day School of the Sacred Heart
Washington Episcopal School
Washington International School
Washington Waldorf School
Westbrook Elementary School
Woods Academy

Over 250

The Barrie School
Beauvoir
Browne Academy
Capitol Hill Cluster (Watkins)
Charles E. Smith Jewish Day School
Chevy Chase Elementary School
Congressional School of Virginia
John Eaton Elementary School
Georgetown Day School
Green Acres School
Holy Trinity School
Janney Elementary School
Lafayette Elementary School
The Langley School
Murch Elementary School
Oyster Bilingual Elementary School
Rosemary Hills Elementary School
St. Agnes School
St. Jane Frances de Chantal School
St. Patrick's Episcopal Day School
St. Peter's Interparish School
The Sidwell Friends School
Somerset Elementary School
Wood Acres Elementary School
Wyngate Elementary School

Catholic Elementary and Special Schools in the District Of Columbia

Elementary Schools

Annunciation, 3825 Klingle Place NW. Grades K–8. 362-1408.

Assumption, 220 Highview Place SE. Grades K–8. 562-7088.

Blessed Sacrament, 5841 Chevy Chase Parkway NW. Grades K–8. 966-6682.

Holy Comforter, 15th & East Capitol streets. Grades PreK–8. 547-7556.

Holy Name, 1217 West Virginia Avenue NE. Grades K–8. 397-1614.

Holy Redeemer, 1135 New Jersey Avenue NW. Grades K–8. 638-5789.

Holy Trinity. 1325 36th Street NW. Grades N–8. 337-2339.

Immaculate Conception. 711 N Street NW. Grades PreK–6. 234-1093.

Nativity Catholic Academy, 6008 Georgia Avenue NW. Grades PreK–8. 723-3322.

Our Lady of Perpetual Help, 1409 V Street SE. Grades K–4, 889-1662.

Our Lady of Perpetual Help, 1604 Morris Road SE. Grades 5–8. 678-0211.

Our Lady Queen of Peace, 3740 Ely Place SE, Grades K–8. 584-4278.

Our Lady of Victory, 4755 Whitehaven Parkway NW, Grades PreK–8. 337-1421.

Sacred Heart, 1625 Park Road NW. Grades K–8. 265-4828.

St. Ann's Academy, 4404 Wisconsin Avenue NW. Grades PreK–8. 363-4460.

St. Anselm's Abbey School, 4501 South Dakota Avenue NE. Grades K–8. 269-2350.

St. Anthony's School, 12th & Lawrence streets NE. Grades K–8. 526-4657.

St. Augustine, 1421 V Street NW. Grades PreK–8. 667-2608.

St. Benedict the Moor, 330 21st Street NE. Grades K–8. 397-3897.

St. Francis De Sales, 2019 Rhode Island Avenue NE. Grades K–8. 529-5394.

St. Francis Xavier, 2700 O Street NE. Grades K–5. 581-2010.

St. Gabriel's, 510 Webster Street NW, Grades K–8. 726-9212.

St. John's College Middle School, 2607 Military Road NW. Grades 7–8. 363-2316.

St. Peter's Interparish, 422 Third Street SE. Grades PreK–8. 544-1618.

St. Thomas More, 4265 Fourth Street SE. Grades K–8. 561-1189.

Special Institutions

Lt. Joseph P. Kennedy Institute, 801 Buchanan Street NE. 529-7600. Program for people ages 5 through 65 with developmental disabilities.

St. Joseph's Center, P.O. Box 10038. 526-0100. Day nursery.

St. Gertrude's School, 4801 Sargent Road NE. 526-7676.

Jewish Day Schools

Charles E. Smith Jewish Day School, 1901 E. Jefferson Street, Rockville, MD 20852. Grades K–12. 301/881-1400.

Gesher Jewish Day School, 2908 Valley Drive, Alexandria, VA 22302. Grades K–5. 703/998-6733.

Hebrew Academy of Greater Washington, 2010 Linden Lane, Silver Spring, MD 20910. Grades N–12. 301/587-4100.

Hebrew Day Institute, 1710 Hunters Lane, Rockville, MD 20852. Grades N–6. 301/984-2111

Hebrew Day School of Montgomery County, 1401 Arcola Avenue, Silver Spring, MD 20902. Grades K–6. 301/649-5400.

Jewish Primary Day School, 2850 Quebec Street, NW, Washington, DC 20008. Grades K–3. 202/722-0199.

A Sampling of Individuals Who Test and/or Tutor

Carol Abert, 2850 Davenport Street NW, Washington, DC 20008. 202/244-6052. Specialty: mathematics.

Ann Bennet, 5912 Kirby Road, Bethesda, MD 20817. 301/320-5995. Specialty: young children, study skills, learning disabilities.

Roberta Bien, 9913 Hall Road, Potomac, MD 20854. 301/299-6920. Tutors in all academic subjects.

Judy Israel, 7012 Wolftree Lane, Rockville, MD 20852. 301/881-8643. Testing and tutoring for all ages.

Michael Kirchberg, 4545 42nd Street NW, Suite 212, Washington, DC

20016. 202/244-4017. Specialty: long-term difficult problems for adolescents and adults.

Patricia Lemer, 6701 Fairfax Road, Chevy Chase, MD 20815. 301/654-0944. Testing only; specialty: preschool and primary, learning disabilities, public school advocacy.

Ellen Nannis, 19261 Montgomery Village Avenue, Gaithersburg, MD 20879. 301/948-3238. Psychologist.

Patricia Quinn, 3268 Arcadia Place NW, Washington, DC 20015. 202/244-8530. Specialty: developmental evaluations of infants and young children.

Pamela Smith, 5209 MacArthur Terrace NW, Washington, DC 20016. 202/362-1891. Tutoring only—young children; specialty: self-esteem problems.

Annette Spector, 6845 Elm Street, Suite 709, McLean, VA 22101. 703/241-1653. Testing and tutoring for all ages and subjects.

Sybil Wolin, 5410 Connecticut Avenue NW, Washington, DC 20015. 202/966-8171. Testing and tutoring for all ages and subjects; specialty: advocacy in public schools.

A Sampling of Agencies That Test and/or Tutor

Kingsbury Center, 2138 Bancroft Place NW, Washington, DC 20008. 202/232-5877. Testing and tutoring: all ages and subjects.

The Learning Laboratory, 8417 Bradley Boulevard, Bethesda, MD 20817. 301/365-7700. Diagnostic testing, learning style analysis; teach how to learn so not dependent on tutoring; videotaped learning style analysis.

The Learning Workshop, 8280 Greensboro Drive, Suite 470, McLean, VA 22102. 703/749-2981. Testing and tutoring: all ages and subjects.

The Math Center, 3311 Macomb Street NW, Washington, DC 20008. 202/244-6853. Testing and tutoring: mathematics for all ages.

Reading Center, George Washington University, 2201 G Street NW, Washington, DC 20052. 202/994-6286. Testing and tutoring for all ages; special programs: after-school program for gifted students; logical thinking courses.

Specific Diagnostics, 11600 Neset Street, Suite 130, Rockville, MD 20852. 301/468-6616. Testing and tutoring: all subjects and ages.

Traveling Tutors, P.O. Box 7175, Silver Spring, MD 20907. 301/585-0650 (MD); 703/893-9010 (VA). Tutoring only—all subjects; SAT preparation.

A Sampling of School Placement Counselors

Susan Dranitzke 202/544-5222
Resources for Children
124 12th Street SE
Washington, DC 20003

Comments: specializes in Capitol Hill and Virginia, low-key.

Ethna Hopper 202/686-1774
Ethna Hopper Associates
5100 Wisconsin Avenue NW
Washington, DC 20016

Comments: specializes in "desperate" and newcomers, business-like, expensive.

Georgia K. Irvin 301/951-0131
Georgia K. Irvin and Associates, Inc.
4701 Willard Avenue, Suite 227
Chevy Chase, MD 20815

Comments: ex-director of admissions for Sidwell Friends, motherly, expensive.

Patricia S. Lemer, M.Ed. 301/654-0944
6701 Fairfax Road
Chevy Chase, MD 20815

Comments: focuses on the match between learning style and school, low-key, moderate.

Sidney Manning, Ph.D. 301/681-3500
11227 Lockwood Drive
Silver Spring, MD 20910

Comments: hard-to-place special education children.

Bernice Wilson Munsey, Ed.D., NCC 202/895-1515
4801 Massachusetts Avenue NW, Suite 400
Washington, DC 20016

Comments: special education a specialty.

Margaret Schatzow, Ph.D. 301/652-3766
3218 Brooklawn Court
Chevy Chase, MD 20815

Comments: developmental psychologist, good on local public schools and for very young children.

Frances Turner 301/299-2012
11137 Hurdle Hill Drive
Potomac, MD 20854

Comments: ex-director, admissions, McLean School.

Private Schools for Learning-Disabled Children

Accotink Academy, Elaine McConnell, Head
8519 Tuttle Road, Springfield, VA 22152. 703/451-8041
Ages 6–20, ungraded

Chelsea School, Margaret Gray, Director
711 Pershing Drive, Silver Spring, MD 20910. 301/585-1430
Small junior high and high school for learning disabled
Just adding 6th, 7th, and 8th grade, fall '89
About 50 students
Both private tuition and publicly funded
Mostly college prep

Commonwealth Learning Center and Academy, run by Leary (see below)
7515 Lee Highway, Falls Church, VA. 703/573-5400

Ivymount School, Shari Gelman, Director
11614 Seven Locks Road, Rockville, MD 20854. 301/469-0223
Ungraded—infant–age 12
Mostly severely handicapped
A few classes of learning disabled
Mostly funded
Superb occupational therapy, related services
May be worth being in too restricted an environment to obtain good services

Kingsbury Day School, Judy Zangwill, Director
2138 Bancroft Place NW, Washington, DC 20008. 202/232-5877
DC primary school for "high risk"
Age 5–10
Approximately 40 students
Associated with Kingsbury Center
Range of problems
Most parents pay tuition
Contracted out occupational therapy and speech on site
Developmental sequential program
Academic tutoring included

The Lab School of Washington, DC, Sally Smith, Director
4759 Reservoir Road NW, Washington, DC 20007. 202/965-6600
Ages 5 through high school
About 300 students
Wide range of abilities and disabilities
Many students funded by DC and PG County
Excellent occupational therapy, speech and language, counseling on site
Teaches academics through the arts

Leary School, Albert D. Leary, Director
6349 Uncalnia Road, Alexandria, VA 22312. 703/941-8150
Ages 6–16

McLean School of Maryland, Hamilton Bishop, Head
8224 Lochinver Lane, Potomac, MD 20854. 301/299-8277
Catch-up classes, grades 2–9

Oakwood School, Robert McIntyre, Director
7210 Braddock Road, Annandale, VA 22003. 703/941-5788
Grades 1–9
Small classes
Bright students with unique learning needs
Mostly boys
Good for students who need a smaller class

Books, Magazines, and Articles

General Books

Ames, Louise Bates. *Is Your Child in the Wrong Grade?* Lumberville, Pa.: Modern Learning Press, 1978.

Ames, Louise Bates, and Joan Bates Chase. *Don't Push Your Pre-Schooler*. New York: Harper and Row, 1980.

Beeby, Lauren Carlisle. *Quick Check of Your Children's Learning Styles*. Stillwater, Okla.: Champ Publishing, 1985. (Available from Champ Publishing, 2911 N. Crescent Drive, P.O. Box 1714, Stillwater, OK 74076.)

Cohen, Dorothy. *The Learning Child*. New York: Vintage Books, 1972.

Elkind, David. *The Hurried Child*. Reading, Mass.: Addison-Wesley, 1981.

———. *Miseducation: Preschoolers at Risk*. New York: Alfred Knopf, 1987.

Frith, Terry. *Secrets Parents Should Know About Public Schools*. New York: Simon and Schuster, 1985.

Healy, Jane M. *Your Child's Growing Mind*. Garden City, N.Y.: Doubleday, 1987.

Lawrence, Gordon. *People Types and Tiger Stripes: A Practical Guide to Learning Styles*. Gainesville, Fla.: Center for Applications of Psychological Type, Inc., 1982. (Available from Center for Applications of Psychological Type, Inc., 414 7th Terrace, Gainesville, FL 32601.)

Nemko, Marty. *How to Get Your Child a "Private School" Education in a Public School*. Washington, D.C.: Acropolis Books, 1986.

Vail, Priscilla. *Smart Kids with School Problems: Things to Know and Ways to Help*. New York: Dutton, 1987.

Gifted Children

Alvino, James. *Parent's Guide to Raising a Gifted Child: Recognizing and Developing Your Child's Potential*. Boston: Little, Brown, 1985.

Saunders, Jacquelyn. *Bringing Out the Best: A Resource Guide for Parents of Young Gifted Children*. Minneapolis: Free Spirit Publishers, 1986.

Vail, Priscilla. *The World of the Gifted Child*. New York: Walker Books, 1979.

Directories

The Black Student Fund Independent School Directory. Washington, D.C.: The Black Student Fund, 1990. (Available from The Black

Student Fund, 3636 16th Street NW, Washington DC 20010, 202/387-1414; no charge.)

Cavanaugh, Merry M. *The Preschool and Day Care Book*. Washington, D.C.: The Preschool Book, 1988. (Available from The Preschool Book, 3833 Calvert Street NW, Washington, DC 20007; $6.98 plus $1.20 handling.)

Coerper, Lois H., and Shirley W. Mersereau. *Independent School Guide*. Chevy Chase, Md.: Independent School Guides, 1989. (Available from Independent School Guides, 7315 Brookville Road, Chevy Chase, MD 20815, 301/652-8635; $10.00 plus $1.50 handling.)

Learning Disabilities Directory, Learning Disabilities Council, P.O. Box 8451, Richmond, VA, 804/740-7124.

Maryland Non-Public Schools. Baltimore: Maryland State Department of Education, 1981.

Montgomery County Public Schools: Schools at a Glance. Rockville: The Department of Educational Accountability, December 1988.

Washington Small Schools. Silver Spring, Md.: Washington Small Schools Association, 1990. (Available from Washington Small Schools Association, 13925 New Hampshire Avenue, Silver Spring, MD 20904; no charge.)

Magazines and Articles

Parent and Child Magazine
7048 Wilson Lane, Bethesda, MD 20817. 301/229-2216
$12.95/year, 6x/year
Informative articles on school-related and other issues.

Washington Parent
The Parent Connection, 5606 Knollwood Road, Bethesda, MD 20816. 301/320-2321
$10/year, 6x/year

Gifted Child Monthly
P.O. Box 115, Sewell, NJ 08080
$25/year, sample issue $1
Games, articles, contests, programs for gifted kids of all ages.

Johnson, Betsey, and Pat Froelicher. "Is Your Child Ready for Kindergarten?" *Connection*, Winter 1986.

Organizations, Associations, and Parent Support Groups

There are many local groups that offer information, advocacy, publications, lectures, workshops, and other varieties of support for parents and educators. These range in size and scope from small and grassroots to chapters of large national associations. Many will put parents on their mailing list for no charge; some have small membership fees. All provide valuable resources.

Arlington County Association of Children with Learning Disabilities (ACACLD)
P.O. Box 1255
Arlington, Virginia 22210
703/538-6314
Similar programs to DCACLD and MCACLD.

Associates for Renewal in Education
Brenda Strong-Nixon, Executive Director
45 P Street NW
Washington, DC 20001
202/483-9424
Information on day care, after school, and summer programs.

Black Student Fund
Barbara Patterson, Director
3636 16th Street NW
Washington, DC 20010
202/387-1414
Gives scholarships to qualified black students to attend independent schools. Publishes directory of membership schools. Has city-wide fair each fall with representative families from each membership school.

Closer Look
1201 16th Street NW
Washington, DC 20036
202/822-7900
Referral source for parents for a variety of resources. Publishes directory of community resources for the learning disabled.

District of Columbia Association of Children with Learning Disabilities (DCACLD)
P.O. Box 6350
Washington, DC 20015
202/244-5177
Monthly program meetings, newsletter, advocacy, and support. Published handbook on obtaining appropriate services in the DC Public Schools.

Gifted Child Society
190 Rock Road
Glen Rock, New Jersey 07452
201/444-6520
Publishes national newsletter with resources for gifted children, including camps and schools. Also has games, articles, and other areas of interest for both parents and children.

Home and School Institute
Dorothy Rich, Director
1201 16th Street NW
Washington, DC 20036
202/466-3633
Workshops and materials on home instruction.

Independent Educational Counselors Association (IECA)
38 Cove Road, P.O. Box 125
Forestdale, MA 02644
617/477-2127
Free national directory of certified school counselors

Montgomery County Association of Children with Learning Disabilities (MCACLD)
P.O. Box 623
Rockville, Maryland 20851
301/933-1076
Monthly newsletter with information about legislation, local and national programs, new books, etc. Valuable even if not a Montgomery County resident. Advocacy, tutor list, summer programs.

National Association for the Education of Young Children (NAEYC)
1834 Connecticut Avenue NW
Washington, DC 20009
202/232-8777
Publishes pamphlets and booklets on all aspects of preschool and primary education.

The Parent Connection
5606 Knollwood Road
Bethesda, MD 20816
301/320-2321
Support for new parents, computer-assisted day care location, matches families with similar needs, parenting workshops, newsletter.

Parent Educational Advocacy Training Center (PEATC)
228 S. Pitt Street, Suite 300
Alexandria, VA 22314
703/836-2953
Similar to entry below.

Parent Information and Training Center
Pat Coffin, Director
Lynbrook Center
8001 Lynbrook Drive
Bethesda, MD 20814
301/654-4043
Helps Montgomery County residents understand the special education process. Publishes newsletter and provides telephone advisory.

Tips on Trips and Camps
8202 Spring Bottom Way
Baltimore, MD 21208
301/530-3313
Free advisory service on summer programs including camps, travel, and academic support—local, national, and international.

Washington Independent Services and Educational Resources (WISER)
P.O. Box 11504
Washington, DC 20008
202/686-9239
Publishes free directory of local professionals in a variety of disciplines with private practices in fields relating to education. Monthly program meetings open to the public. Annual fair in fall to meet members.

About the Authors

Blythe Lyons, a native of Pittsburgh, Pennsylvania, is a graduate of the Edmund A. Walsh School of Foreign Service at Georgetown University. She has been employed as a researcher and writer at the Atlantic Council of the United States and as a Senior Consultant at International Energy Associates, Limited. She currently resides in Washington, D. C. with her husband and two sons.

Missy Janes, a native of Middleburg, Virginia, earned a degree in Elementary Education from Goucher College in Baltimore. Her teaching experience includes work with children with communication disorders, hospitalized infants, and toddlers. She was the Art Coordinator at the National Geographic Society until leaving to start her own company in children's wear. She lives in Washington, D.C. with her husband and two small children.